Becoming a Translator

By integrating translation theory and the practical skills required by the working translator, Douglas Robinson presents an innovative approach to translation.

Becoming a Translator draws on a broad range of contemporary translation theories and integrates the latest trends in learning theory, memorization skills, and brain science. In addition, the book provides the type of practical information and advice that novice translators need:

- how to translate faster and more accurately
- how to deal with arising problems
- how to deal with stress
- how the market works

A wide variety of lively activities and exercises are included to facilitate the learning of both theory and practice. In addition, the book includes a detailed "Appendix for teachers." This contains suggestions for discussion, activities, and hints for the teaching of translation.

Becoming a Translator has been specifically designed for introductory undergraduate courses in the theory and practice of translation. It will also be of interest to professional translators and scholars of translation and language.

Douglas Robinson is currently Associate Professor of English at the University of Mississippi. His previous publications include *The Translator's Turn* (1991), *Translation and Taboo* (1996), *What is Translation?* (1997).

Becoming a Translator

An Accelerated Course

Douglas Robinson

LONDON AND NEW YORK

First published 1997
by Routledge
11 New Fetter Lane, London EC4P 4EE

Simultaneously published in the USA
and Canada
by Routledge
29 West 35th Street, New York,
NY 10001

Reprinted 1998, 1999

*Routledge is an imprint of the
Taylor & Francis Group*

Typeset in Times by J&L Composition
Ltd, Filey, North Yorkshire

Printed and bound in Great Britain by
TJ International Ltd, Padstow, Cornwall

*British Library Cataloguing in
Publication Data*
A catalogue record for this book is
available from the British Library

*Library of Congress Cataloguing in
Publication Data*
Robinson, Douglas,
  Becoming a translator: an accelerated
course / Douglas Robinson.
    p. cm.
  1. Translating and
interpreting. I. Title.
P306.R6   1997
418'.02–dc21   97–7057

ISBN 0–415–14860–X (hbk)
ISBN 0–415–14861–8 (pbk)

Contents

List of figures   ix
Acknowledgements   x

Introduction   1

1 External knowledge: the user's view   5

Internal and external knowledge   6
Reliability   7
Textual reliability   8
The translator's reliability   12
Timeliness   16
Cost   19
Trade-offs   19
Discussion   21
Exercises   22
Suggestions for further reading   23

2 Internal knowledge: the translator's view   25

Who are translators?   26
Professional pride   28
Reliability   29
Involvement in the profession   30
Ethics   30
Income   33
Speed   34
Project management   39

Raising the status of the profession   39
Enjoyment   40
Discussion   44
Exercises   45
Suggestions for further reading   46

3 The translator as learner   47

The translator's intelligence   49
The translator's memory   51
Representational and procedural memory   52
Intellectual and emotional memory   53
Context, relevance, multiple encoding   54
The translator's learning styles   57
Context   62
Field-dependent/independent   62
Flexible/structured environment   63
Independence/dependence/interdependence   64
Relationship-/content-driven   65
Input   66
Visual   66
Auditory   68
Kinesthetic   70
Processing   73
Contextual-global   73
Sequential-detailed/linear   74
Conceptual (abstract)   75
Concrete (objects and feelings)   76
Response   76
Externally/internally referenced   77
Matching/mismatching   79
Impulsive-experimental/analytical-reflective   80
Discussion   82
Exercises   83
Suggestions for further reading   91

4 The process of translation   93

The shuttle: experience and habit   94
Charles Sanders Peirce on instinct, experience, and habit 96
Abduction, induction, deduction   98
Karl Weick on enactment, selection, and retention   100

The process of translation   102
Discussion   107
Exercises   108
Suggestions for further reading   108

5 Experience   109

What experience?   110
Intuitive leaps (abduction)   113
Pattern-building (induction)   118
Rules and theories (deduction)   120
Discussion   123
Exercises   124
Suggestions for further reading   125

6 People   127

The meaning of a word   128
Experiencing people   130
First impressions (abduction)   132
Deeper acquaintance (induction)   133
Psychology (deduction)   138
Discussion   140
Exercises   141
Suggestions for further reading   143

7 Working people   145

A new look at terminology   146
Faking it (abduction)   148
Working (induction)   152
Terminology studies (deduction)   156
Discussion   158
Exercises   159
Suggestions for further reading   160

8 Languages   161

Translation and linguistics   162
What could that be? (abduction)   164
Laying down tracks (induction)   167
Teaching transfer patterns (deduction)   172

Discussion 182
Exercises 182
Suggestions for further reading 189

9 Social networks 191

The translator as social being 192
Pretending (abduction) 194
Pretending to be a translator 194
Pretending to be a source-language reader and target-language writer 197
Pretending to belong to a language-use community 198
Learning to be a translator (induction) 202
Teaching and theorizing translation as a social activity (deduction) 204
Discussion 212
Exercises 213
Suggestions for further reading 219

10 Cultures 221

Cultural knowledge 222
Self-projection into the foreign (abduction) 225
Immersion in cultures (induction) 228
Intercultural awareness (deduction) 231
Discussion 238
Exercises 239
Suggestions for further reading 244

11 When habit fails 245

The importance of analysis 246
The reticular activation system: alarm bells 249
Checking the rules (deduction) 253
Checking synonyms, alternatives (induction) 259
Picking the rendition that feels right (abduction) 260
Discussion 262
Exercise 262
Suggestions for further reading 262

Appendix for teachers 263
Works cited 317
Index 325

Figures

1 Learning styles   60–61
2 Peirce's instinct/experience/habit triad in
   translation   97
3 Peirce's instinct/experience/habit and
   abduction/induction/deduction triads in
   translation   100
4 The wheel of experience   104
5 The translator's experience of terminology   158
6 Charting the dynamic progress of linguistic
   theorizing   178
7 The "basic situation for translatorial activity"   216
8 The systematic assessment of flow in daily
   experience   251
9 Channels of learning   273

Acknowledgements

This book has taken shape in interaction with teachers and students of translation in the United States, Mexico, Puerto Rico, Brazil, and England. Eileen Sullivan's invitation to tour central Mexico in the fall of 1994 first got me started on the series of interactive hands-on experiences that eventually turned into these chapters; and while many of the participants in my seminars in Guadalajara, Mexico D.F., Tlaxcala, Xalapa, and Veracruz were enthusiastic, I owe even more to the skeptics, who forced me to recognize such things as the importance of the "slow" or analytical side of the shuttle movement explored here. Thanks especially to Richard Finks Whitaker, Teresa Moreno, Lourdes Arencibo, Adriana Menassé, and Pat Reidy in Mexico; Marshall Morris, Angel Arzán, Yvette Torres, and Sara Irizarry in Puerto Rico; John Milton, Rosemary Arrojo, John Schmidt, Regina Alfarano, Maria Paula Frota, and Peter Lenny in Brazil; Peter Bush, Mona Baker, and Terry Hale in England.

Several people read early drafts of the book in part or in whole, and made helpful comments: Anthony Pym, Beverly Adab, and Marla O'Neill. Bill Kaul's pictorial and other comments were as usual least helpful and most enjoyable.

I owe a special debt of gratitude to my friends and fellow translators on Lantra-L, the translators' on-line discussion group, who have graciously consented to being quoted repeatedly in these pages. A lonely translator could not ask for more dedicated help, support, advice, and argument!

For the innovative pedagogical material in the book I owe the greatest debt of all to my wife Heljä Robinson, who got every bit as excited about my (our) applications of brain science, suggestopedia, neurolinguistic programming, and learning-styles theory to translator training as I did. She not only fed me books and articles and ideas;

she read every chapter, some several times over, suggested new points to stress, invented exercises or helped me adapt ones that she had used in her own teacher education classrooms, and generally engaged me in a bracing and heady dialogue out on the leading edges of pedagogical insight.

Introduction

The present-day rapid development of science and technology, as well as the continuous growth of cultural, economic, and political relations between nations, have confronted humanity with exceptional difficulties in the assimilation of useful and necessary information. No way has yet been found to solve the problems in overcoming language barriers and of accelerated assimilation of scientific and technological achievements by either the traditional or modern methods of teaching. A new approach to the process of teaching and learning is, therefore, required if the world is to meet the needs of today and tomorrow.

Georgi Lozanov, *Suggestology and Outlines of Suggestopedy* (1971)

The study of translation and the training of professional translators is without question an integral part of the explosion of both intercultural relations and the transmission of scientific and technological knowledge; the need for a new approach to the process of teaching and learning is certainly felt in translator and interpreter training programs around the world as well. How best to bring student translators up to speed, in the literal sense of helping them to learn and to translate rapidly and effectively? How best to get them both to retain the linguistic and cultural knowledge and to master the learning and translation skills they will need to be effective professionals?

1

At present the prevailing pedagogical assumptions in translator training programs are (1) that there is no substitute for practical experience – to learn how to translate one must translate, translate, translate – and (2) that there is no way to accelerate that process without damaging students' ability to detect errors in their own work. Faster is generally better in the professional world, where faster translators – provided that they continue to translate accurately – earn more money; but it is generally not considered better in the pedagogical world, where faster learners are thought to be necessarily careless, sloppy, or superficial.

This book is grounded in a simultaneous acceptance of assumption (1) *and* rejection of assumption (2). There is no substitute for practical experience, and translator training programs should continue to provide their students with as much of it as they can. But there are ways of accelerating that process that do not simply foster bad work habits.

The methodological shift involved is from a pedagogy that places primary emphasis on conscious analysis to a pedagogy that balances conscious analysis with subliminal discovery and assimilation. The more consciously, analytically, rationally, logically, systematically a subject is presented to students, and the more consciously and analytically they are expected to process the materials presented, the more slowly those materials are internalized.

And this is often a good thing. Professional translators need to be able to slow down to examine a problematic word or phrase or syntactic structure or cultural assumption painstakingly, with full analytical awareness of the problem and its possible solutions. Slow analysis is also a powerful source of new knowledge. Without the kinds of problems that slow the translation process down to a snail's pace, the translator would quickly fall into a rut.

The premise of this book is, however, that in the professional world slow, painstaking, analytical learning is the exception rather than the rule – and should be in the academic world of translator training as well. All humans learn better, faster, more effectively, more naturally, and more enjoyably through rapid and holistic subliminal channels. Conscious, analytical learning is a useful *check* on more efficient learning channels; it is not, or at least it should not be, the only or even main channel through which material is presented.

This book, therefore, is set up to shuttle between the two extremes of subliminal or unconscious learning, the "natural" way people learn outside of class, and conscious, analytical learning, the "artificial" way people are traditionally taught in class. As teaching methods move away from traditional analytical modes, learning speeds up and becomes more enjoyable and more effective; as it approaches the subliminal extreme, students learn enormous quantities of material at up to ten times the speed of traditional methods while hardly even noticing that they're learning anything. Because learning is unconscious, it seems they haven't learned anything; to their surprise, however, they can perform complicated tasks much more rapidly and confidently and accurately than they ever believed possible.

Effective as these subliminal methods are, however, they are also somewhat mindless, in the sense of involving very little critical reflection, metathinking, testing of material against experience or reason. Translators need to be able to process linguistic materials quickly and efficiently; but they also need to be able to recognize problem areas and to slow down to solve them in complex analytical ways. The main reason for integrating conscious with subliminal teaching methods is that learners need to be able to test and challenge the materials and patterns that they sublimate so quickly and effectively. Translators need to be able to shuttle back and forth between rapid subliminal translating and slow, painstaking critical analysis – which means not only that they should be trained to do both, but that their training should embody the shuttle movement between the two, subliminal-becoming-analytical, analytical-becoming-subliminal. Translators need to be able not only to perform both subliminal speed-translating and conscious analytical problem-solving, but also to shift from one to the other when the situation requires it (and also to recognize when the situation does require it).

Hence the rather strange look of some of the chapters, and especially the exercises at the end of the chapters. Teachers and students accustomed to traditional analytical pedagogies will probably shy away at first from critical perspectives and hands-on exercises designed to develop subliminal skills. And this critical caution is a good thing: it is part of the shuttle movement from subliminal to conscious processing. The topics for discussion that precede the exercises at the end of every chapter are in fact designed to foster just this sort of critical skepticism about the claims made in the chapter. Students should be given a chance both to experience the power of subliminal learning and translating and to question the nature and impact of what they are experiencing. Subliminal functioning without critical self-awareness quickly becomes mind-numbing mechanical routine; analytical critiques without rich playful experience quickly become inert scholasticism.

The primary course for which this textbook is intended is the introduction to the theory and practice of translation. Such introductory courses are designed to give undergraduate (and, in some cases, graduate) students an overall view of what translators do and how translation is studied. To these ends the book is full of practical details regarding the professional activities of translators, and in Chapters 6–10 it offers ways of integrating a whole series of theoretical perspectives on translation, from psychological theories in Chapter 6 through terminological theories in Chapter 7, linguistic theories in Chapter 8, and social theories in Chapter 9 to cultural theories in Chapter 10.

In addition, however, the exercises are designed not only to teach *about* translation but to help students translate better as well; and the book might also be used as supplementary material in practical translation seminars. Since the book is not written for a specific language combination, the teacher will have to do some work to adapt the exercises to the specific language combination in which the students are working; while suggestions are given on how this might be done, it would be impossible to anticipate the specific needs of individual students in countries around the world. If this requires more active and creative input from teachers, it also allows teachers more latitude to adapt the book's exercises to their students' needs. A teacher's guide at the end of the book provides some additional suggestions for adapting these exercises to individual classrooms.

Since most translators traditionally (myself included) were not trained for the job, and many still undergo no formal training even today, I have also set up the book for self-study. Readers not currently enrolled in, or employed to teach in, translator training programs can benefit from the book by reading the chapters and doing the exercises that do not require group work. Many of the exercises designed for group work can easily be adapted for individuals. The main thing is *doing* the exercises and not just thinking about them. Thought experiments work only when they are truly experiments and not just reflection upon what this or that experiment might be like.

Chapter 1

External knowledge:
the user's view

- **Internal and external knowledge**   6
- **Reliability**   7
- Textual reliability   8
- The translator's reliability   12
- **Timeliness**   16
- **Cost**   19
- **Trade-offs**   19
  - **Discussion**   21
  - **Exercises**   22
  - **Suggestions for further reading**   23

THESIS: Translation can be perceived from the outside, from the client's or other user's point of view, or from the inside, from the translator's point of view; and while this book takes the translator's perspective, it is useful to begin with a sense of what our clients and users need and why.

Internal and external knowledge

Translation is different things for different groups of people. For people who are not translators, it is primarily a text; for people who are, it is primarily an activity. Or, as Anthony Pym (1993: 131, 149–50) puts it, translation is a text from the perspective of "external knowledge," but an activity (aiming at the production of a text) from the perspective of "internal knowledge."

INTERNAL	EXTERNAL
A translator thinks and talks about translation from inside the process, knowing how it's done, possessing a practical real-world sense of the problems involved, some solutions to those problems, and the limitations on those solutions (the translator knows, for example, that no translation will ever be a perfectly reliable guide to the original).	A non-translator (especially a monolingual reader in the target language who directly or indirectly pays for the translation – a client, a book-buyer) thinks and talks about translation from outside the process, not knowing how it's done but knowing, as Samuel Johnson once said of the non-carpenter, a well-made cabinet when s/he sees one.

From the translator's internal perspective, the activity is most important: the process of becoming a translator, receiving and handling requests to do specific translations, doing research, networking, translating words, phrases, and registers, editing the translation, delivering the finished text to the employer or client, billing the client for work completed, getting paid. The text is an important part of that process, of course – even, perhaps, the most important part – but it is never the whole thing.

From the non-translator's external perspective, the text as product or commodity is most important. And while this book is primarily concerned with (and certainly written from and for) the translator's internal knowledge, and thus with the activity of translating – it is, after all, a textbook for student translators – it will be useful to project an external perspective briefly here in Chapter 1, if only to distinguish it clearly from the more translator-oriented approach of the rest of the book. A great deal of thinking and teaching about translation in the past has been controlled by what is essentially external knowledge, text-oriented approaches that one might have thought of greater interest to non-translators than translators – so much, in fact, that these external perspectives have in many ways come to dominate the field.

Ironically enough, traditional approaches to translation based on the non-translating user's need for a certain kind of text have only tended to focus on one of the user's needs: reliability (often called "equivalence" or "fidelity"). A fully user-oriented approach to translation would recognize that *timeliness* and *cost* are equally important factors. Let us consider these three aspects of translation as perceived from the outside – translation users' desire to have a text translated *reliably*, *rapidly*, and *cheaply* – in turn.

Reliability

Translation users need to be able to rely on translation. They need to be able to use the translation as a reliable basis for action, in the sense that if they take action on the belief that the translation gives them the kind of information they need about the original, that action will not fail *because* of the translation. And they need to be able to trust the translator to act in reliable ways, delivering reliable translations by deadlines, getting whatever help is needed to meet those deadlines, and being flexible and versatile in serving the user's needs. Let's look at these two aspects of translation reliability separately.

Textual reliability

A text's reliability consists in the trust a user can place in it, or encourage others to place in it, as a representation or reproduction of the original. To put that differently, a text's reliability consists in the user's willingness to base future actions on an assumed relation between the original and the translation.

For example, if the translation is of a tender, the user is most likely the company to which the tender has been made. "Reliability" in this case would mean that the translation accurately represents the exact nature of the tender; what the company needs from the translation is a reliable basis for action, i.e., a rendition that meticulously details every aspect of the tender that is relevant to deciding whether to accept it. If the translation is done in-house, or if the client gives an agency or freelancer specific instructions, the translator may be in a position to summarize certain paragraphs of lesser importance, while doing painstakingly close readings of certain other paragraphs of key importance.

Or again, if the translation is of a literary classic, the user may be a teacher or student in a class that is reading and discussing the text. If the class is taught in a mother-tongue or comparative literature department, "reliability" may mean that the users agree to act as if the translation really were the original text. For this purpose a translation that reads as if it had originally been written in the target language will probably suffice. If the class is an upper-division or graduate course taught in a modern-language or classics department, "reliability" may mean that the translation follows the exact syntactic contours of the original, and thus helps students to read a difficult text in a foreign language. For this purpose, various "cribs" or "interlinears" are best – like those New Testament translations published for the benefit of seminary students of Greek who want to follow the original Greek text word for word, with the translation of each word printed directly under the word it renders.

Or if the translation is of advertising copy, the user may be the marketing department in the mother company or a local dealer, both of whom will presumably expect the translation "reliably" to sell products or services without making impossible or implausible or illegal claims; or it may be prospective customers, who may expect the translation to represent the product or service advertised reliably, in the sense that, if they should purchase one, they would not feel that the translation had misrepresented the actual service or product obtained.

As we saw above, this discussion of a text's reliability is venturing into the territory traditionally called "accuracy" or "equivalence" or "fidelity." These terms are in fact shorthand for a wide variety of reliabilities that govern the user's external perspectives on translation. There are many different types of textual reliability; there is no single touchstone for a reliable translation, certainly no single simple formula for abstract semantic (let alone syntactic) "equivalence" that can be applied easily and unproblematically in every case. All that matters to the non-translating user is that the translation be reliable in more or less the way s/he expects (sometimes unconsciously): accurate or effective or some combination of the two; painfully literal or easily readable in the target language or somewhere in the middle; reliable for her or his specific purposes.

A text that meets those demands will be called a "good" or "successful" translation, period, even if another user, with different expectations, might consider it bad or unsuccessful; a text considered a failure by some users, because it doesn't meet their reliability needs, might well be hailed as brilliant, innovative, sensitive, or highly accurate by others.

It is perhaps unfortunate, but probably inevitable, that the norms and standards appropriate for one group of users or use situations should be generalized to apply to all. Because some users demand literal translations, for example, the idea spreads that a translation that is not literal is no translation at all; and because some users demand semantic (sense-for-sense) equivalence, the idea spreads that a translation that charts its own semantic path is no translation at all.

Thus a free retelling of a children's classic may be classified as an "adaptation" rather than a translation; and an advertising translation that deviates strikingly from the original in order to have the desired impact on target readers or viewers (i.e., selling products or services) may be thought of as a "new text" rather than as an advertising translation.

Each translation user, limited to the perspective of her or his own situational needs, may quite casually fall into the belief that those needs aren't situational at all, indeed aren't her or his needs at all, but simply the nature of translation itself. *All* translation is thus-and-such – because *this* translation needs to be, and how different can different translations be? The fact that they can be very different indeed is often lost on users who believe their own expectations to be the same as everyone else's.

This mistaken belief is almost certainly the source of the quite widespread notion that "fidelity," in the sense of an exact one-to-one correspondence between original and translation, is the only goal of translation. The notion arises when translation is thought of exclusively as a product or commodity (rather than as an activity or process), and when the reliability of that product is thought of narrowly in terms of exact correspondence between texts (rather than as a whole spectrum of possible exchanges).

TYPES OF TEXT RELIABILITY

1 Literalism

The translation follows the original word for word, or as close to that ideal as possible. The syntactic structure of the source text is painfully evident in the translation.

2 Foreignism

The translation reads fairly fluently but has a slightly alien feel. One can tell, reading it, that it is a translation, not an original work.

3 Fluency

The translation is so accessible and readable for the target-language reader as to seem like an original in the target language. It never makes the reader stop and reflect that this is in fact a translation.

4 Summary

The translation covers the main points or "gist" of the original.

5 Commentary

The translation unpacks or unfolds the hidden complexities of the ori-

Reliably translated texts cover a wide range from the lightly edited to the substantially rewritten, with the "accurate" or "faithful" translation somewhere in the middle; there is no room in the world of professional translation for the theoretical stance that only straight sense-for-sense translation *is* translation, therefore as a translator I should never be expected to edit, summarize, annotate, or re-create a text.

While some effort at user education is probably worthwhile, it is usually easier for translators simply to shift gears, find out (or figure out) what the user wants or needs or expects, and provide that – without attempting to enlighten the user about the variability and volatility of such expectations. Many times clients' demands are unreasonable, unrealistic, even impossible – as when the marketing manager of a company going international demands that an advertising campaign in fourteen different languages be identical to the

---

ginal, exploring at length implications that remain unstated or half-stated in the original.

6 Summary-commentary

The translation summarizes some passages briefly while commenting closely on others. The passages in the original that most concern the user are unpacked; the less important passages are summarized.

7 Adaptation

The translation recasts the original so as to have the desired impact on an audience that is substantially different from that of the original; as when an adult text is adapted for children, a written text is adapted for television, or an advertising campaign designed to associate a product with sophistication uses entirely different images of sophistication in the source and target languages.

8 Encryption

The translation recasts the original so as to hide its meaning or message from one group while still making it accessible to another group, which possesses the key.

original, and that the translators in all fourteen languages show that this demand has been met by providing literal backtranslations of their work. Then the translators have to decide whether they are willing to undertake the job at all; and if so, whether they can figure out a way to do it that satisfies the client without quite meeting her or his unreasonable demands.

For the hard fact is that translators, with all their internal knowledge, can rarely afford to ignore the external perspectives of nontranslators, who are, after all, the source of our income. As Anthony Pym (1993: 149) notes wryly, in conversation with a client it makes little sense to stress the element of creative interpretation present in all translation; this will only create misunderstandings. From the client's external point of view, "creative interpretation" spells flagrant distortion of the original, and thus an unreliable text; from the translator's internal point of view, "creative interpretation" signals the undeniable fact that all text-processing involves some degree of interpretation and thus some degree of creativity, and beyond that, the translator's sense that every target language is more or less resistant to his or her activities.

The translator's reliability

But the text is not the only important element of reliability for the user; the translator too must be reliable.

ASPECTS OF TRANSLATOR RELIABILITY

Reliability with regard to the text

1 Attention to detail

The translator is meticulous in her attention to the contextual and collocational nuances of each word and phrase she uses.

2 Sensitivity to the user's needs

The translator listens closely to the user's special instructions regarding the type of translation desired, understands those instructions quickly and fully, and strives to carry them out exactly and flexibly.

3 Research

The translator does not simply "work around" words she doesn't know, by using a vague phrase that avoids the problem or leaving a question mark where the word would go, but does careful research, in reference books and Internet databases, and through phone calls, faxes, and e-mail inquiries.

4 Checking

The translator checks her work closely, and if there is any doubt (as when she translates into a foreign language) has a translation checked by an expert before delivery to the client. (The translator also knows when there is any doubt.)

Reliability with regard to the client

5 Versatility

The translator is versatile enough to translate texts outside her area of specialization, out of languages she doesn't feel entirely competent in (always having such work checked, of course), in manners she has never tried. (The translator also knows when she can handle a novel task and when something is simply beyond her abilities and needs to be politely refused.)

6 Promises

The translator knows her own abilities and schedule and working habits well enough to make realistic promises to clients or agencies regarding delivery dates and times, and then keeps those promises; or, if pressing circumstances make it impossible to meet a deadline, calls the client or agency and renegotiates the time frame or arranges for someone else to finish the job.

7 Friendliness

The translator is friendly and helpful on the phone or in person, is pleasant to speak or be with, has a sense of humor, offers helpful advice (such as who to call for that one page of Estonian or Urdu), doesn't offer unhelpful advice (such as how to talk to the client), and so on.

8 Confidentiality

The translator will not disclose confidential matters learned through the process of translation (or negotiation) to third parties.

Reliability with regard to technology

9 Hardware and software

The translator owns a late-model computer, a recent version of a major word-processing program, a fax machine, and a modem (or a fax/modem), and knows how to use them (including in-house bulletin board systems, e-mail, and the like).

Notice that this list is closely related to the traditional demand that the translator be "accurate," and indeed contains that demand within it, under "Attention to detail," but that it is a much more demanding conception of reliability than merely the expectation that the translator's work be "correct." The best synonym for the translator's reliability would not be "correctness" but "professionalism": the reliable translator in every way comports himself or herself like a professional. A client that asks for a summary and receives a "correct" or "faithful" translation will not call the translator reliable – in fact will probably not call the translator ever again. A sensitive and versatile translator will recognize when a given task requires something besides straight "accuracy" – various forms of summary or commentary or adaptation, various kinds of imaginative re-creation – and, if the client has not made these instructions explicit, will confirm this hunch before beginning work.

Clearly, however, the translator's reliability greatly exceeds the specific operations performed on texts. Clients and agencies want freelancers who will produce *reliable texts*, texts that they won't have to edit substantially after they arrive; but they also want freelancers who will produce *texts reliably*, on time and otherwise as promised, modemed if they were supposed to be modemed, camera-ready and express-mailed if that was the plan, and so on. They want to work with people who are pleasant and professional and helpful on the phone, asking competent, knowledgeable questions, making quick and businesslike decisions, even making reasonable demands that cause extra work for them, such as "fax me the whole thing, including illustrations, and I'll call you within ten minutes to let you know whether I can do it." A freelancer who can't take a job but can suggest someone else for the client or agency to call will probably get another job from the same client or agency later; an abrupt, impatient freelancer who treats the caller as an unwanted interruption and just barely has time to say "No" before hanging up may not. Given a choice between two producers of reliable texts in a given language combination, who would not rather call someone pleasant than someone unpleasant?

Just to speak from the agency end of things: I have on file plenty of resumes of translators in all kinds of languages. Who do I send the work to?

1 the person who keeps phoning up and nudging me if I have any work for him. He shows he wants to do work for me so that means more to me than someone who just sends a resume who I never hear from again.
2 the person who accepts a reasonable rate and doesn't badger for higher prices.
3 the person who does (a) great work, (b) quickly, and (c) needs little if no editing work on his translation.
4 the person who has the main wordprocessing programs used by most clients, a fax and preferably a modem.
5 a pleasant, nice to deal with person.

(1) is usually important for me to take notice of a translator. (2,3,4,5) are necessary for me to keep going back to that person. Of course, if you need a certain translation combination in a certain topic and have few translators who can handle it, you'll turn to those translators notwithstanding their faults.

Miriam Samsonowitz

* * * * *

We might work differently, Miriam, but I would hate to be disturbed by someone who calls me continuously. I could tell fairly well how good the person is as a translator, and if I want to use her/his services, I would often send her/him a sample (and pay for it).

Sincerely
Gloria Wong

* * * * *

Maybe it's a cultural question. In some countries, Miriam's position is not only dead on, but essential for the survival of the person doing the nudging. In such cultures, both parties accept that and are used (or resigned) to it. In others, such ''nudging'' would definitely be seen by both parties as pestering, and you'll get further by using the ''humble'' approach. I think Canada is somewhere near the middle – you can nudge a bit, but not too much. The U.S. is perhaps a bit more towards the nudging end – you have to really go after what you want, and persistence is considered a virtue and tends to get a positive response. But even there, there is such a word as obnoxious.

Werner Maurer[1]

Timeliness

But it is not enough for the user of a translation that both it and its creator be reliable; it must also be timely, in the sense of not arriving past the time of its usefulness or value. Timeliness is most flexible in the case of literary or Biblical translations, which are supposedly timeless; in fact, of course, they are not timeless but simply exist in a greatly extended time frame. The King James Version of the Bible is still in use after almost four centuries; but even it is not timeless. It has been replaced in many churches with newer translations; and even in the most conservative churches it is difficult to imagine it still in use a thousand or two thousand years hence. Sooner or later the time will come when it too will have had its day.

Timeliness is least flexible when the translation is tied to a specific dated use situation.

---

[1] All of the boxed translator discussions in this book are taken from Lantra-L, an Internet discussion group for translators. To subscribe to it, send a message to listserv@segate.sunet.se saying only SUBSCRIBE LANTRA-L YOUR NAME. The Lantra-L archives are stored on the World Wide Web at http: //segate.sunet.se/archives/lantra-l.html, and all of the passages quoted here with permission from their authors can be found there.

Other Internet discussion forums for translation scholars include Translat and ATSA-L. To join the former, send a message to listproc@wugate.wustl.edu saying only SUBSCRIBE TRANSLAT YOUR NAME. To join the latter, send a message to listserv @ olemiss.edu saying only SUBSCRIBE ATSA-L YOUR NAME.

If you are a CompuServe subscriber, you may also want to join FLEFO, the foreign-language forum that also has several translation sections. At the CompuServe prompt, type GO FLEFO, or follow the instructions in the CompuServe access software.

A provincial governor in Finland is entertaining guests from Kenya, and wants to address them in English; his English is inadequate to the task, so he writes up a one-page speech in Finnish and has it translated into English. Clearly, if the translation is not timely, if it is made after the luncheon engagement, it is useless. As often happens, the governor is too busy to write up the speech in good time before it is to be read; he finishes it on the morning of the luncheon, and his staff immediately start calling around to local translators to find one who can translate the one-page document before noon. An English lecturer at the university promises to do the job; a courier brings him the text and sits in his office while he translates, waiting to carry the finished text back to the governor's office.

A Chinese iron foundry is seeking to modernize its operations, and in response to its queries receives five bids: one from Japan, two from the United States, one from Spain, and one from Egypt. As requested, all five bids are in English, which the directors can read adequately. When the bids arrive, however, the directors discover that their English is not sufficient; especially the bids from Japan, Spain, and Egypt, since they were written by nonnative speakers of English, pose insuperable difficulties for the directors. With a ten-day deadline looming before them, they decide to have the five bids translated into Mandarin. Since they will need at least four days to read and assess the bids, they need to find enough translators to translate a total of over 20,000 words in six days. A team of English professors and their students from the university undertake the task, with time off their teaching and studying.

One of the most common complaints translators make about this quite reasonable demand of timeliness is that all too often clients are unaware of the time it takes to do a translation. Since they have written proposals or bids themselves, they think nothing of allowing their own people two weeks to write a forty-page document; since they have never translated anything, they expect a translator to translate this document in two days.

The frustrating slowness of translation (as of all text-production) is one of several factors that fuel dreams of machine translation: just as computers can do calculations in nanoseconds that it would take humans hours, days, weeks to do, so too would the ideal translation machine translate in minutes a text that took five people two weeks to write. User-oriented thought about translation is product-driven: one begins with the desired end result, in this case meeting a very short deadline, and then orders it done. How it is done, at what human cost, is a secondary issue. If in-house translators regularly complain about ungodly workloads before critical deadlines, if agencies keep trying to educate you regarding the difficulty and slowness of translation, you begin to shop around for machine translation software, or perhaps commission a university to build one especially for your company. The main thing is that the translations be done reliably and quickly (and cheaply – more of that in a moment). If human translators take too long, explore computer solutions.

It is not often recognized that the demand for timeliness is very similar to the demand for reliability, and thus to the theoretical norm of equivalence or fidelity. Indeed, timeliness is itself a form of reliability: when one's conception of translation is product-driven, all one asks of the process is that it be reliable, in the complex sense of creating a solidly trustworthy product on demand (and not costing too much). We need it *now*. And it has to be *good*. If a human translator can do it rapidly and reliably, fine; if not, make me a machine that can.

This is not to say that a product-driven user-orientation is pernicious or evil. It often seems callous to the translator who is asked to perform like a machine, working long hours at repetitive and uninspiring tasks, and expected not to complain (indeed, to be grateful for the work). But it is important not to become narcissistic in this. Translators are not the only ones working long hours at uninspiring tasks. Indeed the people who expect translations to be done reliably and rapidly are often putting in long exhausting hours themselves. The reality of any given situation, especially but not exclusively in the business world, is typically that an enormous quantity of work needs to be done immediately, preferably yesterday, and there are never enough hands or eyes or brains to do it. Yes, in an ideal world no one would have to do boring, uninspiring work; until someone builds a world like that, however, we are stuck in this one, where deadlines all too often seem impossible to meet.

What we can do, as translators and translation teachers, is to reframe the question of speed from an internal viewpoint, a translator-orientation. How can we enhance the translator's speed without simply mechanizing it? More on this in the next chapter.

Cost

Reliably, rapidly – and above all *cheaply*. Cost controls virtually all translation. A translation that the client considers too expensive will not be done. A translation that the translator considers too cheap may not get done either, if the translator has a strong enough sense of self-worth, or an accurate enough sense of the market, to refuse to work virtually for free. Private persons with a book they would like translated and no knowledge of the market may call a translator and ask how much it would cost to have the book translated; when they hear the ballpark figure they are typically shocked. "I was thinking maybe a couple hundred! Certainly not five thousand!" Where translators are professionally unorganized – as they are in most of the world – a small group of quasi-professional translators can undercut professional translators' fees and make those fees seem exorbitant, even when by translating at those market rates 40–60 hours per week a translator can just barely stay above the poverty line. When "quality" or reliability suffers as a result (and it almost always does), it is easy to blame the result on all translators, on the profession as a whole.

Trade-offs

From a user's "external" point of view, obviously, the ideal translation would be utterly reliable, available immediately, and free. Like most ideals, this one is impossible. Nothing is utterly reliable, everything takes time, and there ain't no such thing as a free lunch.

Even in a less than ideal world, however, one can still hope for the best possible *realistic* outcome: a translation that is reasonably reliable, delivered in good time before the deadline, and relatively inexpensive. Unfortunately, even these lowered expectations are often unreasonable, and trade-offs have to be considered:

- *The closer one attempts to come to perfect reliability, the more the translation will cost and the longer it will take* (two or three translators, each of whom checks the others' work, will improve reliability and speed while adding cost and time).

- *The shorter the time span allowed for the translation, the more it will cost and the harder it will be to guarantee reliability* (one translator who puts aside all other work to do a job quickly will charge a rush fee, and in her rush and mounting exhaustion may make – and fail to catch – stupid mistakes; a group of translators will cost more, and may introduce terminological inconsistencies).

- *The less one is willing to pay for a translation, the harder it will be to ensure reliability and to protect against costly delays* (the only translators willing to work at a cut rate are non-professionals whose language, research, translation, and editing skills may be wholly inadequate to the job; a non-professional working alone may also take ill and not be able to tell another translator how to pick up where s/he left off, or may lack the professional discipline needed to set and maintain a pace that will ensure timely completion).

I wonder if anyone on the list has had an experience similar to mine. I work at a large company on a contract basis. I've been with them, off and on, for over 2.5 years now. At present, I work full-time, some part-time, and often – overtime. The work load is steady, and they see that the need in my services is constant. They refuse to hire me permanently, though. Moreover, they often hire people who are engineers, bilingual, but without linguistic skills or translator credentials, or abilities. The management doesn't seem to care about the quality of translation, even though they have had a chance to find out the difference between accurate translation and sloppy language, because it has cost them time and money to unravel some of the mistakes of those pseudo-translators. I know that I will be extraordinarily lucky if they ever decide to hire me on a permanent basis.

Ethically, I can't tell them that the work of other people is . . . hm . . . substandard. Most engineers with whom I have been working closely know what care I take to convey the material as accurately as possible, and how much more efficient the communication becomes when they have a good translator.

I also know that it is supposed to be a part of translator's job to educate his/her clients. I tried that . . . . <sigh.>

Rina

These real-world limitations on the user's dream of instant reliable translation free of charge are the translator's professional salvation. If users could get exactly what they wanted, they either would not need us or would be able to dictate the nature and cost of our labor without the slightest consideration for our needs. Because we need to get paid for doing work that we enjoy, we must be willing to meet nontranslating users' expectations wherever possible; but because those expectations can never be met perfectly, users must be willing to meet us halfway as well. Any user who wants a reliable translation will have to pay market rates for it and allow a reasonable time period for its completion; anyone who wants a reliable translation faster than that will have to pay above market rates. This is simple economics; and users understand economics. We provide an essential service; the products we create are crucial for the smooth functioning of the world economy, politics, the law, medicine, and so on; much as users may dream of bypassing the trade-offs of real-world translating, then, they remain dependent on what we do, and must adjust to the realities of that situation.

This is not to say that we are in charge, that we are in a position to dictate terms, or that we can ever afford to ignore users' dreams and expectations. If users want to enhance reliability while increasing speed and decreasing cost, we had better be aware of those longings and plan for them. This book doesn't necessarily offer such a plan; such a plan may not even exist yet. What it offers instead is a translator-oriented approach to the field, one that begins with what translators actually do and how they feel about doing it – without ever forgetting the realities of meeting users' needs. In Chapter 2 I will be redefining from the translator's perspective the territory we have been exploring here in Chapter 1: the importance of reliability, income, and *enjoyment*, that last a subjective translator experience that is completely irrelevant to users but may mean the difference between a productive career and burnout.

Discussion

1   The ethics of translation has often been thought to consist of the translator assuming an entirely external perspective on his or her work, thinking about it purely from the user's point of view:

thinking, for example, that accuracy is the only possible goal of translation; that the translator has no right to a personal opinion or interpretation; that the finished product, the translated text, is the only thing that matters. What other ethical considerations are important? Is it possible to allow translators their full humanity – their opinions, interpretations, likes and dislikes, enthusiasms and boredoms – while still insisting on ethical professional behavior that meets users' expectations?

2   Translators are usually, and understandably, hostile toward machine translation systems, which promise clients enormous increases in speed at a fraction of the cost of human translation. Translators typically point to the low quality or reliability of machine-translated texts, but in some technical fields, where style is not a high priority, the use of constrained source languages (specially written so as to be unambiguous for machine parsing) makes reliability possible along with speed and low cost. How should translators meet this challenge? Translate faster and charge less? Retrain to become pre- and post-editors of machine translation texts? Learn to translate literature?

Exercises

1   List the stereotyped character traits of your country, your region, your group (gender, class, race, education level, etc.). Next list user-oriented ideals for the translator – the personal characteristics that would make a translator "good" or "reliable" in the eyes of a non-translating employer or client. Now compare the lists, paying special attention to the mismatches – the character traits that would make people like you "unqualified" for the translation field – and discuss the transformations that would be required in either the people who want to be translators or in society's thinking about translation to make you a good translator.

2   Dramatize a scene in the conference room of a large international corporation that needs a text translated into the executives' native language by a certain date. What are the parameters of the discussion? What are the main issues? What are the pressures and the

worries? Try to perceive translation as much as possible from this "external" point of view.

3   Work in small groups to list as many different types of translation user (including the same user in different use situations) as you can. Then identify the type of text reliability that each would be likely to favor – what each would want a "good" translation to do, or be like.

4   Break up into groups of three, in each group a source-language user, a target-language user, and a translator. Take a translation use-situation from this chapter and try to negotiate (a) who is going to commission and pay for the translation, the source or target user or both (who stands to benefit most from it? which user has economic power over the other?) and (b) how much money is available to pay the translator (will the translator, who is a pro-fessional, do it for that money?).

Suggestions for further reading

Gutt (1992), Hewson and Martin (1991), Holz-Mänttäri (1984), Pym (1992a, 1993, 1995)

Chapter 2

Internal knowledge:
the translator's view

- **Who are translators?** 26
- **Professional pride** 28
- Reliability 29
- Involvement in the profession 30
- Ethics 30
- **Income** 33
- Speed 34
- Project management 39
- Raising the status of the profession 39
- **Enjoyment** 40
  - **Discussion** 44
  - **Exercises** 45
  - **Suggestions for further reading** 46

T HESIS: While translators must meet the needs of translation users in order to make a living, it is also important for them to integrate those needs into a translator-oriented perspective on the work, seeing the reliability that users demand in the larger context of professional pride (including also involvement in the profession and ethics); seeing the timeliness users want in terms of enhanced income, requiring speed but also connected to project management and raising the status of the profession; and insisting on the importance of actually enjoying the work.

Who are translators?

What does it take to be a translator or interpreter? What kind of person would even want to, let alone be able to, sit at a computer or in court day after day turning words and phrases in one language into words and phrases in another? Isn't this an awfully tedious and unrewarding profession?

It can be. For many people it is. Some people who love it initially get tired of it, burn out on it, and move on to other endeavors. Others can only do it on the side, a few hours a day or a week or even a month: they are writers or teachers or editors by day, but for an hour every evening, or for an afternoon one or two Saturdays a month, they translate, sometimes for money, sometimes for fun, mostly (one hopes) for both. If a really big job comes along and the timing and money are right, they will spend a whole week translating, eight to ten hours a day; but at the end of that week they feel completely drained and are ready to go back to their regular work.

Other people, possibly even the majority (though to my knowledge there are no statistics on this), translate full time – and don't burn out. How do they do it? What skills do they possess that makes it possible for them to "become" doctors, lawyers, engineers, poets, business executives, even if only briefly and on the computer screen? Are they talented actors who feel comfortable shifting from role to role? How do they know so much about specialized vocabularies? Are they walking dictionaries and encyclopedias? Are they whizzes at *Trivial Pursuit*?

These are the questions we'll be exploring throughout the book; but briefly, yes, translators and (especially) interpreters do all have something of the actor in them, the mimic, the impersonator, and they do develop remarkable recall skills that will enable them to remember a word (often in a foreign language) that they have heard only once. Translators and interpreters are voracious and omnivorous readers, people who are typically in the middle of four books at once, in several languages, fiction and nonfiction, technical and humanistic subjects, anything and everything. They are hungry for real-world experience as well, through travel, living abroad for extended periods, learning foreign languages and cultures, and above all paying attention to how people use language all around them: the plumber, the kids' teachers, the convenience store clerk, the doctor, the bartender, friends and colleagues from this or that region or social class, and so on. Translation is often called a profession of second choice: many translators were first professionals in other fields, sometimes several other fields in succession, and only turned to translation when they lost or quit those jobs or moved to a country where they were unable to practice them; as translators they often mediate between former colleagues in two or more different language communities. Any gathering of translators is certain to be a diverse group, not only because well over half of the people there will be from different countries, and almost all will have lived abroad, and all will shift effortlessly in conversation from language to language, but because by necessity translators and interpreters carry a wealth of different "selves" or "personalities" around inside them, ready to be reconstructed on the computer screen whenever a new text arrives, or out into the airwaves whenever a new speaker steps up to the podium. A crowd of translators always seems much bigger than the actual bodies present.

But then there are non-translators who share many of these same characteristics: diplomats, language teachers, world travelers . . . What special skills make a well-traveled, well-read language lover a translator?

My father worked for the international area of a major
Brazilian bank. As a consequence, I lived in 8 countries
and 10 cities between the ages of 1 and 19. My parents
learned the languages of the places we lived in ''on loca-
tion''. My father never wanted us (my 3 brothers and I) to
study in American or French schools (which can be found anywhere), but instead forced us to learn and study in the language of the place. My parents encouraged travel and
language studies, and since I was 14, I traveled alone
throughout Europe. I learned the 3Rs in Spanish, did high
school in Italian and Portuguese. In Luxembourg, I studied
at the European School in three languages at the same time
(French, English and Italian) and spoke Portuguese at home.
Italian used to be choice for girlfriends:-)

The outcome: I speak Portuguese, English, Spanish, Italian, and French and translate from one into the other.

I have always worked with the set of languages I learned in
my youth. I have started learning Russian, but I didn't like
my teacher's accent. For the future, I plan to study Chinese
(I have a brother who lives in Taiwan and a nephew who speaks
it fluently).

Renato Beninatto

Not surprisingly, perhaps, the primary characteristics of a good
translator are similar to the expectations translation users have for the
ideal translation: a good translator is reliable and fast, and will work
for the going rate. From an internal point of view, however, the
expectations for translation are rather different than they look from
the outside. For the translator, reliability is important mainly as a
source of professional pride, which also includes elements that are of
little or no significance to translation users; speed is important mainly
as a source of increased income, which can be enhanced through
other channels as well; and it is extremely important, perhaps even
most important of all, that the translator enjoy the work, a factor
that is of little significance to outsiders. Let's consider these three
"internal" requirements in order: professional pride, income, and
enjoyment.

Professional pride

From the user's point of view, it is essential to be able to rely on
translation – not only on the text, but on the translator as well, and

generally on the entire translation process. Because this is important to the people who pay the bills, it will be important to the translator as well; the pragmatic considerations of keeping your job (for in-house people) or continuing to get offered jobs (for freelancers) will mandate a willingness to satisfy an employer's or client's needs.

But for the translator or interpreter a higher consideration than money or continued employability is professional pride, professional integrity, professional self-esteem. We all want to feel that the job we are doing is important, that we do it well, and that the people we do it for appreciate our work. Most people, in fact, would rather take professional pride in a job that pays less than get rich doing things they don't believe in. Despite the high value placed on making a lot of money (and certainly it would be nice!), a high salary gives little pleasure without pride in the work.

The areas in and through which translators typically take professional pride are reliability, involvement in the profession, and ethics.

Reliability

As we saw in Chapter 1, reliability in translation is largely a matter of meeting the user's needs: translating the texts the user needs translated, in the way the user wants them translated, by the user's deadline. The demands placed on the translator by the attempt to be reliable from the user's point of view are sometimes impossible; sometimes disruptive to the translator's private life; sometimes morally repugnant; often physically and mentally exhausting. If the demands are at all possible, however, in many or even most cases the translator's desire to take professional pride in reliability will override these other considerations, and s/he will stay up all night doing a rush job, cancel a pleasant evening outing with a friend, or translate a text reliably that s/he finds morally or politically loathsome.

Professional pride in reliability is the main reason we will spend hours hunting down a single term. What is our pay for that time? Virtually nothing. But it feels enormously important to get just the right word.

Involvement in the profession

It is a matter of little or no concern to translation users, but of great importance to translators, what translator associations or unions we belong to, what translator conferences we go to, what courses we take in the field, how we network with other translators in our region and language pair(s). These "involvements" sometimes help translators translate better, which is important for users and thus for the pride we take in reliability. More crucially, however, they help us feel better about being translators; they enhance our professional self-esteem, which will often sustain us emotionally through boring and repetitive and low-paid jobs. Reading about translation, talking about translation with other translators, discussing problems and solutions related to linguistic transfer, user demands, nonpayment, and the like, taking classes on translation, attending translator conferences – all this gives us the strong sense that we are are not isolated underpaid flunkies but professionals surrounded by other professionals who share our concerns. Involvement in the translation profession may even give us the intellectual tools and professional courage to stand up to unreasonable demands, to educate clients and employers rather than submit meekly and seethe inwardly. Involvement in the profession helps us realize that translation users need us as much as we need them: they have the money we need; we have the skills they need. And we will sell those skills to them, not abjectly, submissively, wholly on their terms, but from a position of professional confidence and strength.

Ethics

The professional ethics of translation have traditionally been defined very narrowly: it is unethical for the translator to distort the meaning of the source text. As we have seen, this conception of translator ethics is far too narrow even from the user's point of view: there are many cases when the translator is explicitly asked to "distort" the meaning of the source text in specific ways, as when adapting a text for television, a children's book, or an advertising campaign.

From the translator's internal point of view, the ethics of translation are more complicated still. What is the translator to do, for example, when asked to translate a text that s/he finds offensive? Or, to put that differently, how does the translator proceed when professional ethics (loyalty to the person paying for the translation) clash with personal ethics (one's own political and moral beliefs)? What does the feminist translator do when asked to translate a blatantly sexist text? What does the liberal translator do when asked to translate a neo-Nazi text? What does the environmentalist translator do when asked to translate an advertising campaign for an environmentally irresponsible chemical company?

As long as thinking about translation has been entirely dominated by an external (nontranslator) point of view, these have been nonquestions – questions that have not been asked, indeed that have been unaskable. The translator translates whatever texts s/he is asked to translate, and does so in a way that satisfies the translation user's needs. The translator *has* no personal point of view that has any relevance at all to the act of translation.

From an internal point of view, however, these questions must be asked. Translators are human beings, with opinions, attitudes, beliefs, and feelings. Translators who are regularly required to translate texts that they find abhorrent may be able to suppress their revulsion for a few weeks, or months, possibly even years; but they will not be able to continue suppressing those negative feelings forever. Translators, like all professionals, want to take pride in what they do; if a serious clash between their personal ethics and an externally defined professional ethics makes it difficult or impossible to feel that pride, they will eventually be forced to make dramatic decisions about where and under what conditions they want to work.

And so increasingly translators are beginning to explore new avenues by which to reconcile their ethics as human beings with their work as translators. The Québécoise feminist translator Susanne Lotbinière-Harwood (1991), for example, tells us that she no longer translates works by men: the pressure is too great to adopt a male voice, and she refuses to be coopted. In her literary translations of works by women she works very hard to help them create a woman-centered language in the target culture as well. In *The Subversive Scribe* Suzanne Jill Levine (1992) tells us that in her translations of flagrantly sexist Latin American male authors, she works – often with the approval and even collaboration of the authors themselves – to subvert their sexism.

This broader "internal" definition of translator ethics is highly controversial. For many translators it is unthinkable to do anything that might harm the interests of the person or group that is paying for the translation (the translation "commissioner" or "initiator"). For other translators, the thought of being rendered utterly powerless to make ethical decisions based on personal commitments or belief structures is equally abhorrent; it feels to some like the Nürnberg "ethics" of the SS, the claim that "we were just obeying orders." When the translator's private ethics clash substantially with the interests of the commissioner, to what extent can the translator afford to live by those ethics and still go on earning a living? And on the other hand, to what extent can the translator afford to compromise with those ethics and still go on taking professional pride in his or her work?

A British translator living in Brazil who is very active in local and international environmentalist groups is called by an agency with an ongoing job, translating into English everything published in Brazil on smoking. Every week a packet of photocopies arrives, almost all of it based on scientific research in Brazil and elsewhere on the harmful effects of smoking. As a fervent nonsmoker and opponent of the tobacco industry, she is pleased to be translating these texts. The texts are also relatively easy, many of them are slight variations on a single press release, and the money is good.

Gradually, however, ethical doubts begin to gnaw at her. Who in the English-speaking world is so interested in what Brazilians write about smoking, and so rich, as to pay her all this money to have it all in English? And surely this person or group isn't just interested in Brazil; surely she is one of hundreds of translators around the world, one in each country, hired by a local agency to translate everything written on smoking in their countries as well. Who could the ultimate user be but one of the large tobacco companies in the United States or England? She starts paying closer attention, and by reading between the lines is finally able to determine that the commission comes from the biggest tobacco company in the world, one responsible for the destruction of thousands of acres of the Amazon rain forest for the drying of tobacco leaves, a neocolonialist enterprise that has disrupted not only the ecosystem of the rain forest but the economy of the Amazonian Indians. Gradually her ethical doubts turn into distaste for her work: she

Income

Professionals do their work because they enjoy it, because they take pride in it – and also, of course, to earn a living. Professional translators translate for money. And most professional translators (like most professionals of any field) feel that they don't make enough money, and would like to make more. There are at least three ways to do this, two of them short-term strategies, the third long-term: translate faster (especially but not exclusively if you are a freelancer); create your own agency and farm translation jobs out to other freelancers (take a cut for project management); and (the long-term strategy) work to educate clients and the general public

---

is essentially helping the largest tobacco company in the world spy on the opposition.

One week, then, a sixty-page booklet comes to her, written by a Brazilian antitobacco activist group. It is well researched and wonderfully written; it is a joy to translate. It ends on a plea for support, detailing several ways in which the tobacco industry has undermined its work. Suddenly she realizes what she has to do: she has to give her translation of this booklet, paid for by the tobacco industry, to this group that is fighting this rather lucrative source of her income. Not only would that help them disseminate their research to the English-speaking world; sales of the booklet would provide them with a much-needed source of funding.

So she calls the group, and sets up a meeting; worried about the legality of her action, she also asks their lawyer to determine what if any legal risks she and they might be taking, and be present at the meeting. When at the meeting she is reassured that it is perfectly legal for her to give them the translation, she hands over the diskette and leaves.

No legal action is ever taken against her, but she never gets another packet in the mail from the agency; that source of income dries up entirely, and instantly. It seems likely that the tobacco company has a spy in the antitobacco group, because she is cut off immediately, the same week, perhaps even the same day – not, for instance, months later when the booklet is published in English.

about the importance of translation, so that money managers will be more willing to pay premium fees for translation.

Speed

Speed and income are not directly related for all translators. They are for freelancers. The situation is somewhat more complex than this, but basically the faster a freelancer translates, the more money s/he makes. (Obviously, this requires a large volume of incoming jobs; if, having done a job quickly, you have no other work to do, translating faster will not increase your income.)

For in-house translators the links between speed and money are considerably less obvious. Most in-house translators are expected to translate fast, so that employability, and thus income, is complexly related to translation speed. Translation speed is enforced in a variety of unofficial ways, mostly though phone calls and visits from engineers, editors, bosses, and other irate people who want their job done instantly and can't understand why you haven't done it yet. Some in-house translators, however, do translations for other companies in a larger concern, and submit records of billable hours to their company's bookkeeping department; in these cases monthly targets may be set (200 billable hours per month, invoices worth three times your monthly income, etc.) and translators who exceed those targets may be given bonuses. Some translation agencies also set such targets for their in-house people.

A translator's translating speed is controlled by a number of factors:

1 typing speed

2 the level of text difficulty

3 personal preferences or style

4 job stress, general mental state.

(1) and (2) should be obvious: the faster one types, the faster one will (potentially) be able to translate; the harder the text, the slower it will be to translate. (4) is also relatively straightforward: if you work under great pressure, with minimum reward or praise, your general

state of mind may begin to erode your motivation, which may in turn slow you down.

(3) is perhaps less obvious. Who would "prefer" to translate slowly? Don't all translators want to translate as rapidly as possible? After all, isn't that what our clients want?

The first thing to remember is that not everyone translates for clients. There is no financial motivation for rapid translation when one translates for fun. The second is that not all clients need a translation next week. The acquisitions editor at a university press who has commissioned a literary or scholarly translation may want it done quickly, for example, but "quickly" may mean in six months rather than a year, or one year rather than two.

And the third thing to remember is that not everyone is willing or able to force personal preferences into conformity with market demands. Some people just do prefer to translate slowly, taking their time, savoring each word and phrase, working on a single paragraph for an hour, perfecting each sentence before moving on to the next. Such people will probably never make a living as freelancers; but not all translators *are* freelancers, and not all translators need to make a living at it. People with day jobs, high-earning spouses, or family money can afford to translate just as slowly as they please. Many literary translators are academics who teach and do research for a salary and translate in their free time, often for little or no money, out of sheer love for the original text; in such situations rapid-fire translation may even feel vaguely sacrilegious.

There can be no doubt, however, that in most areas of professional translation, speed is a major virtue. I once heard a freelancer tell a gathering of student translators, "If you're fast, go freelance; if you're slow, get an in-house job." But translation divisions in large corporations are not havens for slow translators either. The instruction would be more realistic like this: "If you're fast, get an in-house job; if you're really fast, so your fingers are a blur on the keyboard, go freelance. If you're slow, get a day job and translate in the evenings."

Above all, work to increase your speed. How? The simplest step is to improve your typing skills. If you're not using all ten fingers, teach yourself to, or take a typing class at a community college or other adult education institute. If you're using all ten fingers but looking at the keyboard rather than the screen while you type, train yourself to type without looking at the keys. Take time out from translating to practice typing faster.

— —

Well Richard, maybe it's different for your language pair, but we don't consider 600 [words per hour, wph] to be any great shakes – it's rather normal. For most of our folks, 600 is a good rate when some resarch is required, and 1000 to 1500 wph is not unusual for some for the historical or legal texts we do when the translators are highly familiar with the subject matter. Some of our star translators manage – seriously – daily production of 10 to 15 thousand words. And have been doing so for years. I personally consider 7500 to 9500 to be a good day's work. Perhaps if we were translating great literature it would take longer, but for reference materials, legal briefs, and piles of government documents, you would starve to death at 200 wph.

Sincerely,
Vladimir Hindrichs

* * * * *

I also reacted to Ryszard's remark saying that 600 words per hour is not a big deal. But come on, guys, be sensible. 1,500 words per hour? For 10 hours a day? For five days a week?

Assuming that a star translator of yours has a daily production output of 10,000 words, s/he works only four days a week and 48 weeks a year, then her/his annual output would run into something like four volumes of Britannica (I mean size, not contents).

Is it possible at all, even if one works exclusively with "reference materials, legal briefs, and piles of government documents"? Or maybe I was sluggish and lazy with ca. 3,000 pages (1,800 keystrokes per page) last year?

JK

* * * * *

The figures being bandied about here are possible but very rare and not on a sustained basis, nor is it likely that they are for checked and revised output, but raw characters in a first draft. They will also only apply to very experienced translators who generally translate the same subject matter all the time. That's the path to high productivity and one path to high income as a translator.

Association surveys and agency statistics indicate that most translators (full-time professionals) average around 2,000 checked and completed per day.

Talk about more tends to be boasting or else comes from "characters" trying to pursuade people they should accept low rates, because "if you average the normal 12,000 a day that means you'll be a millionaire by next Christmas".

Even repetitive work like patents with long claims and abstracts done using TM cannot be reasonably done at that sort of rate all the time.

I'm considered fast and have managed 10,000+ in a day, but my output falls noticeably for a few days after that. The other "known-for-being-fast" translators I know all say the same thing. So anyone out there feeling inferior because they don't constantly achieve figures anywhere near this can cheer up.

Michael Benis

* * * * *

If you allow me my 2 centavos, the output will depend highly on the material to be translated. When I worked with technical translations for IBM, my output was constant: 15,000 words per day during 2 years in a row.

But I got tired of IBM, and started doing what I really love: movies, training videos, TV shows.

When I work with training videos (hardware and software training), I don't have texts to work with, but I have to listen to the tape and write the translation. It is a mix of interpreter and translator job. In this case, my normal output is 6,000 words per day. But it can fall to 3,000 or 2,000 if the speaker does not have a good pronunciation. Even so, I will still be doing a very fast job.

Now, talking about movies, it is impossible to determine how many words per day, because movies are a Pandora box. A 100-minute movie can have 5,000 words or 17,000 words. I can translate a 17,000 words movie as simple as Hearts and Souls (104 min.) in 8 hours, but a more complex movie like The Doors (140 min.), with less than 14,000 words, took me 14 hours to translate. And my clients say I am fast (I don't know many movie translators to make comparisons).

So I guess that the diversity of subjects must be taken into account. Depending on the subject, an average of 6,000 words a day can be much better than an average of 15,000 words a day in a completely different (but much easier and repetitive) subject.

XXXXXX
Jussara Simoes

- -

The other factors governing translating speed are harder to change. The speed with which you process difficult vocabulary and syntactic structures depends partly on practice and experience. The more you translate, the more well-trodden synaptic pathways are laid in your brain from the source to the target language, so that the translating of certain source-language structures begins to work like a macro on the computer: zip, the target-language equivalent practically leaps through

37

your fingers to the screen. Partly also it depends on subliminal reconstruction skills that we will be exploring in the rest of the book.

The hardest thing to change is a personal preference for slow translation. Translating faster than feels comfortable increases stress, decreases enjoyment (for which see below), and speeds up translator burnout. It is therefore more beneficial to let translating speeds increase slowly, and as naturally as possible, growing out of practice and experience rather than a determination to translate as fast as possible right now.

In addition, with translating speed as with other things, variety is the spice of life. Even the fastest translators cannot comfortably translate at top speed all day, all week, all month, year-round. In this sense it is fortunate, in fact, that research, networking, and editing slow the translator down; for most translators a "broken" or varied rhythm is preferable to the high stress of marathon top-speed translating. You translate at top speed for an hour or two, and the phone rings; it is an agency offering you a job. You go back to your translation while they fax it to you, then stop again to look the new job over and call back to say yes or no. Another hour or two of high-speed translating and a first draft of the morning job is done; but there are eight or ten words that you didn't find in your dictionaries, so you get on the phone or the fax or e-mail, trying to find someone who knows. Phone calls get immediate answers; faxes and e-mail messages take time. While you're waiting, you pick up the new translation job, start glancing through it, and before you know it (some sort of automatism clicks in) you're translating it, top speed. An hour later the fax machine rings; it's a fax from a friend overseas who has found some of your words. You stop translating to look through the fax. You're unsure about one of the words, so you get back on e-mail and send out a message over a listserver, asking other subscribers whether this seems right to them; back in your home computer, you jump over to the morning translation and make the other changes. You notice you're hungry, so you walk to the kitchen and make a quick lunch, which you eat while looking over the fax one more time. Then back to the afternoon translation, top speed. If the fax machine hasn't rung in an hour or two, you find a good stopping place and check your e-mail; nothing for you, but there's a debate going on about a group of words you know something about, so you type out a message and send it. Then you edit the morning translation for a while, a boring job that has to be done some time; and back to the afternoon translation.

And all this keeps you from burning out on your own translating speed. Interruptions may cut into your earnings; but they may also prolong your professional life (and your sanity).

Project management

Another effective way to increase your income is to create your own agency: farm out some of your work to other freelancers and take a cut of the fee for project management, including interfacing with the client, editing, desktop publishing, etc. Most agency-owners do not, in fact, immediately begin earning more money than they did as freelancers; building up a substantial clientele takes time, often years. A successful agency-owner may earn three or four times what a freelancer earns; but that sort of success only comes after many years of just getting by, struggling to make payroll (and sometimes earning *less* than you did before), and dealing with all the added headaches of complicated bookkeeping, difficult clients, unreliable freelancers, insurance, etc.

There is, of course, much more to be said on the subject of creating your own agency; but perhaps a textbook on "becoming a translator" is not the place to say it.

Raising the status of the profession

This long-range goal is equally difficult to deal with in a textbook of this sort, but it should not be forgotten in discussions of enhancing the translator's income. Some business consultants become millionaires by providing corporate services that are not substantially different from the services provided by translators. Other business consultants are paid virtually nothing. The difference lies in the general perception of the relative value of the services offered. The higher the value placed on the service, the more money a company will be willing to budget for it. Many small companies (and even some large ones) value translation so little that they are not willing to pay anything for it, and do it themselves; others grudgingly admit that they need outside help, but are unwilling to pay the going rate, so they hire anyone they can find who is willing to do the work for almost nothing. One of the desired outcomes of the work done by translator associations and unions, translator training programs, and translation scholars to raise the general awareness of translation and its importance to society is, in fact, to raise translator income.

Enjoyment

One would think that burnout rates would be high among translators. The job is not only underpaid and undervalued by society; it involves long hours spent alone with uninspiring texts working under the stress of short deadlines. One would think, in fact, that most translators would burn out on the job after about three weeks.

And maybe some do. That most don't, that one meets freelance translators who are still content in their jobs after thirty years, says something about the operation of the greatest motivator of all: they enjoy their work. They must – for what else would sustain them? Not the fame and fortune; not the immortal brilliance of the texts they translate. It must be that somehow they find a sustaining pleasure in the work itself.

In what, precisely? And why? Is it a matter of personal style: some people just happen to love translating, others don't? Or are there ways to teach oneself to find enhanced enjoyment in translation?

Not all translators enjoy every aspect of the work; fortunately, the field is diverse enough to allow individuals to minimize their displeasure. Some translators dislike dealing with clients, and so tend to gravitate toward work with agencies, which are staffed by other translators who understand the difficulties translators face. Some translators go stir-crazy all alone at home, and long for adult company; they tend to get in-house jobs, in translation divisions of large corporations or translation agencies or elsewhere, so that they are surrounded by other people, who help relieve the tedium with social interaction. Some translators get tired of translating all day; they take breaks to write poetry, or attend a class at the local college, or go for a swim, or find other sources of income to pursue every third hour of the day, or every other day of the week. Some translators get tired of the repetitiveness of their jobs, translating the same kind of text day in, day out; they develop other areas of specialization, actively seek out different kinds of texts, perhaps try their hand at translating poetry or drama. (We will be dealing with these preferences in greater detail in Chapter 3.)

Still, no matter how one diversifies one's professional life, translating (like most jobs) involves a good deal of repetitive drudgery that will simply never go away. And the bottom line to that is: if you can't learn to enjoy even the drudgery, you won't last long in the profession. There is both drudgery and pleasure to be found in reliability, in painstaking research into the right word, in brain-wracking attempts to recall a word that you know you've heard, in working on a translation until it feels just right. There is both drudgery and pleasure to be found in speed, in translating as fast as you can go, so that the keyboard hums. There is both drudgery and pleasure to be found in taking it slowly, staring dreamily at (and through) the source text, letting your mind roam, rolling target-language words and phrases around on your tongue. There are ways of making a mind-numbingly boring text come alive in your imagination, of turning technical documentation into epic poems, weather reports into songs.

In fact in some sense it is not too much to say that the translator's most important skill is the ability to learn to enjoy everything about the job. This is not the translator's most important skill from the user's point of view, certainly; the user wants a reliable text rapidly and cheaply, and if a translator provides it while hating every minute of the work, so be it. If as a result of hating the work the translator burns out, so be that too. There are plenty of translators in the world; if one burns out and quits the profession, ten others will be clamoring for the privilege to take his or her place.

But it is the most important skill for the translators themselves. Yes, the ability to produce reliable texts is essential; yes, speed is important. But a fast and reliable translator who hates the work, or who is bored with it, feels it is a waste of time, will not last long in the profession – and what good are speed and reliability to the ex-translator? "Boy, I used to be *fast*." Pleasure in the work will motivate a mediocre translator to enhance her or his reliability and speed; boredom or distaste in the work will make even a highly competent translator sloppy and unreliable.

And in some sense this textbook is an attempt to teach translators to enjoy their work more – to drill not specific translation or vocabulary skills but what we might call "pretranslation" skills, attitudinal skills that (should) precede and undergird every "verbal" or "linguistic" approach to a text: intrinsic motivation, openness, receptivity, a desire to constantly be growing and changing and learning new things, a commitment to the profession, and a delight in words, images, intellectual challenges, and people.

In fact the fundamental assumptions underlying the book's approach to translation might be summed up in the following list of axioms:

1   Translation is more about people than about words.

2   Translation is more about the jobs people do and the way they see their world than it is about registers or sign systems.

3   Translation is more about the creative imagination than it is about rule-governed text analysis.

4   The translator is more like an actor or a musician (a performer)

The structure of flow. The autotelic [self-rewarding] experience is described in very similar terms regardless of its context . . . Artists, athletes, composers, dancers, scientists, and people from all walks of life, when they describe how it feels when they are doing something that is worth doing for its own sake, use terms that are interchangeable in the minutest details. This unanimity suggests that order in consciousness produces a very specific experiential state, so desirable that one wishes to replicate it as often as possible. To this state we have given the name of "flow," using a term that many respondents used in their interviews to explain what the optimal experience felt like.

Challenges and skills. The universal precondition for flow is that a person should perceive that there is something for him or her to do, and that he or she is capable of doing it. In other words, optimal experience requires a balance between the challenges perceived in a given situation and the skills a person brings to it. The "challenge" includes any opportunity for action that humans are able to respond to: the vastness of the sea, the possibility of rhyming words, concluding a business deal, or winning the friendship of another person are all classic challenges that set many flow experiences in motion. But any possibility for action to which a skill corresponds can produce an autotelic experience.

It is this feature that makes flow such a dynamic force in evolution.

than like a tape recorder.

5   The translator, even of highly technical texts, is more like a poet or a novelist than like a machine translation system.

Which is not to say that translation is not about words, or phrases, or registers, or sign systems. Clearly those things are important in translation. It is to say rather that it is more productive for the translator to think of such abstractions in larger human contexts, as a part of what people do and say.

Nor is it to say that human translation is utterly unlike the operation of a tape recorder or machine translation system. Those analogies can be usefully drawn. It is merely to say that machine analogies may be counterproductive for the translator in her or his

---

For every activity might engender it, but at the same time no activity can sustain it for long unless both the challenges and the skills become more complex . . . For example, a tennis player who enjoys the game will want to reproduce the state of enjoyment by playing as much as possible. But the more such individuals play, the more their skills improve. Now if they continue to play against opponents of the same level as before, they will be bored. This always happens when skills surpass challenges. To return in flow and replicate the enjoyment they desire, they will have to find stronger opposition.

To remain in flow, one must increase the complexity of the activity by developing new skills and taking on new challenges. This holds just as true for enjoying business, for playing the piano, or for enjoying one's marriage, as for the game of tennis. Heraclitus's dictum about not being able to step in the same stream twice holds especially true for flow. This inner dynamic of the optimal experience is what drives the self to higher and higher levels of complexity. It is because of this spiraling compexity that people describe flow as a process of "discovering something new," whether they are shepherds telling how they enjoy caring for their flocks, mothers telling how they enjoy playing with their children, or artists, describing the enjoyment of painting. Flow forces people to stretch themselves, to always take on another challenge, to improve on their abilities.

(Mihaly Csikszentmihalyi, "The Flow Experience and Its Significance for Human Psychology" (1995: 29–30) (with permission))

work, which to be enjoyable must be not mechanical but richly human. Machine analogies fuel formal, systematic thought; they do not succor the translator, alone in a room with a computer and a text, as do more vibrant and imaginative analogies from the world of artistic performance or other humanistic endeavors.

Is this, then, a book of panaceas, a book of pretty lies for translators to use in the rather pathetic pretense that their work is really more interesting than it seems?

No. It is a book about how translators actually view their work; how translating actually feels to successful professionals in the field.

Besides, it is not that thinking about translation in more human terms, more artistic and imaginative terms, simply makes the work *seem* more interesting. Such is the power of the human imagination that it actually makes it *become* more interesting. Imagine yourself bored and you quickly become bored. Imagine yourself a machine with no feelings, a computer processing inert words, and you quickly begin to feel dead, inert, lifeless. Imagine yourself in a movie or a play (or an actual use situation) with other users of the machine whose technical documentation you're translating, all of you using the machine, walking around it, picking it up, pushing buttons and flipping levers, and you begin to feel more alive.

Discussion

1 Should translators be willing to do any kind of text-processing requested, such as editing, summarizing, annotating, desktop publishing? Or should translators be allowed to stick to translating? Explore the borderlines or gray areas between translating and doing something else; discuss the ways in which those gray areas are different for different people.

2 When and how is it ethical or professional to improve a badly written source text in translation? Are there limits to the improvements that the translator can ethically make? (Tightening up sentence structure; combining or splitting up sentences; rearranging sentences; rearranging paragraphs . . .) Is there a limit to the improvements a translator should make without calling the client or agency for approval? A reliable translator is someone who on

the one hand doesn't make unauthorized changes – but who on the other hand doesn't pester the client or agency with queries about every minute little detail. Where should the line of "reliability" be drawn?

Exercises

1   Set up a translating speed test. Translate first 10 words in five minutes; then 20 words in five minutes; then 30, 40, 50, and so on. Stick with the five-minute period each time, but add 10 more words. Try to pace yourself as you proceed through each text segment: when you do 10 words in five minutes, translate two words the first minute, two more the second, etc. When you are trying to do 100 words in five minutes, try to translate 20 words each minute.

   Pay attention to your "comfort zone" as the speed increases. How does it feel to translate slowly? Medium-speed? Fast? When the pace gets too fast for your comfort, stop. Discuss or reflect on what this test tells you about your attitudes toward translation speed.

2   Reflect on times in your studies or a previous career when you were close to burnout – when the stress levels seemed intolerable, when nothing in your work gave you pleasure. Feel again all those feelings. Now direct them to a translation task, for this class or another. Sit and stare at the source text, feeling the stress rising: it's due tomorrow and you haven't started working on it yet; it looks so boring that you want to scream; the person you're doing it for (a client, your teacher) is going to hate your translation; you haven't had time for yourself, time to put your feet up and laugh freely at some silly TV show, in months. Pay attention to your bodily responses: what do you feel?

   Now shake your head and shoulders and relax; put all thought of deadlines and critiques out of your head. Give yourself ten minutes to do nothing; then look through the source text with an eye to doing the silliest translation you can imagine. Start doing the silly translation in your head; imagine a group of friends laughing together over the translation. Work with another person to come up with the funniest bad translation of the text, and laugh together while you work. Now imagine yourself doing the "straight" or serious translation – and compare your feelings about the task now with your feelings under stress.

Suggestions for further reading

Duff (1989), Finlay (1971), Picken (1989), Robinson (1991), Samuelsson-Brown (1993)

Chapter 3

The translator as learner

- **The translator's intelligence**   49
- **The translator's memory**   51
- Representational and procedural memory   52
- Intellectual and emotional memory   53
- Context, relevance, multiple encoding   54
- **The translator's learning styles**   57
- **Context**   62
- Field-dependent/independent   62
- Flexible/structured environment   63
- Independence/dependence/interdependence   64
- Relationship-/content-driven   65
- **Input**   66
- Visual   66
- Auditory   68
- Kinesthetic   70
- **Processing**   73
- Contextual-global   73
- Sequential-detailed/linear   74

- Conceptual (abstract)   75
- Concrete (objects and feelings)   76
- **Response**   76
- Externally/internally referenced   77
- Matching/mismatching   79
- Impulsive-experimental/analytical-reflective   80
  - **Discussion**   82
  - **Exercises**   83
  - **Suggestions for further reading**   91

T HESIS: translation is intelligent activity involving complex processes of conscious and unconscious learning; we all learn in
different ways, and institutional learning should therefore be as flexible and as complex and rich as possible, so as to activate the
channels through which each student learns best.

The translator's intelligence

The question posed by Chapter 2 was: how can the translator maximize speed and enjoyment while not minimizing (indeed if possible
while enhancing) reliability? How can the translator translate faster
and have more fun doing it, while gaining and maintaining a deserved
reputation as a good translator?

At first glance the desires to translate faster and to translate
reliably might seem to be at odds with one another. One common-
sensical assumption says that the faster you do something, the more
likely you are to make mistakes; the more slowly you work, the more
likely that work is to be reliable. The reliable translator shouldn't
make (major) mistakes, so s/he shouldn't try to translate fast.

But increased speed, at least up to a point, really only damages
reliability when you are doing something new or unfamiliar, something that requires concentration, which always takes time. "Old"
and "familiar" actions, especially habitual actions, can be performed
both quickly and reliably because habit takes over. You're late in the
morning, so you brush your teeth, tie your shoes, throw on your coat,
grab your keys and wallet or purse and run for the door, start the car
and get on the road, all in about two minutes – and you don't forget
anything, you don't mistie your shoes, you don't grab a fork and a
spoon instead of your keys, because you've done all these things so
many times before that your body knows what to do, and does it.

And there are important parallels between this "bodily memory" and translation. Experienced translators are fast because they

have translated so much that it often seems as if their "brain" isn't doing the translating – their fingers are. They recognize a familiar source-language structure and they barely pause before their fingers are racing across the keyboard, rendering it into a well-worn target-language structural equivalent, fitted with lexical items that seem to come to them automatically, without conscious thought or logical analysis. Simultaneous interpreters don't seem to be thinking at all – who, the astonished observer wonders, could possibly think that fast? No, it is impossible; the words must be coming to the interpreter from somewhere else, some subliminal or even mystical part of the brain that ordinary people lack.

It should be clear, however, that even at its most "habitual" or "subliminal," translation is not the same sort of activity as tying your shoes or brushing your teeth. Translation is always *intelligent* behavior – even when it seems least conscious or analytical. Translation is a highly complicated process requiring rapid multilayered analyses of semantic fields, syntactic structures, the sociology and psychology of reader- or listener-response, and cultural difference. Like all language use, translation is constantly creative, constantly new. Even translators of the most formulaic source texts, like weather reports, repeatedly face novel situations and must engage in unexpected problem-solving. And most translation tasks are enormously more complex than those. As William H. Calvin writes in *How Brains Think* (1996: 1, 13):

> Piaget used to say that intelligence is what you use when you don't know what to do . . . If you're good at finding the one right answer to life's multiple-choice questions, you're *smart*. But there's more to being *intelligent* – a creative aspect, whereby you invent something new "on the fly." . . . This captures the element of novelty, the coping and groping ability needed when there is no "right answer," when business as usual isn't likely to suffice. Intelligent improvising. Think of jazz improvisations rather than a highly polished finished product, such as a Mozart or Bach concerto. Intelligence is about the *process* of improvising and polishing on the timescale of thought and action.

This book is about such intelligence as it is utilized in professional translation. It seeks both to teach you *about* that intelligence, and to get you to *use* that intelligence in faster, more reliable, and more enjoyable ways. This will entail both developing your analytical skills and learning to sublimate them, becoming both better and faster at analyzing texts and contexts, people and moods: better because more accurate, faster because less aware of your own specific analytical processes. In this chapter we will be exploring the complex learning processes by which novices gradually become experienced professionals; in Chapter 4 we will be developing a theoretical model for the translation process; and in Chapters 5 through 11 we will be moving through a series of thematic fields within translation – people, language, social networks, cultural difference – in which this process must be applied.

The translator's memory

Translation is an intelligent activity, requiring creative problem-solving in novel textual, social, and cultural conditions. As we have seen, this intelligent activity is sometimes very conscious; most of the time it is subconscious, "beneath" our conscious awareness. It is no less intelligent when we are not aware of it – no less creative, and no less analytical. This is not a "mystical" model of translation. The sublimated intelligence that makes it possible for us to translate rapidly, reliably, and enjoyably is the product of learning – which is to say, of experience stored in memory in ways that enable its effective recall and flexible and versatile use.

This does not mean that good translators must *memorize* vast quantities of linguistic and cultural knowledge; in fact, insofar as we take "memorization" to mean the conscious, determined, and rote or mechanical stuffing of facts into our brains, it is quite the opposite. Translators must be good at storing experiences in memory, and at retrieving those experiences whenever needed to solve complex translation problems; but they do not do this by memorizing things. Memory as *learning* works differently. Learning is what happens when you're doing something else – especially something enjoyable, but even something unpleasant, if your experience leaves a strong enough impression on you. Translators learn words and phrases, styles and tones and registers, linguistic and cultural strategies while translating, while interpreting, while reading a book or surfing the Internet, while talking to people, while sitting quietly and thinking about something that happened. Communicating with people in a foreign country, they learn the language, internalize tens of thousands of words and phrases and learn to use them flexibly and creatively in ways that make sense to the people around them, without noticing themselves "memorizing." Translating the texts they are sent, interpreting the words that come out of a source speaker's mouth, they learn transfer patterns, and those patterns are etched on their brains for easy and intelligent access, sometimes without their even being aware that they have such things, let alone being able to articulate them in analytical, rule-governed ways. All they know is that certain words and phrases activate a flurry of finger activity on the keyboard, and the translation seems to write itself; or they open their mouths and a steady stream of target text comes out, propelled by some force that they do not always recognize as their own.

Representational and procedural memory

Memory experts distinguish between *representational memory* and *procedural memory*. Representational memory records what you had for breakfast this morning, or what your spouse just told you to get at the store: specific events. Procedural memory helps you check your e-mail, or drive to work: helps you perform skills or activities that are quickly sublimated as unconscious habits.

And translators and interpreters need both. They need representational memory when they need to remember a specific word: "What *was* the German for 'word-wrap'?" Or, better, because more complexly contextualized in terms of person and event (see below): "What *did* that German computer guy last summer in Frankfurt call 'word-wrap'?" They need procedural memory for everything else: typing and computer skills, linguistic and cultural analytical skills for source-text processing, linguistic and cultural production skills for target-text creation, and transfer patterns between the two.

Representational memory might help a translator define a word s/he once looked up in a dictionary; procedural memory might help a translator use the word effectively in a translation. Representational memory might help a student to reproduce a translation rule on an exam; procedural memory might help a student to use that rule in an actual translation exercise with little or no awareness of actually doing so.

While both forms of memory are essential for translation, their importance is relatively specialized. Procedural memory is most useful when things go well: when the source text makes sense, is well-formed grammatically and lexically; when the translation job is well-defined, its purpose and target audience clearly understood; when editors and users and critics either like the translation or do not voice their criticisms. Representational memory is most useful when things go less well: when a poorly written source text requires a conscious memory of grammatical rules and fine lexical distinctions; when the translation commissioner is so vague about a job that it cannot be done until the translator has coaxed out of her or him a clear definition of what is to be done; when rules, regularities, patterns, and theories must be spelled out to an irate but ill-informed client, who must be educated to see that what seems like a bad translation is in fact a good one.

To put that in the terms we'll be using in the remainder of this book: procedural memory is part of the translator's subliminal processing; representational memory is a part of the translator's conscious processing. Procedural memory helps the translator translate rapidly; representational memory is often needed when perceived problems make rapid translation impossible or inadvisable.

Intellectual and emotional memory

Brain scientists also draw a distinction between two different neural pathways for memory, one through the hippocampus, recording the facts, the other through the amygdala, recording how we feel about the facts. As Goleman (1995: 20) writes:

> If we try to pass a car on a two-lane highway and narrowly miss having a head-on collision, the hippocampus retains the specifics of the incident, like what stretch of road we were on, who was with us, what the other car looked like. But it is the amygdala that ever after will send a surge of anxiety through us whenever we try to pass a car in similar circumstances. As [Joseph] LeDoux [a neuroscientist at New York University] put it to me, "The hippocampus is crucial in recognizing a face as that of your cousin. But it is the amygdala that adds you don't really like her."

The point to note here is that amygdala arousal – "emotional memory" – adds force to all learning. This is why it is always easier to remember things that we care about, why things we enjoy (or even despise) always stick better in our memories than things about which we are indifferent. The strongest memories in our lives are always the ones that had the most powerful emotional impact on us: first kiss, wedding day, the births of our children, various exciting or traumatic events that transform our lives.

This also has important consequences for translators. The more you enjoy learning, the better you will learn. The more pleasurable you find translating, editing, hunting for obscure words and phrases, the more rapidly you will become proficient at those activities. (Really hating the work will also engrave the activities indelibly on your memory, but will not encourage you to work harder at them.) Hence the emphasis placed throughout this book on enjoyment: it is one of the most important "pretranslation skills," one of the areas of attitudinal readiness or receptivity that will help you most in becoming – and remaining – a translator.

Context, relevance, multiple encoding

Students of memory have also shown that what you remember well depends heavily on the context in which you are exposed to it, how relevant it is to your life (practical use-value, emotional and intellectual associations), and the sensory channels through which it comes to you (the more the better).

Context

The setting in which a thing is found or occurs is extremely important for the associations that are so crucial to memory. Without that context it is just an isolated item; in context, it is part of a whole interlocking network of meaningful things. For example, in Chapter 7 we will be taking a new look at terminology studies, based not on individual words and phrases, or even on larger contexts like "register," but on working people in their workplaces. Contextualizing a word or phrase as part of what a person doing a job says or writes to a colleague makes it much easier to remember than attempting to remember it as an independent item.

The physical and cultural context in which the learner learns a thing can also be helpful in building an associative network for later recall. Everyone has had the experience of going in search of something and forgetting what they were looking for – then having to return to the exact spot in which the need for the thing was first conceived, and remembering it instantly. The *place* in which the item was initially moved to long-term memory jogged that memory and the item was recalled. Students tested on material in the room where they learned it tend to do better on the test than those tested in another room. "It seems that the place in which we master information helps recreate the state necessary to retrieve it, probably by stimulating the right emotions, which are very important influences on memory" (Gallagher 1994: 132).

This phenomenon involves what is called "state-dependent learning" – the peculiar fact that memories retained in a given mental or physical state are most easily recalled in that state. People who learn a fact while intoxicated may have great difficulty remembering it while sober, and it will come to them immediately, almost miraculously, when under the influence again. It may be difficult to remember the most obvious and ordinary everyday facts about work while relaxing in the back yard on Saturday; when someone calls from work and you have to switch "states" rapidly, the transition from a Saturday-relaxation state to a workday-efficiency state may be disturbingly difficult.

Winifred Gallagher comments in *The Power of Place* (1994: 132):

> The basic principle that links our places and states is simple: a good or bad environment promotes good or bad memories, which inspire a good or bad mood, which inclines us toward good or bad behavior. We needn't even be consciously aware of a pleasant or unpleasant environmental stimulus for it to shape our states. The mere presence of sunlight increases our willingness to help strangers and tip waiters, and people working in a room slowly permeated by the odor of burnt dust lose their appetites, even though they don't notice the smell. On some level, states and places are internal and external versions of each other.

Interpreters have to be able to work anywhere, requiring them to develop the ability to create a productive mental state regardless of external conditions; translators tend to be more place-dependent. Their work station at home or at the office is set up not only for maximum efficiency, dictionaries and telephone close at hand, but also for maximum familiarity, at-homeness. They settle into it at the beginning of any work period *in order to* recreate the proper working frame of mind, going through little rituals (stacking paper, tidying piles, flipping through a dictionary, sharpening pencils) that put them in a translating mood. What they learn there they remember best there; thus the notorious difficulty of translating while on vacation, or at someone else's work station. It's not so much that the computer keyboard is different; it's that *everything* is different. All the little subliminal cues that put you in the proper frame of mind are absent – with the result that it is often very difficult to get the creative juices flowing. Translators who travel extensively now rely increasingly on portable work stations, especially laptop computers; the computer and other related paraphernalia then become like magic amulets that psychologically transform any place – an airport gate area, an airplane tray table, a hotel bed – into the external version of the internal state needed to translate effectively.

A group of translation scholars from various places in North and South America have gathered in Tlaxcala, Mexico, for a conference on scientific-technical translation. One night at dinner talk turns to travel, and to everyone's surprise the Cuban interpreter who has told stories of the collapse of the societal infrastructure in Cuba has been to more exotic places than anyone else present: Bali, Saudi Arabia, etc., always on official (interpreting) business. She starts describing the places she's seen, the people she's met, the words she's learned – and is disturbed to discover that she has forgotten an Arabic word she learned in Riyadh. Playfully, a dinner companion from the US unfolds a paper napkin off the table and holds it in front of her mouth like a veil. Her eyes fly open in astonishment and the word she was looking for bursts out of her mouth; she laughs and claps her hands over her mouth as if to prevent further surprises.

Relevance

The less relevant a thing is to you, the harder it will be for you to remember it. The more involved you are with it, the easier it will be for you to remember it. Things that do not impinge on our life experience "go in one ear and out the other." This is why it is generally easier to learn to translate or interpret by doing it, in the real world, for money, than it is in artificial classroom environments – and why the most successful translation and interpretation (T&I) programs always incorporate real-world experience into their curricula, in the form of internships, apprenticeships, and independent projects. It is why it is generally easier to remember a word or phrase that you needed to know for some purpose – to communicate some really important point to a friend or acquaintance, to finish a translation job – than one you were expected to memorize for a test. And it is why it is easier to remember a translation theory that you worked out on your own, in response to a complex translation problem or a series of similar translation jobs, than one that you read in a book or saw diagrammed on the blackboard. This will be the subject of Chapters 5–10.

Multiple encoding

The general rule for memory is that the more senses you use to register and rehearse something, the more easily you will remember it. This is called multiple encoding: each word, fact, idea, or other item is encoded through more than one sensory channel – visual, auditory, tactile, kinesthetic, gustatory, olfactory – which provides a complex support network for memory that is exponentially more effective than a single channel. This principle, as the rest of this chapter will show, underlies the heavy emphasis on "multimodal" exercises in this book – exercises drawing on several senses at once.

The translator's learning styles

Translation is intelligent activity. But what *kind* of intelligence does it utilize?

Howard Gardner (1985, 1993), director of Project Zero at Harvard University, has been exploring the multiplicity of intelligences since the early 1980s. He argues that, in addition to the linguistic and logical/mathematical intelligence measured by IQ tests, there are at least four other intelligences (probably more):

- *musical intelligence*: the ability to hear, perform, and compose music with complex skill and attention to detail; musical intelligence is often closely related to, but distinct from, mathematical intelligence
- *spatial intelligence*: the ability to discern, differentiate, manipulate, and produce spatial shapes and relations; to "sense" or "grasp" (or produce) relations of tension or balance in paintings, sculptures, architecture, and dance; to create and transform fruitful analogies between verbal or musical or other forms and spatial form; related to mathematical intelligence through geometry, but once again distinct
- *bodily-kinesthetic intelligence*: the ability to understand, produce, and caricature bodily states and actions (the intelligence of actors, mimes, dancers, many eloquent speakers); to sculpt bodily motion to perfected ideals of fluidity, harmony, and balance (the intelligence of dancers, athletes, musical performers)
- *personal intelligence*, also called "emotional intelligence" (see Chapter 6): the ability to track, sort out, and articulate *one's own* and *others'* emotional states ("intrapersonal" and "interpersonal" intelligence, respectively; the intelligences of psychoanalysts, good parents, good teachers, good friends); to motivate oneself and others to direct activity toward a desired goal (the intelligence of all successful professionals, especially leaders).

And, of course:

- *logical/mathematical intelligence*: the ability to perceive, sort out, and manipulate order and relation in the world of objects and the abstract symbols used to represent them (the intelligence of mathematicians, philosophers, grammarians)
- *linguistic intelligence*: the ability to hear, sort out, produce, and manipulate the complexities of a single language (the intelligence of poets, novelists, all good writers, eloquent speakers, effective teachers); the ability to learn foreign languages, and to hear, sort out, produce, and manipulate the complexities of transfer among them (the intelligence of translators and interpreters)

This last connection, the obvious one between translators and interpreters and linguistic intelligence, may make it seem as if translators and interpreters were intelligent *only* linguistically; as if the only intelligence they ever brought to bear on their work as translators were the ability to understand and manipulate language.

It is not. Technical translators need high spatial and logical/mathematical intelligence as well. Interpreters and film dubbers need high bodily-kinesthetic and personal intelligence. Translators of song lyrics need high musical intelligence.

Indeed one of the most striking discoveries made by educational research in recent years is that different people learn in an almost infinite variety of different ways or "styles." And since good translators are always in the process of "becoming" translators – which is to say, learning to translate better, learning more about language and culture and translation – it can be very useful for both student translators and professional translators to be aware of this variety of learning styles.

An awareness of learning styles can be helpful in several ways. For the learner, it can mean discovering one's own strengths, and learning to structure one's working environment so as to maximize those strengths. It is hard for most of us to notice causal relationships between certain semiconscious actions, like finding just the right kind of music on the radio and our effectiveness as translators. We don't have the time or the energy, normally, to run tests on ourselves to determine just what effect a certain kind of noise or silence has on us while performing specific tasks, or whether (and when) we prefer to work in groups or alone, or whether we like to jump into a new situation feet first without thinking much about it or hang back to figure things out first. Studying intelligences and learning styles can help us to recognize ourselves, our semiconscious reactions and behaviors and preferences, and thus to structure our professional lives more effectively around them.

An awareness of learning styles may also help the learner expand his or her repertoire, however: having discovered that you tend to rush into new situations impulsively, using trial and error, for example, you might decide that it could be professionally useful to develop more analytical and reflective abilities as well, to increase your versatility in responding to novelty. Discovering that you tend to prefer kinesthetic input may encourage you to work on enhancing your receptiveness to visual and auditory input as well.

In *Brain-Based Learning and Teaching*, Eric Jensen (1995a) outlines four general areas in which individual learning styles differ: *context, input, processing*, and *response* (see Figure 1). Let us consider each in turn, bearing in mind that your overall learning style will not only be a combination of many of these preferences but will vary from task to task and from learning situation to learning

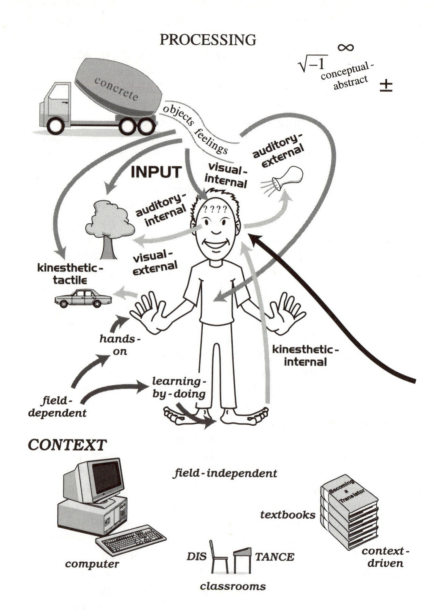

FIGURE 1 Learning styles

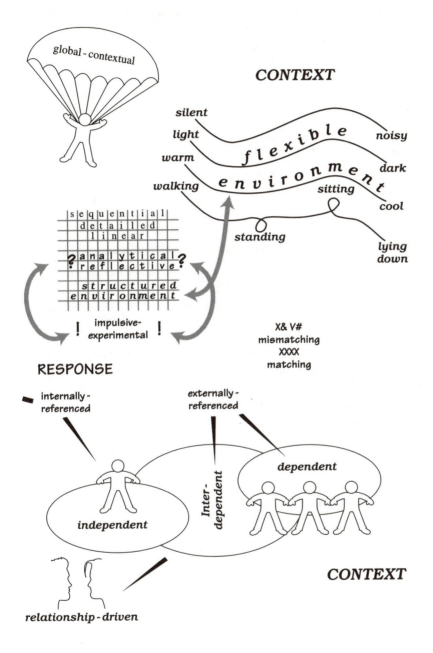

global - contextual

CONTEXT

silent

light

warm

walking

flexible

environment

noisy

dark

cool

sitting

standing

lying down

sequential

detailed

linear

?analytical?

reflective?

structured

environment

! impulsive-experimental !

X& V#
mismatching
XXXX
matching

RESPONSE

internally - referenced

externally - referenced

dependent

Inter-dependent

independent

CONTEXT

relationship - driven

situation. What follows is not a series of categorical straitjackets; it is a list of general tendencies that flow more or less freely through every one of us. You may even recognize yourself, in certain moods or while performing certain tasks, in each of the categories below.

Context

It makes a great deal of difference to learners *where* they learn – what sort of physical and social environment they inhabit while learning. Some different variables, as presented in Jensen (1995a: 134–8), are discussed below.

Field-dependent/independent

Just how heavily do you depend on your immediate physical environment or context when you learn?

Field-dependent learners learn best in "natural" contexts, the contexts in which they would learn something without really trying because learning and experiencing are so closely tied together. This sort of learner prefers learning-by-doing, hands-on work, on-the-job training to school work or learning-by-reading. Field-dependent language-learners learn best in the foreign country, by mingling with native speakers and trying to understand and speak; they will learn worst in a traditional foreign-language classroom, with its grammatical rules and vocabulary lists and artificial contexts, and marginally better in a progressive classroom employing methodologies from suggestopedia (accelerated learning (Lozanov 1971/1992)), total physical response (Asher 1985), or the natural method (Krashen and Terrell 1983). Field-dependent translators will learn to translate by translating – and, of course, by living and traveling in foreign cultures, visiting factories and other workplaces where specialized terminology is used, etc. They will shun translator-training programs and abstract academic translation theories; but may feel they are getting something worthwhile from a more hands-on, holistic, contextually based translator-training methodology.[1]

---

[1] Note that the connections between specific learning styles and preferences among language-learners, translators, and interpreters offered in this chapter are best guesses, not research-based. The primary research in this fascinating branch of translation studies remains to be done.

Field-independent learners learn best in artificial or "irrelevant" contexts. They prefer to learn *about* things, usually from a distance. They love to learn in classrooms, from textbooks and other textual materials (including the World Wide Web or CD-ROM encyclopedias), or from teachers' lectures. They find it easiest to internalize predigested materials, and greatly appreciate being offered summaries, outlines, diagrams and flowcharts. (In this book, field-independent learners will prefer the chapters to the exercises.) Field-independent language-learners will learn well in traditional grammar-and-vocabulary classrooms; but given the slow pace of such classrooms, they may prefer to learn a foreign language by buying three books, a grammar, a dictionary, and a novel. Field-independent translators will gravitate toward the classroom, both as students and as teachers (indeed they may well prefer teaching, studying, and theorizing translation to actually doing it). As translation teachers and theorists they will tend to generate elaborate systems models of translational or cultural processes, and will find the pure structures of these models more interesting than real-life examples.

Flexible/structured environment

Flexible-environment learners like variety in their learning environments, and move easily and comfortably from one to another: various degrees of noisiness or silence, heat or cold, light or darkness; while standing up and walking around, sitting in comfortable or hard chairs, or lying down; in different types of terrain, natural or artificial, rough or smooth, chaotic or structured (e.g., in a classroom, with people every which way or sitting quietly in desks arranged in rows and columns). Flexible-environment language-learners will learn well both in the foreign country and in various kinds of foreign-language classroom. Flexible-environment translators will prefer to work in a number of different contexts every day: at an office, at home, and in a client's conference room; at fixed work stations and on the move with a laptop. They will gravitate toward working situations that allow them to work in noise and chaos some of the time and in peace and quiet at other times. Flexible-environment learners will often combine translator and interpreter careers.

Structured-environment learners tend to have very specific requirements for the type of environment in which they work best:

in absolute silence, or with a TV or radio on. If they prefer to work with music playing, they will usually have to play the same type of music whenever they work. Structured-environment translators will typically work at a single work station, at the office *or* at home, and will feel extremely uncomfortable and incompetent (slow typing speed, bad memory) if forced temporarily to work anywhere else. Many structured-environment translators will keep their work stations neat and organized, and will feel uncomfortable and incompetent if there are extra papers or books on the desk, or if the piles aren't neat; some, however, prefer a messy work station and feel uncomfortable and incompetent if someone else cleans it up.

Independence/dependence/interdependence

Independent learners learn best alone. Most can work temporarily with another person, or in larger groups, but they do not feel comfortable doing so, and will typically be much less effective in groups. They are often high in intrapersonal intelligence. Independent translators make ideal freelancers, sitting home alone all day with their computer, telephone, fax/modem, and reference works. Other people exist for them (while they work) at the end of a telephone line, as a voice or typed words in a fax or e-mail message. They may be quite sociable after work, and will happily spend hours with friends over dinner and drinks; but during the hours they have set aside for work, they have to be alone, and will quickly grow anxious and irritable if someone else (a spouse, a child) enters their work area.

Dependent learners, typically people high in interpersonal intelligence, learn best in pairs, teams, other groups. Most can work alone for short periods, but they do not feel comfortable doing so, and will be less effective than in groups. They like large offices where many people are working together on the same project or on similar projects and often confer together noisily. Dependent translators work best in highly collaborative or cooperative in-house situations, with several translators/editors/managers working on the same project together. They enjoy meeting with clients for consultation. Dependent translators often gravitate toward interpreting as well, and may prefer escort interpreting or *chuchotage* (whispered interpreting) over solitary booth work – though working in a booth may be quite enjoyable if there are other interpreters working in the same booth.

Interdependent learners work well both in groups and alone; in either case, however, they perceive their own personal success and competence in terms of larger group goals. They are typically high in both intrapersonal and interpersonal intelligence. Interdependent translators in in-house situations will feel like part of a family, and will enjoy helping others solve problems or develop new approaches. Interdependent freelancers will imagine themselves as forming an essential link in a long chain moving from the source-text producer through various client, agency, and freelance people to generate an effective target text. Interdependent freelancers will often make friends with the people at clients or agencies who call them with translation jobs, making friendly conversation on the phone and/or meeting them in person in their offices or at conferences; phone conversations with one of them will give the freelancer a feeling of belonging to a supportive and interactive group.

Relationship-/content-driven

Relationship-driven learners are typically strong in personal intelligence; they learn best when they like and trust the presenter. "WHO delivers the information is more important than WHAT the information is" (Jensen 1995a: 134). Relationship-driven learners will learn poorly from teachers they dislike or mistrust; with them, teachers will need to devote time and energy to building an atmosphere of mutual trust and respect before attempting to teach a subject; and these learners will typically take teaching and learning to be primarily a matter of communication, dialogue, the exchange of ideas and feelings, only secondarily the transmission of inert facts. Relationship-driven language-learners tend also to be field-dependent, and learn foreign languages best in the countries where they are natively spoken; and there prefer to learn from a close friend or group of friends, or from a spouse or family. The focus on "people" and "working people" in Chapters 6 and 7 of this book will be especially crucial for this sort of learner. Relationship-driven translators often become interpreters, so that cross-cultural communication is always in a context of interpersonal relationship as well. When they work with written texts, they like to know the source-language writer and even the target-language end-user personally; like interdependent translators, they love to collaborate on translations, preferably with the writer and various other experts and resource people present. Relationship-driven freelancers imagine themselves in personal interaction with the source-language writer and target-language reader. It will feel essential to them to see the writer's face in their mind's eye, to hear the writer speaking the text in their mind's ear; to feel the rhythms and the tonalizations of the source text as the writer's personal speech to them, and of the target text as their personal speech to the reader. Robinson (1991) addresses an explicitly relationship-driven theory of translation as embodied dialogue.

Content-driven learners are typically stronger in linguistic and logical/mathematic than in personal intelligence; they focus most fruitfully on the information content of a written or spoken text. Learning is dependent on the effective presentation of information, not on the learner's feelings about the presenter. Content-driven language-learners prefer to learn a foreign language as a logical syntactic, semantic, and pragmatic system; content-driven student translators prefer to learn about translation through rules, precepts, and systems diagrams (deduction: see Chapter 4). Content-driven translators focus their attention on specialized terms and terminologies and the object worlds they represent; syntactic structures and cross-linguistic transfer patterns; stylistic registers and their equivalencies across linguistic barriers. Content-driven translation theorists tend to gravitate toward linguistics in all its forms, descriptive translation studies, and systematic cultural studies.

Input

The sensory form of information when it enters the brain is also important. Drawing on the psychotherapeutic methodology of Neuro-Linguistic Programming, Jensen (1995a: 135–6) identifies three different sensory forms in which we typically receive information, the visual, the auditory, and the kinesthetic (movement and touch), and distinguishes in each between an internal and an external component.

Visual

Visual learners learn through visualizing, either seeking out external images or creating mental images of the thing they're learning. They score high in spatial intelligence. They may need to sketch a diagram of an abstract idea or cluster of ideas before they can understand or appreciate it. They tend to be good spellers, because they can see the word they want to spell in their mind's eye. People with "photographic memory" are visual learners; and even when their memory is not quite photographic, visual learners remember words, numbers, and graphic images that they have seen much better than conversations they have had or lectures they have heard.

Visual-external learners learn things best by seeing them, or seeing pictures of them; they like drawings on the blackboard or overhead projector, slides and videos, handouts, or computer graphics. Visual-external language-learners remember new words and phrases best by writing them down or seeing them written; a visual-external learner in a foreign country will spend hours walking the streets and pronouncing every street and shop sign. Visual-external learners may feel thwarted at first by a different script: Cyrillic or Greek characters, Hebrew or Arabic characters, Japanese or Chinese characters, for much of the world Roman characters – these "foreign" scripts do not at first carry visual meaning, and so do not lend themselves to visual memory. As long as the visual-external learner has to sound out words character by character, it will be impossible to memorize them by seeing them written in the foreign script; they will have to be transliterated into the native script for visual memory to work. Visual-external translators usually do not become interpreters; in fact, it may seem to them as if interpreters have no "source text" at all, because they can't see it. If diagrams or drawings are available for a translation job, they insist on having them; even better, when possible, is a visit to the factory or other real-world context described in the text. Translation for these people is often a process of visualizing source-text syntax as a spatial array and rearranging specific textual segments to meet target-language syntactic requirements, as with this Finnish–English example (since visual-external learners will want a diagram):

[Karttaan] [on merkitty] [punaisella symbolilla] [tienrakennustyöt] ja [sinisellä] [päällystystyöt]

[New road construction] [is marked] [on the map] [in red], [resurfacing] [in blue]

This sort of translator may well be drawn to contrastive linguistics, which attempts to construct such comparisons for whole languages.

Visual-internal learners learn best by creating visual images of things in their heads. As a result, they are often thought of as daydreamers or, when they are able to verbalize their images for others, as poets or mystics. Visual-internal learners learn new foreign words and phrases best by picturing them in their heads – creating a visual image of the object described, if there is one, or creating images by association with the sound or look or "color" of a word if there is not. Some visual-internal language-learners associate whole languages with a single color; every image they generate for individual words or phrases in a given language will be tinged a certain shade of blue or yellow or whatever. Visual-internal translators also constantly visualize the words and phrases they translate. If there is no diagram or drawing of a machine or process, they imagine one. If the words and phrases they are translating have no obvious visual representation – in a mathematics text, for example – they create one, based on the look of an equation or some other associative connection.

Auditory

Auditory learners learn best by listening and responding orally, either to other people or to the voices in their own heads. Learning for them is almost always accompanied by self-talk: "What do I know about this? Does this make sense? What can I do with this?" They are often highly intelligent musically. They are excellent mimics and can remember jokes and whole conversations with uncanny precision. They pay close attention to the prosodic features of a spoken or written text: its pitch, tone, volume, tempo. Their memorization processes tend to be more linear than those of visual learners: where a visual learner will take in an idea all at once, in the form of a spatial picture, an auditory learner will learn it in a series of steps that must be followed in precisely the same order ever after.

Auditory-external learners prefer to hear someone describe a thing before they can remember it. Given a diagram or a statistical table, they will say, "Can you explain this to me?" or "Can you talk me through this?" Auditory-external language-learners learn well in natural situations in the foreign culture, but also do well in language

labs and classroom conversation or dialogue practice. They are typically very little interested in any sort of "reading knowledge" of the
language; they want to hear it and speak it, not read it or write it.
Grammars and dictionaries may occasionally seem useful, but will
most often seem irrelevant. "Native" pronunciation is typically very
important for these learners. It is not enough to communicate in the
foreign language; they want to sound like natives. Auditory-external
learners tend to gravitate toward interpreting, for obvious reasons;
when they translate written texts, they usually voice both the source
text and their emerging translation to themselves, either in their heads
or aloud. They make excellent film-dubbers for this reason: they can
hear the rhythm of their translation as it will sound in the actors'
voices. The rhythm and flow of a written text is always extremely
important to them; a text with a "flat" or monotonous rhythm will
bore them quickly, and a choppy or stumbly rhythm will irritate or
disgust them. They often shake their heads in amazement at people
who don't care about the rhythm of a text – at source-text authors
who write "badly" (meaning, for them, with awkward rhythms), or at
target-text editors who "fix up" their translation and in the process
render it rhythmically ungainly. Auditory-external translators work
well in collaborative groups that rely on members' ability to articulate their thought processes; they also enjoy working in offices where
several translators working on similar texts constantly consult with
each other, compare notes, parody badly written texts out loud, etc.

Auditory-internal learners learn best by talking to themselves.
Because they have a constant debate going on in their heads, they
sometimes have a hard time making up their minds, but they are
also much more self-aware than other types of learners. Like visual-
internal learners, they have a tendency to daydream; instead of
seeing mental pictures, however, they daydream with snippets of
remembered or imagined conversation. Auditory-internal language-
learners also learn well in conversational contexts and language
labs, but typically need to rehearse what they've learned in silent
speech. Like auditory-external learners, they too want to sound like
natives when they speak the foreign language; they rely much more
heavily, however, on "mental" pronunciation, practicing the sounds
and rhythms and tones of the foreign language in their "mind's
ear." Auditory-internal learners are much less likely to become
interpreters than auditory-external learners, since the pressure to
voice their internal speech out loud is much weaker in them.

Auditory-internal translators also care enormously about rhythms, and constantly hear both the source text and the emerging target text internally. In addition, auditory-internal translators may prefer to have instrumental music playing softly in the background while they work, and will typically save one part of their mental processing for a running internal commentary: "What an idiot this writer is, can't even keep number and gender straight, hmm, what was that word, I know I know it, no, don't get the dictionary, it'll come, wonder whether the mail's come yet, Jutta hasn't written in weeks, hope she's all right . . ." Not only is this constant silent self-talk not distracting; it actually helps the auditory-internal translator work faster, more effectively, and more enjoyably.

Kinesthetic

Kinesthetic learners learn best by doing. As the name suggests, they score high in bodily-kinesthetic intelligence. Their favorite method of learning is to jump right into a thing without quite knowing how to do it and figure it out in the process of doing it. Having bought a new machine, visual learners will open the owner's manual to the diagrams; auditory learners will read the instructions "in their own words," constantly converting the words on the page into descriptions that fit their own mind better, and when they hit a snag will call technical support; kinesthetic learners will plug it in and start fiddling with the buttons. Kinesthetic learners typically talk less and act more; they are in touch with their feelings and always check to see how they feel about something before entering into it; but they are less able to articulate their feelings, and also less able to "see the big picture" (visual learners) or to "think something through and draw the right conclusions" (auditory learners).

(But remember that we all learn in all these different ways; we are all visual, auditory, and kinesthetic learners. These categories are ways of describing tendencies and preferences in a complex field of overlapping styles. As we have seen before, you may recognize yourself in some small way in *every* category listed here.)

Kinesthetic-tactile learners need to hold things in their hands; they typically learn with their bodies, with touch and motion. They are the ones who are constantly being warned not to touch things in museums; they can't stand to hang back and look at something from a distance, or to listen to a guide drone on and on about it. They want to *feel* it. Kinesthetic-tactile language-learners learn best in the foreign country, and in the classroom in dramatizations, skits, enacted dialogues, and the like. They find it easiest to learn a phrase like "Open the window" if they walk to a window and open it while saying it. In the student population, it is the kinesthetic-tactile learners who are most often neglected in traditional classrooms geared toward auditory and visual learning (and an estimated 15 percent of all adults learn best tactilely). Kinesthetic-tactile translators and interpreters feel the movement of language while they are rendering it into another language: as for auditory learners, rhythm and tone are extremely important for them, but they feel those prosodic features as ripples or turbulence in a river of language flowing from one language to the other, as bumps or curves in a road (see Robinson 1991: 104–9). To them it seems as if texts translate themselves; they have a momentum of their own, they flow out of groups of people off the page into their bodies and out through their mouths or fingers with great force. The translator's or interpreter's job feels more like "steering" or "channeling" the flow than like producing a target-language equivalent for source-language words and phrases. Problem words or phrases stop or hinder the flow, act like a bottleneck or a rocky snag; when this happens kinesthetic-tactile translators may well check dictionaries or list synonyms in their heads, but their primary sensation is one of trying to restart the flow. The analytical processes that help translators determine the nature of a source-language problem and develop a target-language solution are important to kinesthetic-tactile translators too, but those processes are usually much more deeply sublimated in them than they are in visual and auditory learners, and it may seem to them as if the problems simply disappear, or as if the solutions come to them from some external source. When they "visualize" individual words and phrases, they do so in terms of touch and movement: they can imagine their hands touching a thing, picking it up, turning it over, hefting it, feeling its contours; they "feel" themselves moving toward or around or away from it.

Kinesthetic-internal learners use their feelings or "experiences" as a filter for what they learn. Things or ideas that "feel good" or give the learner "good vibes" are easy to learn; a negative or suspicious gut-reaction may make it virtually impossible to keep an open mind.

A translator whose native language is English, but who lived for many years in Finland, is sitting at home in Illinois, translating a chainsaw manual from English into Finnish. While he translates, subconsciously he recreates in his mind scenes from his life in Finland, memories of cutting firewood with a chainsaw. Though it is summer in Illinois, the scenes in his head are wintry; he can almost feel the crunch of snow under his boots, the sensation of a gloved hand rubbing crusty snow off a log. He is with a male friend or brother-in-law, the owners of chainsaws who have asked for his help in sawing up some firewood. (His father first taught him to use a chainsaw in rural Washington State; but somehow, because he is translating into Finnish, his subconscious mind only recreates Finnish chainsaw memories.) He can feel the heft of the chainsaw as he works it into position to start cutting, applies pressure to the trigger, and saws through the log with a rocking motion; he can see his friend or brother-in-law with the chainsaw in his lap, sharpening the individual blades on the chain. The "daydreams" or "reveries" are largely wordless, and almost entirely kinesthetic, involving motion and touch rather than elaborate visual images; but miraculously, technical terms for parts of the apparatus – the trigger, the choke, the handle, the protective shield, the chain bar – come to him as if from nowhere. Not all of them; he spends hours faxing and phoning friends in Finland, who help him find equivalents for words he has never heard. But words that he hasn't heard in seven or eight years, in some cases words that he only heard once or twice, come to him on the wings of a semiconscious kinesthetic daydream.

How a thing is presented is much more important than the thing itself: smoothly or roughly, easily or awkwardly, tamely or wildly, monotonously or with rich emotional textures. Kinesthetic-internal language-learners are so powerfully affected by the emotional charge of language that they are easily bored by the artificial tonalizations of teachers, fellow students, and the native speakers on language-lab tapes who work hard to make their voices unnaturally clear for the foreign learner. It is extremely important for them that a sentence like "John is late" be charged emotionally – with anger or irritation, with sadness or resignation, with secret malicious glee – and the sentence will feel significantly different to them depending on how it is charged. If it is read or uttered in a monotone in class or on a tape, it will not seem like language at all. Hence this sort of learner will always learn a foreign language best in the country where it is spoken natively, or from a lover or close friend who speaks it natively, or in a classroom where students are taught to dramatize the language they are learning with their whole bodies. (This is the kind of language-learner who loves being laughed at when s/he makes a mistake: the laughter signals not only the error itself but how native speakers feel about the error, and thus provides valuable clues to how to say it properly.) Kinesthetic-internal learners are far more likely to become translators than interpreters, as they are often not very expressive orally. They too, like kinesthetic-tactile translators, feel language flowing from the source text into the target language, almost on its own power; but they are more likely to be aware of that flow than kinesthetic-tactile translators, to experience it as a pleasurable feeling that they want to intensify and prolong. They too "visualize" indi-vidual words and phrases in terms of touch and movement, but the kinesthetic images are much more likely to be imaginary, associated more closely with feelings than with concrete tactile experience.

Processing

Different learners also process information in strikingly different ways. Jensen (1995a: 136–7) sorts the various processing models into four main types: *contextual-global*, *sequential-detailed/linear*, *conceptual*, and *concrete*.

Contextual-global

Contextual-global learners are sometimes described as "parachu-tists": they see the big picture, as if they were floating high above it, and often care less about the minute details. They want to grasp the main points quickly and build a general sense of the whole, and only later, if at all, fill in the details. They first want to know what something means and how it relates to their experience – its rele-vance, its purpose – and only then feel motivated to find out what it's like, what its precise nature is. They are "multitaskers" who like to work on many things at once, jumping from one problem to another as they grow bored with each and crave a change. They process information intuitively and inferentially, and often get a "gut-feeling" for the answer or solution or conclusion halfway through a procedure.

Contextual-global translators and interpreters tend to prefer jobs where minute accuracy is less important than a general overall "fit" or target-cultural appropriateness: escort interpreting over court interpreting; literary and commercial translating over scientific and technical translating. They want to get a general "feel" for the source text and then create a target text that feels more or less the same, or seems to work in more or less the same way. When they are required by the nature of the job to be more minutely accurate, contextual-global translators prefer to do a rough translation quickly (for them the enjoyable part) and then go back over it slowly, editing for errors (for them the drudgery). Contextual-global freelancers tend to be somewhat sloppy with their bookkeeping, and often lose track of who has paid and who hasn't. They own dictionaries and other reference works, but have a hard time remembering to update them, and often prefer to call an expert on the phone or check a word with Internet friends than own exactly the right dictionary. When contextual-global translators and interpreters become theorists, they tend to build loosely knit, highly intuitive theories based on the translator's subjectivity (see Robinson 1991, Pym 1993) and/or activity as guided by target-cultural purpose (see Reiß and Vermeer 1984, Holz-Mänttäri 1984; see also Chapters 9–10 below).

Sequential-detailed/linear

Sequential-detailed or linear learners prefer to control the learning process as much as possible by doing only one thing at a time: focusing on a single task until it is finished, and proceeding through that task one step at a time. These learners always want to know how to proceed in advance; they want a map, a formula, a menu, a checklist. They are analytical, logical, sequential, linear thinkers, typically high in logical/mathematical intelligence, who believe in being systematic and thorough in all things.

Sequential-detailed or linear translators and interpreters will typically gravitate toward highly structured working situations and texts. Stable employment with a steady salary is preferable to the uncertainties of freelancing. If possible, these people want to know far in advance what they will be translating tomorrow, next week, next month, so they can read up on it, learn vocabularies and registers, be prepared before the job begins. They are much more likely to specialize in a certain subject area, such as biomedical or patents or software localization, so they can learn all about their field. Sequential-detailed interpreters will gravitate toward academic and political meetings where speakers read from prepared scripts, and wherever possible will avoid more spontaneous contexts like court interpreting, where one never knows what the speaker is going to say next. (Contextual-global translators and interpreters, who prefer to render texts as spontaneously as possible, would go crazy with boredom if they were forced to translate or interpret familiar texts in the same narrowly defined field week after week, month after month, year after year.) If any professional translator ever does a detailed textual analysis of the source text before beginning to translate, it will be the sequential-detailed translator. Sequential-detailed translators own all the latest dictionaries in their field, and tend to trust dictionaries more than contextual-global translators; they also meticulously maintain their own private (and possibly also a corporate) terminological database, updating it whenever they happen upon a new word in a source text or other reading material. When sequential-detailed translators and interpreters become theorists, they tend to build comprehensive and minutely detailed models that aim to account for (or guide the translator's choices in) every single aspect of the translation process. They are drawn to linguistic, psycholinguistic, and sociolinguistic models (see Nida and Taber 1969, Catford 1965, Wilss 1977/1982), and when they study the larger cultural patterns controlling translation they prefer large descriptive systems models (see Lefevere 1992, Toury 1995).

Conceptual (abstract)

Conceptual or abstract learners process information most effectively at high levels of generality and at a great distance from the distractions of practical experience. They prefer talking and thinking to doing, and love to build elaborate and elegant systems that bear little resemblance to the complexities of real life.

Conceptual or abstract translators and interpreters quickly lose patience with the practical drudgery of translating and interpreting, and gravitate toward universities, where they teach translators (or, where translator training programs are not common, language and literature students) and write translation theory. Their theoretical work tends to be much more solidly grounded in fascinating intellectual traditions (especially German romanticism and French poststructuralism) than in the vicissitudes of translation experience; it is often rich in detail and highly productive for innovative thought but difficult to apply to the professional world (see Steiner 1975, Berman 1984/1992, Venuti 1995).

Concrete (objects and feelings)

Concrete learners prefer to process information by handling it in as tangible a way as possible. They are suspicious of theories, abstract models, conceptualizations – generally of academic knowledge that strays too far from their sense of the hands-on realities of practical experience.

Concrete translators and interpreters are usually hostile toward or wary of translator training, and would prefer to learn to translate on their own, by doing it. Within translator-training programs, they openly express their impatience or disgust with theoretical models and approaches that do not directly help them translate or interpret specific passages better. When concrete translators and interpreters become theorists, they gravitate toward contrastive linguistics, either describing specific transfer patterns between specific languages (for French and English, see Vinay and Darbelnet 1958/1977) or telling readers the correct way to translate a wealth of examples in a number of common linguistic categories, like titles, sentence modifiers, and tag questions (for French, German, and English, see Newmark 1987).

Response

In any interaction, your response to the information you've taken in and processed will be the action you take; that action, learning-styles theorists like Bernice McCarthy (1987) suggest, is filtered by such considerations as other people's attitudes, conformity to rules, and time. Jensen (1995a: 137–8) offers six types of response filter: externally and internally referenced, matching and mismatching, impulsive-experimental and analytical-reflective.

Externally/internally referenced

Externally referenced learners respond to informational input largely on the basis of other people's expectations and attitudes. Societal norms and values control their behavior to a great extent. "What is the right thing to do?" implies questions like "What would my parents expect me to do?" or "What would all right-thinking people do in my situation?"

Externally referenced translators and interpreters almost certainly form the large majority of the profession. They predicate their entire professional activity and self-image on subordination to the various social authorities controlling translation: the source author, the translation commissioner (who initiates the translation process and pays the translator's fee), and the target reader. Their reasoning runs like this: The source author has something important to say. The importance of that message is validated by social authorities who decide that it should be made available to readers in other languages as well. The message is important enough to make it imperative that it be transferred across linguistic and cultural barriers without substantial change. The translator is the chosen instrument in this process. In order to facilitate this transfer-without-change, the translator must submit his or her will entirely to the source text and its meanings, as well as to the social authorities that have selected it for translation and will pay the translator for the work. This submission means the complete emptying out (at least while translating) of the translator's personal opinions, biases, inclinations, and quirks, and especially of any temptation to "interpret" the text based on those idiosyncratic tendencies. The translator can be a fully functioning individual outside the task of translation, but must submit to authority *as* a translator. For externally referenced translators and interpreters this is an ethical as well as a legal issue: a translator who violates this law is not only a bad professional but a bad person.

Internally referenced learners develop a more personal code of ethics or sense of personal integrity, and respond to input based on their internal criteria – which may or may not deviate sharply from societal norms and values, depending on the situation.

It is easy enough to identify various maverick translators as internally referenced: Ezra Pound, Paul Blackburn, and the other literary translators discussed in Venuti (1995: 190–272) are good examples. The difficulty with this identification, however, is that many of these translators only seem internally referenced because the source of their *external* reference is not the one generally accepted by society. Venuti himself, for example, argues that translators should reject the external reference imposed by capitalist society that requires the translator to create a fluent text for the target reader, and replace it with a more traditional (but in capitalist society also dissident) external reference to the textures of the foreign text. The "foreignizing" translator who leaves traces of the source text's foreignness in his or her translation thus seems "internally referenced" by society's standards, but is in fact referring his or her response not to some idiosyncratic position but to an alternative external authority, the source text or source culture, or an ethical ideal for the target culture as positively transformed by contact with foreignness.

Such feminist translators as Barbara Godard, Susanne Lotbinière-Harwood, Myriam Díaz-Diocaretz, and Susanne Jill Levine, too, seem internally referenced by society's standards because they either refuse to translate texts by men and see themselves as intervening radically in the women's texts they translate in order to promote women's issues and a feminist voice, or, when they do translate male texts, are willing to render them propagandistically. And some of these translators write about their decisions to translate as they do as if the pressures to do so came from inside – which they almost certainly do. Lotbinière-Harwood, for example, speaks of the depression and self-loathing she felt while translating Lucien Francœur, and of her consequent decision never to translate another male text again. Levine writes of her personal pain as a feminist translating the works of sexist men. Díaz-Diocaretz (1985: 49ff.) reprints long sections from her translator's log, written while translating the lesbian feminist poet Adrienne Rich into Spanish, and much of her anguish over specific decisions seems internally referenced. Clearly, however, this personal pain and the personal code of ethics that grows out of these women's ongoing attempts to heal that pain are both also externally referenced to the women's movement, to solidarity with other women engaged in the same healing process.

By the same token, the "externally referenced" translator or interpreter who obeys society's norms and submits her or his interpretive will to the target culture's needs *feels* this submission as internally motivated. It rarely feels as if one were being forced to submit; one *wants* to submit. By identifying with social authorities, the translator or interpreter develops an internal reference that is modeled on an external one, but comes to feel like her or his own.

For translators and interpreters, therefore, it may be more useful to speak of conventionally referenced and unconventionally referenced learners – those who are willing to submit to the broadest, most generally accepted social norms and those who, out of whatever combination of personal and shared pain and individual and collective determination to fight the sources of that pain, refer their translational decisions to authorities other than the generally accepted ones. In some cases the other authority might even be the translator herself or himself, with no connection to dissident movements or other external support; in most cases, perhaps, translators and interpreters build their ethics in a confusing field of conflicting external authorities, and may frequently be both praised and attacked for the same translation by different groups.

Matching/mismatching

Matchers respond most strongly to similarities, consistencies, groupings, belongingness. They are likely to agree with a group or an established opinion, because discordance feels wrong to them. Matchers define critical thinking as the process of weeding out things that don't fit: quirky opinions from a body of recognized fact, novelties in a well-established tradition, radical departures from a generally accepted trend.

In the field of translation and interpretation, matchers love the concept of equivalence. For them the entire purpose of translation is achieving equivalence. The target text must match the source text as fully as possible. Every deviation from the source text generates anxiety in them, and they want either to fix it, if they are the translator or an editor, or to attack it, if they are outsiders in the position of critic.

Mismatchers respond most strongly to dissimilarities, inconsistencies, deviations, individuality. They are likely to disagree with a group or an established opinion, because there is something profoundly suspicious about so many people toeing the same line. Mismatchers define critical thinking as the process of seeking out and cherishing things that don't fit: quirky opinions in a body of recognized fact, novelties in a well-established tradition, radical departures from a generally accepted trend.

In the field of translation and interpretation, mismatchers may feel uncomfortable with the concept of equivalence. It may feel like a straitjacket to them. As a result, they tend to gravitate toward areas of specialization that allow and even encourage creative deviation, such as some forms of advertising and poetic translation, or translating for children. They shun forms of translation in which equivalence is strictly enforced, such as technical, legal, and medical; and to the extent that they associate translation theory with the enforcement of equivalence, they may shun theory as well. When they write translation theory themselves, they tend to ignore equivalence altogether (see Lefevere 1992) or to reframe it in radical ways: Pym (1992a), for example, argues that equivalence is an economic concept that never means an exact match but rather a negotiated equation of two mismatched items, such as a certain quantity of meat for a certain quantity of money; Robinson (1991) sees equivalence as a fiction that helps some translators organize their work so as to turn *away* from the source text toward the target culture.

Impulsive-experimental/analytical-reflective

Impulsive-experimental learners respond to new information through trial and error: rather than reading the instructions or asking for advice, they jump right in and try to make something happen. If at first they fail, they try something else. Failure is nothing to be ashamed of; it is part of the learning process. At every stage of that process, spontaneity is valued above all else: it is essential for these learners to stay fresh, excited, out on the cutting edge of their competence and understanding, and not let themselves sink into tired or jaded repetition.

Impulsive-experimental learners often become interpreters, especially simultaneous and court interpreters, because they love the thrill of always being forced to react rapidly and spontaneously to emerging information. Impulsive-experimental translators find other ways of retaining the spontaneity they crave, as in this quotation from Philip Stratford (Simon 1995: 97):

To know what is coming next is the kiss of death for a reader. It interferes with the creative process also. While novelists and poets do not usually write completely blind, they do rely heavily on a sense of discovery, of advancing into the unknown as they pursue their subject and draw their readers along with them. The challenge for the translator . . . is to find ways to reproduce this excitement, this creative blindness, this sense of discovery, in the translation process. The translator must, like an actor simulating spontaneity, use tricks and certain studied techniques to create an illusion of moving into the unknown. To cultivate creative blindness one should never read a text one is going to translate too carefully at first, and once only. It helps to have a short memory.

Analytical-reflective learners prefer to respond more slowly and cautiously: their motto is "look before you leap." They take in information and reflect on it, test it against everything else they know and believe, check it for problems and pitfalls, ask other people's advice, and only then begin carefully to act on it. They are pragmatic ("What good is this? What effect will it have on me and my environment?") and empirical ("How accurate is this? How far can I trust it?"). Unlike impulsive-experimental learners, who tend to focus on present experience, analytical-reflective learners tend to be focused on the past ("How does this fit with what I know from past experience? How does it match with or deviate from established traditions?") or the future ("What future consequences will this information have on my own and others' actions? How will it transform what we do and how we think and feel about it?").

Analytical-reflective learners gravitate toward translation jobs that allow (and even encourage) them to take the time to think things through carefully before proceeding. The sort of corporate situation where engineers and technicians and editors demand ever greater speed and don't care much about style or idiomatic target-language usage or user impact or other "big picture" considerations will cause analytical-reflective translators great anxiety; if they land such a job, they will not last long there. They will probably feel more at home in a translation agency where, even if speed is important, good, solid, reliable workmanship is of equal or even greater importance. Analytical-reflective translators are probably best suited to freelancing, since working at home enables them to set their own pace, and do whatever pretranslation textual analyses and database searches they feel are necessary to ensure professional-quality work. Because they tend to work more slowly than impulsive-experimental translators, they will have to put in longer hours to earn as much money; but they will also earn the trust and respect of the clients and agencies for whom they work, because the translations they submit will so rarely require additional editing.

Discussion

1   Even if mnemonic devices involving visualization, acting out, and the like are more effective memorization channels than more "intellectual" or analytical approaches, just how appropriate are such activities to a university classroom? Discuss the tensions between traditional assumptions about what sorts of intellectual activities are appropriate in universities and the pedagogical implications of recent research on how the brain learns best – especially in terms of subtle body signals, such as embarrassment or uneasiness at certain "inappropriate" activities, in teacher and students alike.

   In what ways are tacit assumptions about "appropriate" activities controlled by "procedural memories" from earlier classes, in university and before? Discuss the impact of procedural memory on students' *and* teachers' willingness to try new things, enter into new experiences, and apply findings to translation pedagogy.

2   What are some of the procedural memories that already help you to translate? How did you acquire them? How do they work? Which ones don't work very well yet? How might they be improved?

3   Just how useful to the translator is the knowledge about learning styles that is presented in this chapter? Isn't it just as effective, or even more effective, to "prefer" things unconsciously?

4   To what extent does the sequential/analytical presentation of the learning styles in this chapter distort the complexity of human learning? What would be a more global/contextual/intuitive way of thinking about learning styles?

5   While this book was written to appeal to as many different types

of learner as possible, it nevertheless inevitably reflects its author's learning styles in numerous ways. For example, under "relationship-driven learners," above, it was noted that "The focus on 'people' and 'working people' in Chapters 6 and 7 of this book will be especially crucial for this sort of learner" – those chapters argue that relationship-driven (or people-oriented) learning is more effective than content-driven learning, simply because that is how the author learns best. Discussion topic 4 suggests another learning style reflected in this chapter. Exercises 4–5, below, will appeal more to externally referenced and analytical-reflective learners, exercises 6–8 to internally referenced and intuitive-experimental learners. How does this limit the effectiveness of the book's approach? What could or should be changed in the book to make it more effective? What would the book be like if based more on *your* learning styles?

6   What types of teacher and teaching style appeal to you most? Why? Think of examples from your own past experience.

7   What can students do (without angering the teacher!) to liven up a boring class? Discuss some techniques for making yourself more actively engaged in a subject.

Exercises

1   Explore the difference between representational memory and procedural memory by consciously storing the meaning or translation of a new word in long-term memory: open a dictionary to a word that you have never seen before, study the entry, and commit it to memory. Wait a few minutes, and then "represent" it to yourself: review in your mind, or out loud, or on paper, what you have just learned. Now compare that memory with your "procedural" memory of how to get from home to school, or how to translate "how to get from home to school" into another language. What are the major differences between them?

2   Work with two or three other people to translate the following sentence from Gallagher (1994: 129) into another language: "One reason we work so hard to keep our surroundings predictable is that we rely on them to help us segue smoothly from role to role

throughout the day." Now study the translation in relation to the original and try to invent principles or "rules" of relevance that might help you translate a similar passage more easily next time. (For example, are "work so hard to keep" and "rely on them to help" rendered with the same syntactic structure in your target language? What shifts need to be made in word order to make the target text sound natural? "Segue" is a term taken from music; is there an exact equivalent in your target language? If not, what register shifts do you have to make so that it works right? Etc.) Draw on any aspect of your experience – the sound of words, things that have happened to you, places you've heard this or that word or structure – to "personalize" the rule or principle and so make it memorable for you. Note, and discuss with the other members of your group, how your personal "relevance" for any given aspect of the transfer clashes or conflicts with those suggested by other members of the group.

3   Choose a relatively simple technical process (tying your shoe, peeling an orange, brushing your teeth, making a bed) and arrange a "teaching contest": different individuals come up with different ways of teaching it (lecture, small-group work, hands-on exercises, translating a written description of the process, dramatization, etc.) and the class votes on which is the most effective, which "came in second," third, and so on. Then discuss what each ranking means: whether, for example, the other students preferred one teacher more than another because they learned the most from her or him or just because s/he was funny – and whether those two things are necessarily in conflict.

4   This exercise will help you determine whether you prefer to work in a structured or a flexible environment.

On each continuum, draw a vertical line at the spot where you feel most comfortable for each question. If all of your marks are grouped closely together, you probably prefer a structured environment *for that particular variable*; if they are spread out across the continuum, you probably prefer a flexible environment, again for that particular variable. A repeated pattern of closely grouped marks on all or most of the continua indicates a general preference for a structured environment; the more spread-out patterns you have, the stronger your preference for a flexible environment probably is.

(a)   hot   warm   70°F./21°C.   cool   cold

|———|

Make a separate mark on the line for each of the following situations. At roughly what temperature do you prefer to work:

- when you translate?
- when you interpret?
- when you read difficult scholarly works?
- when you read novels?
- when you read the newspaper?
- when you read and write e-mail?
- when you send or read faxes?
- in the winter?
- in the summer?

(b)   noisy,   background music,   fairly quiet,   perfectly quiet,
       busy   movement   peaceful   still

|———|

Make a separate mark on the line for each of the following situations. How much background noise and activity do you like:

- when you translate alone?
- when you translate with someone else?
- when you interpret simultaneously in a booth?
- when you do chuchotage?
- when you interpret consecutively?
- when you read difficult scholarly works?
- when you read novels?
- when you read the newspaper?
- when you read and write e-mail?
- when you send or read faxes?

(c)   standing,   standing   sitting at   sitting in   lying   lying on
       moving   still   a desk   an armchair   in bed   the floor

|———|

Make a separate mark on the line for each of the following situations. In what position do you prefer to work:

- when you translate?
- when you interpret?
- when you read difficult scholarly works?
- when you read novels?
- when you read the newspaper?
- when you read and write e-mail?
- when you send or read faxes?
- when you're alone?
- when you're with other people?

(d)   very bright   bright   light   dim   dark

|—————————————————————————————————|

Make a separate mark on the line for each of the following situations. How light do you like your working environment to be:

- when you translate at home, at your primary work station?
- when you translate at work, at your primary work station?
- when you translate on a laptop, or away from your computer?
- when you interpret?
- when you read difficult scholarly works?
- when you read novels?
- when you read the newspaper?
- when you read and write e-mail?
- when you send or read faxes?

(e)   >2 hours 1–2 hours 45–60 mins 30–45 mins 15–30 mins 0–15 mins

|—————————————————————————————————|

Make a separate mark on the line for each of the following situations. How long do you prefer to work without substantial change in your position, environment, or activity (getting up and walking around, working on something else, more or less noise, etc.):

- when you're translating something interesting?
- when you're translating something boring?
- when you interpret?
- when you read difficult scholarly works?
- when you read novels?
- when you read the newspaper?
- when you read and write e-mail?
- when you send or read faxes?
- when you talk on the phone?

When you look over the five continua and compare the groupings of marks, are the patterns more or less what you expected, or do they come as a surprise? Are some more surprising than others? If this exercise indicates that you prefer a structured environment, does that feel right to you? If it suggests that you prefer a flexible environment, does that feel right?

5 Answer the following questions about processing types (visual, auditory, kinesthetic) by circling the *two* letters that best fit your style – for example, if in a specific question the visual and auditory answers seem to describe your typical behavior, draw a circle around the V and a circle around the A. If only one answer fits your style, draw two circles around the same letter. When you have completed the test, add up the total number of Vs, As, and Ks, and compare. (Based loosely on Rose 1987: 147–9.)

(a) When you try to visualize something, what does your mind generate?
    V   complex and detailed pictures
    A   sounds
    K   dim, vague images in motion

(b) When you're angry, what do you do?
    V   seethe silently with repressed rage
    A   yell and scream
    K   stomp around, kick and throw things, wave your arms

(c) When you're bored, what do you do?
    V   doodle
    A   talk to yourself
    K   pace or fidget

(d) When you have something you need to tell a friend, would you rather

V write a note, letter, fax, e-mail message?
A call him or her on the phone?
K take him or her for a walk?

(e) When you try to remember a phone number, do you
V see the number in your head?
A say it aloud or to yourself?
K dial it, let your fingers remember it?

(f) When you try to remember a person, do you
V remember the face (but often forget the name)?
A remember the name (but often forget the face)?
K remember something you did together?

(g) When you try to "read" a person (mood, opinions, reactions, etc.), what do you "read"?
V facial expressions
A tone of voice
K body movements

(h) When you can't think of the right word, do you
V draw a picture?
A hem and haw?
K gesture or dramatize?

(i) When you dream, do you
V see vivid color pictures?
A hear voices?
K feel yourself moving?

(j) When you think of a friend, do you first think of her or his
V face?
A voice, pet phrases?
K gestures, walk, tone of voice?

(k) When you're learning or teaching in a classroom, what do you like best?
V slides, diagrams, computers, beautifully made textbooks
A talk (lectures, discussions, repeating phrases)
K hands-on exercises, experiences, field trips, dramatization

(l) When you're learning something on your own, what helps you the most?
V illustrations
A a friend's explanation
K refusing all help and just *doing* it, by trial and error

(m) If a fire breaks out, what do you do?
V size up the situation, think, plan, find the exits

      A   shout "Fire!" or scream like mad

      K   run for the exits, help others

(n) When you watch TV or movies, what do you like best?

      V   travel, documentaries

      A   talk shows, news, comedy, drama

      K   sports, adventure, suspense

(o) When you read a novel or watch a movie, what part do you like best?

      V   the description (novel) or the cinematography (movie)

      A   the dialogue

      K   the action

(p) Which art forms do you like to *watch* best?

      V   painting, photography, or sculpture

      A   poetry or music

      K   theater or dance

(q) Which art forms do you like to *do* best?

      V   drawing or painting

      A   writing or singing

      K   acting, dancing, or sculpting

(r) When you want to record a scene, which would you rather do?

      V   take photos

      A   audiotape it

      K   videotape it

(s) When you translate, what do you like best?

      V   written translation

      A   conference or court interpretation

      K   escort interpretation

(t) When you translate, what distracts you most?

      V   messiness, in the source text, on your desk, etc.

      A   noises, music, voices

      K   movement

6   Alone or in groups, create tests like those in exercises 4–5 for one or more of the following pairs of learning styles:

(a) relationship-driven, content-driven

(b) conceptual, concrete

(c) externally referenced, internally referenced

(d) matching, mismatching

(e)   contextual-global, sequential-detailed/linear
(f)   impulsive-experimental, analytical-reflective

Think of everyday learning situations both in the classroom and out, and use the descriptions in the chapter to imagine the different ways in which different types of learners might respond in them. For example, learning to use a computer or new operating system or program: a relationship-driven learner will care enormously about the person teaching him or her, how supportive or impatient s/he is, and will learn more rapidly and enjoyably in a friendly, supportive atmosphere; a content-driven learner will screen out the teacher and focus on the specific instructions s/he receives, and will learn best when those instructions are clear and consistent. A conceptual learner will want an overview of the whole system first; a concrete learner will want to learn to perform a specific function first. Conventionally referenced learners and matchers will want to follow the rules, do things as the programmers intended; unconventionally referenced learners and mismatchers will want to move quickly from the "right" way of using the system to the loopholes, shortcuts, tricks, and gimmicks. Contextual-global and intuitive-experimental learners will want to know generally "what kind" of system it is before diving in and figuring things out on their own (they will read the instruction manual only as a last resort); sequential-detailed/linear and analytical-reflective learners will want to read the instruction manual carefully, take a course on the system, or follow a built-in tutorial program. Ask what sorts of feature will please the different types of learner, which will frustrate or anger them: sequential-detailed/linear learners, for example, will be pleased by clear and concise instructions that work exactly as they are supposed to, and will be frustrated and angered when following the steps precisely as given in the instruction manual does not produce the promised result. Intuitive-experimental learners will be pleased by user-friendly features that guarantee maximum spontaneity and freedom of choice, and will be frustrated and angered by rigid, inflexible features that trap them in loops that they cannot escape without reading the instruction manual or calling technical support.

Since people's preferences vary with the learning situation, make sure you imagine several (at least 5–6) different situations for each pair of learning styles. A person's "learning style" is always a complex composite or numerous different responses; make it possible to take an average as in exercise 1 or 3, or to map different responses onto a grid (a continuum as in exercise 2, a Cartesian grid, etc.).

7 Create or choose an exercise you have used before and modify it using the various learning styles' attributes discussed in this chapter. As you and a group do the modified exercise, pay attention to how it changes the kinds of processes learners go through and the questions that arise.

8 Choose one of the exercises that you've already done in this chapter and express your own learning styles as determined by that exercise in a different format: visually (draw a picture or a diagram), auditorily (have a phone conversation in which you describe yourself as depicted in the exercise to a friend, tell a story about it), or kinesthetically (dramatize it, mime it).

Suggestions for further reading

Alkon (1992), Asher (1985), Buzan (1993), Caine, Nummela Caine and Crowel (1994), Carbo, Dunn and Dunn (1986), Dhority (1992), Dryden and Vos (1993), Gallagher (1994), Gardner (1985, 1993), Grinder (1989), Hampden-Turner (1981), Hart (1975, 1983), Jensen (1988a, 1988b, 1995a), Krashen and Terrell (1983), Margulies (1991), McCarthy (1987), Ostrander and Schroeder (1991), Rose (1987), Rose (1992), Schiffler (1992), Sylwester (1995), Taylor (1988)

Chapter 4

The process of translation

● **The shuttle: experience and habit**   94

● **Charles Sanders Peirce on instinct, experience, and habit**   96

● **Abduction, induction, deduction**   98

● **Karl Weick on enactment, selection, and retention**   100

● **The process of translation**   102

  ● **Discussion**   107

  ● **Exercises**   108

  ● **Suggestions for further reading**   108

T HESIS: Translation for the professional translator is a constant learning cycle that moves through the stages of *instinct* (unfocused readiness), *experience* (engagement with the real world), and *habit* (a "promptitude of action"), and, within experience, through the stages of *abduction* (guesswork), *induction* (pattern-building), and *deduction* (rules, laws, theories); the translator is at once a *professional* for whom complex mental processes have become second nature (and thus subliminal), and a *learner* who must constantly face and solve new problems in conscious analytical ways.

The shuttle: experience and habit

In Chapter 3 we saw some of the astonishing variety of memory patterns and learning styles that undergird all human activities, including translating and interpreting. We remember information and we remember how to perform actions. We remember facts and we remember feelings (and how we feel about certain facts). We remember things better in the context in which we learned them, and relevance or real-world applicability vastly improves our recall. We have preferences for the contexts in which we learn things, the sensory channels through which we are exposed to them, how we process them, and how we respond to them. Some of these patterns and preferences work well with full conscious and analytical awareness of what we are doing; most of them operate most effectively subliminally, beneath our consciousness.

In this chapter we will be focusing this general information about memory and learning into a model for the process by which translators translate: how translators harness their own idiosyncratic preferences and habits into a general procedure for transforming source texts into successful target texts. In brief, the model imagines the translator shuttling between two very different mental states and processes: (1) a subliminal "flow" state in which it seems as if the translator isn't even thinking, as if the translator's fingers or interpreter's mouth is doing the work, so that the translator can daydream while the body translates; and (2) a highly conscious analytical state in which the translator mentally reviews lists of synonyms, looks words up in dictionaries, encyclopedias, and other reference works, checks grammar books, analyzes sentence structures, semantic fields, cultural pragmatics, and so on.

The subliminal state is the one that allows translators to earn a living at the work: in the experienced professional it is very fast, and as we saw in Chapter 2, enhanced speed means enhanced income. It works best when there are no problems in the source text, or when the problems are familiar enough to be solved without conscious analysis. The analytical state is the one that gives the translator a reputation for probity and acumen: it is very slow, and may in some cases diminish a freelancer's income, but without this ability the translator would never be able to finish difficult jobs and would make many mistakes even in easy jobs, so that sooner or later his or her income would dry up anyway.

The shuttle metaphor is taken from weaving, of course: the shuttle is a block of wood thrown back and forth on the loom, carrying the weft or cross-thread between the separated threads of the warp. This metaphor may make the translation process seem mechanical, like throwing a block of wood back and forth – and clearly, it is not. It may also make it seem as if the two states were totally different, perfect opposites, like the left and right side of a loom. The two states are different, but not perfectly or totally so. In fact, they are made up of very much the same experiential and analytical materials, which we will be exploring in detail in Chapters 5–11: experiences of languages, cultures, people, translations; textual, psychological, social, and cultural analyses. The difference between them is largely in the way that experiential/analytical material is stored and retrieved for use: in the subliminal state, it has been transformed into habit, "second nature," procedural memory; in the analytical state, it is brought back out of habit into representational memory and painstakingly conscious analysis.

Experience, especially fresh, novel, even shocking experience, also tough-minded analytical experience, the experience of taking something familiar apart and seeing how it was put together, is in most ways the opposite of habit – even though in another form, processed, repeated, and sublimated, it is the very stuff of habit, the material that habit is made from. Fresh experiences that startle us out of our habitual routines are the goad to learning; without such shocks to the system we would stagnate, become dull and stupefied. Fresh experiences make us feel alive; they roughen the smooth surfaces of our existence, so that we really *feel* things instead of gliding through or past them like ghosts.

Translators need habit in order to speed up the translation process and make it more enjoyable; but they also need new experiences to enrich it and complicate it, slow it down, and, again, to make it more enjoyable. For there is enjoyment to be had in translating on autopilot, in what Mihaly Csikszentmihalyi (1990) calls the "flow" experience, and there is enjoyment to be had in being stopped dead by some enormously difficult problem. There is pleasure in speed and pleasure in slowness; there is pleasure in what is easy and familiar and pleasure in what is new and difficult and challenging. There is pleasure, above all, in variety, in a shuttling back and forth between the new and the old, the familiar and the strange, the conscious and the unconscious, the intuitive and the analytical, the subliminal and the startling.

This back-and-forth movement between habit and fresh experience is one of the most important keys to successful, effective, and enjoyable translation – or to any activity requiring both calm expertise and the ability to grow and learn and deal with unforeseen events. Without habit, life proceeds at a snail's pace; everything takes forever; all the ordinary events in life seem mired in drudgery. Without fresh experience, life sinks into ritualized repetitive sameness, the daily grind, the old rat-race. Life is boring without habit, because habit "handles" all the tedious little routines of day-to-day living while the conscious mind is doing something more interesting; and life is boring without fresh experience, because experience brings novelty and forces us to learn.

Charles Sanders Peirce on instinct, experience, and habit

One useful way of mapping the connections between experience and habit onto the process of translation is through the work of Charles

Sanders Peirce (1857–1913), the American philosopher and founder of semiotics. Peirce addressed the connections between experience and habit in the framework of a triad, or three-step process, moving from instinct through experience to habit. Peirce understood everything in terms of these triadic or three-step movements: *instinct*, in this triad, is a First, or a general unfocused readiness; *experience* is a Second, grounded in real-world activities and events that work on the individual from the outside; and *habit* is a Third, transcending the opposition between general readiness and external experience by incorporating both into a "promptitude of action" (1931–66: 5.477), "a person's tendencies toward action" (5.476), a "readiness to act" (5.480) – to act, specifically, in a certain way under certain circumstances as shaped by experience (see Figure 2). One may be instinctively ready to act, but that instinctive readiness is not yet directed by experience of the world, and so remains vague and undirected; experience of the world is powerfully there, it hits one full in the face, it must be dealt with, but because of its multiplicity it too remains formless and undirected. It is only when an inclination to act is enriched and complicated by experience, and experience is directed and organized by an instinctive inclination to act, that both are sublimated together as habit, a readiness to do specific things under specific conditions – translate certain kinds of texts in certain ways, for example.

The process of translation in Peirce's three terms might be summarized simply like this: the translator begins with a blind, intuitive, instinctive sense in a language, source or target, of what a word or

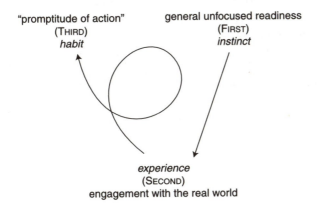

"promptitude of action"   general unfocused readiness
(THIRD)   (FIRST)
habit   instinct

experience
(SECOND)
engagement with the real world

FIGURE 2 Peirce's instinct/experience/habit triad in translation

phrase means, how a syntactic structure works (*instinct*); proceeds by translating those words and phrases, moving back and forth between the two languages, feeling the similarities and dissimilarities between words and phrases and structures (*experience*); and gradually, over time, sublimates specific solutions to specific experiential problems into more or less unconscious behavior patterns (*habit*), which help her or him to translate more rapidly and effectively, decreasing the need to stop and solve troubling problems. Because the problems and their solutions are built into habit, and especially because every problem that intrudes upon the habitualized process is itself soon habitualized, the translator notices the problem-solving process less and less, feels more competent and at ease with a greater variety of source texts, and eventually comes to think of herself or himself as a professional. Still, part of that professional competence remains the ability to slip out of habitual processes whenever necessary and experience the text, and the world, as fully and consciously and analytically as needed to solve difficult problems.

Abduction, induction, deduction

The translator's experience is, of course, infinitely more complicated than simply what s/he experiences in the act of translating. To expand our sense of everything involved in the translator's experience, it will be useful to borrow another triad from Peirce, that of abduction, induction, and deduction. You will recognize the latter two as names for types of logical reasoning, induction beginning with specifics and moving toward generalities, deduction beginning with general principles and deducing individual details from them. "Abduction" is Peirce's coinage, born out of his sense that induction and deduction are not enough. They are limited not only by the either/or dualism in which they were conceived, always a bad thing for Peirce; but also by the fact that on their own neither induction nor deduction is capable of generating new ideas. Both, therefore, remain sterile. Both must be fed raw material for them to have anything to operate on – individual facts for induction, general principles for deduction – and a dualistic logic that recognizes only these two ways of proceeding can never explain where that material comes from.

Hence Peirce posits a third logical process which he calls abduction: the act of making an intuitive leap from unexplained data to a hypothesis. With little or nothing to go on, without even a very clear sense of the data about which s/he is hypothesizing, the thinker entertains a hypothesis that intuitively or instinctively (a First) *seems* right; it then remains to test that hypothesis inductively (a Second) and finally to generalize from it deductively (a Third).

Using these three approaches to processing experience, then, we can begin to expand the middle section of the translator's move from untrained instinct through experience to habit.

The translator's experience begins "abductively" at two places: in (1) a first approach to the foreign language, leaping from incomprehensible sounds (in speech) or marks on the page (in writing) to meaning, or at least to a wild guess at what the words mean; and (2) a first approach to the source text, leaping from an expression that makes sense but seems to resist translation (seems untranslatable) to a target-language equivalent. The abductive experience is one of not knowing how to proceed, being confused, feeling intimidated by the magnitude of the task – but somehow making the leap, making the blind stab at understanding or reformulating an utterance.

As s/he proceeds with the translation, or indeed with successive translation jobs, the translator tests the "abductive" solution "inductively" in a variety of contexts: the language-learner and the novice translator face a wealth of details that must be dealt with one at a time, and the more such details they face as they proceed, the easier it gets. Abduction is hard, because it's the first time; induction is easier because, though it still involves sifting through massive quantities of seemingly unrelated items, patterns begin to emerge through all the specifics.

Deduction begins when the translator has discovered enough "patterns" or "regularities" in the material to feel confident about making generalizations: syntactic structure X in the source language (almost) always becomes syntactic structure Y in the target language; people's names shouldn't be translated; ring the alarm bells whenever the word "even" comes along. Deduction is the source of translation methods, principles, and rules – the leading edge of translation theory (see Figure 3).

And as this diagram shows, the three types of experience, abductive guesses, inductive pattern-building, and deductive laws, bring the translator-as-learner ever closer to the formation of "habit," the creation of an effective procedural memory that will enable the

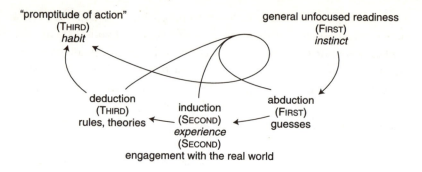

FIGURE 3 Peirce's instinct/experience/habit and abduction/induction/deduction triads in translation

translator to process textual, psychosocial, and cultural material rapidly.

Karl Weick on enactment, selection, and retention

Another formulation of much this same process is Karl Weick's in *The Social Psychology of Organizing*. Weick begins with Darwin's model of natural selection, which moves through stages of variation, selection, retention: a variation or mutation in an individual organism is "selected" to be passed on to the next generation, and thus genetically encoded or "retained" for the species as a whole. In social life, he says, this process might better be described in the three stages of enactment, selection, and retention.

As Em Griffin summarizes Weick's ideas in *A First Look at Communication Theory*, in the first stage, enactment, you simply *do* something; you "wade into the swarm of equivocal events and 'unrandomize' them" (Griffin 1994: 280). This is patently similar to what Charles Sanders Peirce calls "abduction," the leap to a hypothesis (or "unrandomization") from the "swarm of equivocal events" that surround you.

The move from enactment to selection is governed by a principle of "respond now, plan later": "we can only interpret actions that we've already taken. That's why Weick thinks chaotic action is better than orderly inaction. Common ends and shared means are the result of effective organizing, not a prerequisite. Planning comes after enactment" (Griffin 1994: 280).

There are, Weick says, two approaches to selection: rules and cycles. Rules (or what Peirce would call deductions) are often taken to be the key to principled action, but Weick is skeptical. Rules are really only useful in reasonably simple situations. Because rules are formalized for general and usually highly idealized cases, they most often fail to account for the complexity of real cases. Sometimes, in fact, two conflicting rules seem to apply simultaneously to a single situation, which only complicates the "selection" process. One rule will solve one segment of the problem; in attempting to force the remainder of the problem into compliance with that rule, another rule comes into play and undermines the authority of the first. Therefore, Weick says, in most cases "cycles" are more useful in selecting the optimum course of action.

There are many different cycles, but all of them deal in trial and error – or what Peirce calls induction. The value of Weick's formulation is that he draws our attention to the cyclical nature of induction: you cycle out away from the problem in search of a solution, picking up possible courses of action as you go, then cycle back in to the problem to try out what you have learned. You try something and it doesn't work, which seems to bring you right back to where you started, except that now you know *one* solution that won't work; you try something and it does work, so you build it into the loop, to try again in future cycles.

Perhaps the most important cycle for the translator is what Weick calls the act–response–adjustment cycle, involving feedback ("response") from the people on whom your trial-and-error actions have an impact, and a resulting shift ("adjustment") in your actions. This cycle is often called collaborative decision-making; it involves talking to people individually and in small groups, calling them on the phone, sending them faxes and e-mail messages, taking them to lunch, trying out ideas, having them check your work, etc. Each interactive "cycle" not only generates new solutions, one brainstorm igniting another; it also eliminates old and unworkable ones, moving the complicated situation gradually toward clarity and a definite decision. As Em Griffin says, "Like a full turn of the crank on an old-fashioned clothes wringer, each communication cycle squeezes equivocality out of the situation" (Griffin 1994: 281).

The third stage is retention, which corresponds to Peirce's notion of habit. Unlike Peirce, however, Weick refuses to see retention as the stable goal of the whole process. In order for the individual or the group to respond flexibly to new situations, the enactment–

selection–retention process must itself constantly work in a cycle, each "retention" repeatedly being broken up by a new "enactment." Memory, Weick says, should be treated like a pest; while old solutions retained in memory provide stability and some degree of predictability in an uncertain world, that stability – often called "tradition" or "the way things have always been" – can also stifle flexibility. The world remains uncertain no matter what we do to protect ourselves from it; we must always be prepared to leap outside of "retained" solutions to new enactments. In linguistic terms, the meanings and usages of individual words and phrases change, and the translator who refuses to change with them will not last long in the business. "Chaotic action" is the only escape from "orderly inaction." (This is not to say that all action must be chaotic; only that not all action can ever be orderly, and that the need to maintain order at all costs can frequently lead to inaction.) In Griffin's words again, "Weick urges leaders to continually discredit much of what they think they know – to doubt, argue, contradict, disbelieve, counter, challenge, question, vacillate, and even act hypocritically" (Griffin 1994: 283).

The process of translation

What this process model of translation suggests in Peirce's terms, then, is that novice translators begin by approaching a text with an instinctive sense that they know how to do this, that they will be good at it, that it might be fun; with their first actual experience of a text they realize that they don't know how to proceed, but take an abductive guess anyway; and soon are translating away, learning inductively as they go, by trial and error, making mistakes and learning from those mistakes; they gradually deduce patterns and regularities that help them to translate faster and more effectively; and eventually these patterns and regularities become habit or second nature, are incorporated into a subliminal activity of which they are only occasionally aware. In Weick's terms, the enact–select–retain cycle might be reformulated as *translate, edit, sublimate*:

1   *Translate*: act; jump into the text feet first; translate intuitively.

2   *Edit*: think about what you've done; test your intuitive responses against everything you know; but edit intuitively too, allowing an intuitive first translation to challenge (even successfully) a well-

reasoned principle that you believe in deeply; let yourself feel the tension between intuitive certainty and cognitive doubt, and don't automatically choose one over the other; use the act–response–adjustment cycle rather than rigid rules.

3   *Sublimate*: internalize what you've learned through this give-and-take process for later use; make it second nature; make it part of your intuitive repertoire; but sublimate it flexibly, as a directionality that can be redirected in conflictual circumstances; never, however, let subliminal patterns bind your flexibility; always be ready if needed "to doubt, argue, contradict, disbelieve, counter, challenge, question, vacillate, and even act hypocritically."

The model traces a movement from bafflement before a specific problem through a tentative solution to the gradual expansion of such solutions into a habitual pattern of response. The model assumes that the translator is at once:

(a)   a *professional*, for whom many highly advanced problem-solving processes and techniques have become second nature, occurring rapidly enough to enhance especially the freelancer's income and subliminally enough that s/he isn't necessarily able to articulate those processes and techniques to others, or even, perhaps, to herself or himself; and

(b)   a *learner*, who not only confronts and must solve new problems on a daily basis but actually thrives on such problems, since novelties ensure variety, growth, interest, and enjoyment.

Throughout the book, this model of the process of translation will suggest specific recommendations for the translator's "education," in a broad sense that includes both training (and training either in the classroom or on the job) and learning through personal discovery and insight. What *are* the kinds of experiences (abductive intuitive leaps, inductive sifting and testing, deductive generalizing) that will help the translator continue to grow and improve as a working professional? How can they best be habitualized, sublimated, transformed from "novel" experiences or lessons that must be thought about carefully into techniques that seem to come naturally?

As Peirce conceives the movement from instinct through experience to habit, habit is the *end*: instinct and experience are

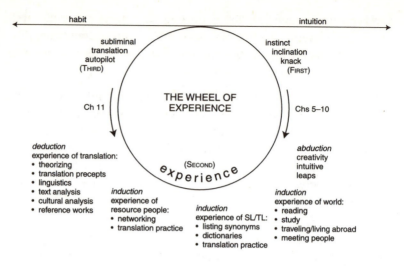

FIGURE 4 The wheel of experience

combined to create habit, and there it stops. Weick's corrective model suggests that in fact Peirce's model must be bent around into a cycle, specifically an act–response–adjustment cycle, in which each adjustment becomes a new act, and each habit comes to seem like "instinct" (see Figure 4).

This diagram can be imagined as the wheel of a car, the line across at the top marking the direction of the car's movement, forward to the right, backward to the left. As long as the wheel is moving in a clockwise direction, the car moves forward, the translation process proceeds smoothly, and the translator/driver is only occasionally aware of the turning of the wheel(s). The line across the top is labeled "habit" *and* "intuition" because, once the experiential processes of abduction, induction, and deduction have been sublimated, they operate sub- or semiconsciously: the smooth movement of the top line from left to right may be taken to indicate the smooth clockwise spinning of the triadic circle beneath it. This movement might be charted as follows:

The translator approaches new texts, new jobs, new situations with an intuitive or *instinctive* readiness, a sense of her or his own knack for languages and translation that is increasingly, with experience, steeped in the automatisms of habit. Instinct and habit for

Peirce were both, you will remember, a readiness to act; the only difference between them is that habit is directed by experience.

Experience begins with general knowledge of the world (Chapter 5), experience of how various people talk and act (Chapter 6), experience of professions (Chapter 7), experience of the vast complexity of languages (Chapter 8), experience of social networks (Chapter 9), and experience of the differences among cultures, norms, values, assumptions (Chapter 10). This knowledge or experience will often need to be actively sought, constructed, consolidated, especially but not exclusively at the beginning of the translator's career; with the passing of years the translator's subliminal repertoire of world experience will expand and operate without her or his conscious knowledge.

On the cutting edge of contact with an actual text or job or situation, the translator has an intuition or image of her or his ability to solve whatever problems come up, to leap *abductively* over obstacles to new solutions. Gradually the "problems" or "difficulties" will begin to recur, and to fall into patterns. This is *induction*. As the translator begins to notice and articulate, or read about, or take classes on, these patterns and regularities, *deduction* begins, and with it the theorizing of translation.

At the simplest level, deduction involves a repertoire of blanket solutions to a certain class of problems – one of the most primitive and yet, for many translators, desirable forms of translation theory. Each translator's deductive principles are typically built up through numerous trips around the circle (abductions and inductions gradually building to deductions, deductions becoming progressively habitualized); each translator will eventually develop a more or less coherent theory of translation, even if s/he isn't quite able to articulate it. (It will probably be mostly subliminal; in fact, whatever inconsistencies in the theory are likely to be conflicts between the subliminal parts, which were developed through practical experience, and the articulate parts, which were most likely learned as precepts.) Because this sort of effective theory arises out of one's own practice, another person's deductive solutions to specific problems, as offered in a theory course or book, for example, will typically be harder to remember, integrate, and implement in practice. At higher levels this deductive work will produce regularities concerning whole registers, text-types, and cultures; thus various linguistic forms of text analysis (Chapter 8), social processes (Chapter 9), and systematic analyses of culture (Chapter 10).

This is the "perfected" model of the translation process, the process as we would all like it to operate all the time. Unfortunately, it doesn't. There are numerous hitches in the process, from bad memory and inadequate dictionaries all the way up through untranslatable words and phrases (*realia*, puns, etc.) to the virtually unsolvable problems of translating across enormous power differentials, between, say, English and various Third World languages. The diagram allows us to imagine these "hitches" kinesthetically: you stop the car, throw it into reverse, back up to avoid an obstacle or to take another road. This might be traced as a counterclockwise movement back around the circle.

The subliminal autopilot fails; something comes up that you cannot solve with existing habitualized repertoires (Chapter 11). In many cases the subliminal process will be stopped automatically by bafflement, an inability to proceed; in other cases you will grow gradually more and more uneasy about the direction the translation is taking, until finally you are no longer able to stand the tension between apparent subliminal "success" and the gnawing vague sense of failure, and throw on the brakes and back up. As we have seen, you can also build an alarm system, perhaps an automatic emergency brake system, into the "habit" or subliminal functioning, so that certain words, phrases, registers, cultural norms, or the like stop the process and force you to deal consciously, alertly, analytically with a problem. This sort of alarm or brake system is particularly important when translating in a politically difficult or sensitive context, as when you feel that your own experience is so alien from the source author's that unconscious error is extremely likely (as when translating across the power differentials generated by gender, race, or colonial experience); or when you find yourself in opposition to the source author's views.

And so, forced out of subliminal translating, you begin to move consciously, analytically, with full intellectual awareness, back around the circle, through deduction and the various aspects of induction to abduction – the intuitive leap to some novel solution that may even fly in the face of everything you know and believe but nevertheless *feels* right. Every time one process fails, you move to another: listing synonyms doesn't help, so you open the dictionary; the word or phrase isn't in the dictionary, or the options offered all look or feel wrong, so you call or fax or e-mail a friend or acquaintance who might be able to help, or send out a query over an Internet listserver; they are no help, so you plow through encyclopedias and other reference materials; if you have no luck there, you call the agency or client; and finally, if nobody knows, you go with your intuitive sense, generate a translation abductively, perhaps marking the spot with a question mark for the agency or client to follow up later. Translating a poem, you may want to jump to abduction almost immediately.

And note that the next step after abduction, moving back around the circle counterclockwise, is once again the subliminal translation autopilot: the solution to this particular problem, whether generated deductively, inductively, or abductively (or through some combination of the three), is incorporated into your habitual repertoire, where it may be used again in future translations, perhaps tested inductively, generalized into a deductive principle, even made the basis of a new theoretical approach to translation.

The rest of this book is structured to follow the circle: first clockwise, in Chapters 5–10, beginning with subliminal translation and moving through the various forms of experience to an enriched subliminality; then (rather more rapidly) counterclockwise, in Chapter 11, exploring the conscious analytical procedures the translator uses when subliminal translation fails. In each case we will be concerned with the tension between experience and habit, the startling and the subliminal – specifically, with how one slides from one to the other, sublimating fresh experiential discoveries into an effective translating "habit," bouncing back out of subliminal translation into various deductive, inductive, and abductive problem-solving procedures.

Discussion

Most theories of translation assume that the translator works consciously, analytically, alertly; the model presented in this chapter assumes that the translator only rarely works consciously, for the most part letting subliminal or habitual processes do the work. Speculate on the nature and origin of this difference of opinion. Are the traditional theories idealizations of the theorist's own conscious processes? Is this chapter an idealization of some real-world translators' bad habits?

Exercises

1 What habits do you rely on in day-to-day living? In what ways do they help you get through the day? When do they become a liability, a straitjacket to be dropped or escaped? Estimate how many minutes a day you are actively conscious of what is happening around you, what you are doing. Scientists of human behavior say it is not a large number: habit runs most of our lives. What about you?

2 What fresh discoveries have you made in your life that have since become "second nature," part of your habitual repertoire? Remember the process by which a new and challenging idea or procedure became old and easy and familiar – for example, the process of changing a habit, replacing a bad habit with a good one. Relive the process in your imagination; jot down the main stages or moments in the change.

3 What are some typical problem areas in your language combination(s)? What are the words or phrases that ought to set off alarm bells when you stumble upon them in a text?

Suggestions for further reading

Gorlée (1994), Lörscher (1991), Peirce (1931–66), Seguinot (1989), Weick (1979)

Chapter 5

Experience

- **What experience?**   110
- **Intuitive leaps (abduction)**   113
- **Pattern-building (induction)**   118
- **Rules and theories (deduction)**   120
  - **Discussion**   123
  - **Exercises**   124
  - **Suggestions for further reading**   125

T HESIS: While it is true that "experience" is the best teacher, experience comes in many shapes and sizes, including wild or educated guesses when faced with an apparently insoluble problem (*abduction*), exposure to a variety of cases over a long period of time, which is what we generally call "practical experience" (*induction*), and theoretical teaching or training based on laws or general principles (*deduction*).

What experience?

Experience of the world is of course essential for all humans. Without experience of other people speaking we would never learn language. Without experience of other people interacting we would never learn our society's behavioral norms. Without experience of written texts and visual media we would never learn about the world beyond our immediate environment.

Without experience of the world – if in fact such a thing is even imaginable – we would never learn anything. Experience of the world is an integral and ongoing part of our being in the world. Without it, we could hardly be said to exist at all.

The real question is, then, not *whether* experience of the world is indispensable for the translator's work, but *what kind of* experience of the world is indispensable for the translator's work.

Is it enough to have profound and extensive experiences of one or more foreign languages? If so, is it enough to have been exposed to that language or those languages in books and classrooms, or is experience of the culture or cultures in which it is natively spoken essential? How important is rich experience of one's mother tongue(s)? And how rich? Is it essential to be exposed to people who speak it in different regions, social classes, and professions? Or is it enough to have read in it widely and attentively?

Alternatively, is extensive experience of a certain subject matter enough, if the translator has a rudimentary working knowledge of at least one foreign language? If so, does that experience need to be hands-on practical experience of the field, experience of the objects and the people who handle them and the way those people speak about the objects? Or is it enough to have experience of books, articles, and coursework on that subject matter?

At a radical extreme that will make professional translators uncomfortable, could it even be sufficient, in certain cases, for the translator to have fleeting and superficial experience of the foreign language and the subject matter but a rich and complex experience with dictionaries? Or, in a slightly less extreme example, would it be enough for a competent professional translator from Spanish and Portuguese to have heard a little Italian and own a good Italian dictionary in order to translate a fairly easy and routine text from the Italian?

One answer to *all* of these questions is: "Yes, in certain cases." A solid experiential grounding in a language can get you through even a difficult specialized text when you have little or no experience of the subject matter; and a good solid experiential grounding in a subject matter can sometimes get you through a difficult text in that field written in a foreign language with which you have little experience. Sometimes knowledge of similar languages and a dictionary can get you through a fairly simple text that you can hardly read at all.

While the ability to compensate for failings in some areas with strengths in others is an important professional skill, however, asking the questions this way is ultimately misleading. While in specific cases a certain level or type of experience (and competence) may be "enough" or "essential," few translators have the luxury of knowing in advance just what will be required to do the job at hand. Thus the translator's key to accumulating experience of the world is not so much what may be "enough" or "essential" for specific translation jobs as it is simply experiencing as much of everything as possible. The more experience of the world, the better; also, the more *of* the world one experiences, the better.

A good translator is someone who has never quite experienced enough to do her or his job well; just one more language, one more degree, one more year abroad, fifty or sixty more books, and s/he'll be ready to start doing the job properly. But that day never comes; not because the translator is incompetent or inexperienced, not because the translator's work is substandard, but because a good translator always wants to know more, always wants to have experienced more, never feels quite satisfied with the job s/he just completed. Expectations stay forever a step or three in front of reality, and keep the translator forever restlessly in search of more experience.

Experience of the world sometimes confirms the translator's habits. There are regularities to social life that make some aspects of our existence predictable. A visit to a city we've visited many times before will confirm many of our memories about that city: a favorite hotel, a favorite restaurant or cafe, a favorite park, areas to avoid, etc. Every attempt to communicate in a foreign language that we know well will similarly confirm many of our memories of that language: familiar words mean more or less the same things that we remember them meaning before, syntactic structures work the same, common phrases are used in situations similar to the ones in which we've encountered them before.

But experience holds constant surprises for us as well. We turn the corner and find that a favorite hotel or restaurant has been torn down, or has changed owners and taken on an entirely new look. Familiar words and phrases are used in unfamiliar ways, so that we wonder how we ever believed ourselves fluent in the language.

If nothing ever stayed the same, obviously, we would find it impossible to function. No one would ever be in a position to give anyone else directions, since nothing would stay the same long enough for anyone to "know" where it was or what it was like. Communication would be impossible.

But if nothing ever changed, our habits would become straitjackets. We would lock into a certain rigid set of worldly experiences and our expectations and predictions based on those experiences, and stop learning. Most of us try to just do that in as many areas of our lives as possible, to become "creatures of habit" (a phrase that is not usually taken as an insult), and so to control our environments in some small way.

But only the extremely insecure crave this "habitual" control over their whole lives; and only the extremely wealthy can afford to achieve anything even approximating that control in reality. The rest of us, fortunately, are forced past our habits in a thousand little ways every day, and so forced to rethink, regroup, shift our understandings and expectations to accord with the new experiences and slowly, sometimes painfully, begin to rebuild broken habits around the changed situation.

As we've seen, the translator's habits make it possible to translate faster, more reliably, and more enjoyably; but when those habits are not broken, twisted, massaged, and reshaped by fresh experience, the enjoyment begins to seep out and speed and reliability stagnate into mechanical tedium. (Player pianos can play fast pieces rapidly and reliably, and for a while it can be enjoyable to listen to their playing; but how long would you enjoy *being* one?)

In Chapters 6–10 we will be considering a sequence of worldly experiences – people, professions, languages, social networks, cultures – and their significance for translators. In each case we will be exploring the relevant experience in terms of Charles Sanders Peirce's triad of abduction, induction, and deduction: intuitive leaps, pattern-building, and the application of general rules or laws or theories. In the rest of this chapter, then, let us examine each of those in turn, asking what role each plays in a translator's engagement with the world.

Intuitive leaps (abduction)

What role should intuition play in translation?

None at all, some say – or as little as possible. Nothing should be left to chance; and since intuition is often equated with guessing, and guessing with randomness or chance, this means that nothing in translation should be left to intuition. But even in its broadest application, this is an extreme position that has little to do with the everyday realities of translation.

It is true that a competent reader would swiftly reject a scientific or technical or legal translation based largely or solely on an ill-informed translator's "intuitions" about the right words and phrases. This kind of "intuition" is the source of the infamous "terrible translations" that one finds in shops and hotels and restaurants and owners' manuals the world around.

From a Brussels shop window: "Come inside and have a fit."

In a hotel in Romania: "The lift is being fixed for the next few days. During that time we regret you will be unbearable."

In a Yugoslavian elevator: "Let us know about an unficiency as well as leaking on the service. Our utmost will improve it."

In a hotel in Budapest: "All rooms not denounced by twelve o'clock will be paid for twicely."

From Prague: "Take one of our horse-driven tours. We guarantee no miscarriages."

In a restaurant in Vienna: "Fried milk, children sandwiches, and boiled sheep."

From Macao: "Utmost of chicken fried in bother."

In a Tokyo hotel: "The flattening of the underwear with pressure is the job of the chambermaid. To get it done, turn her on."

On a Soviet ship in the Black Sea: "Helpsavering apparata in emergings behold many whistles! Associate the stringing apparata about the bosoms and meet behind. Flee then to the indifferent lifesaving shippen obediencing the instructs of the vessel chef."

On a Tokyo map: "Osui Shobunsho (Dirty Water Punishment Place)."

In a hotel in Acapulco: "The manager has personally passed all the water served here."

In an antique shop in Old Delhi: "Curiosities from the backside of India."

In a forest park in Germany: "It is strictly forbidden that people of different sex, for instance men and women, live together in one tent unless they are married with each other for that purpose."

Assembly instructions for an Italian-made baby carriage: "(1) Lead the hind leg in an opened position. (2) Lead the frame of the sack support up. (3) Insert the blushing for blocking in the proper split, push it deeply and wheel in anti time sense till it stops."

But that does not mean that intuition is a bad thing, to be avoided. Intuitive leaps are an essential part of the translation process: essential, but only a part; only a part, but essential.

In the first place, it is often difficult to distinguish intuitive leaps from calm certainty. You are translating along, and stumble briefly on a word. "What *was* that in the target language?" All of a sudden it comes to you, out of nowhere, it seems, and your fingers type it. How do you know it's right? Well, you just know. It *feels* right. It feels intuitively right. Your procedural memory has taken over. In your experience it has always been used in situations or contexts roughly like the one in which the problem word appeared, with roughly the same tone and semantic extension; you turn it around in your head three or four times, sampling it on your tongue, and no matter how you probe it, it still feels right. So you trust your intuition (or your experience) and proceed. You don't check the word in four dictionaries, or fax three friends who might be able to tell you for sure, or send a query out over the Internet. The fact is, if you did that with every word, you would never finish anything. You would certainly never make a living by translating.

Sometimes, of course, your "intuition" or "experience" (and which is it?) tells you that there are serious problems with the word or phrase you've come up with; so you check your dictionaries, and they all confirm your choice, but still you go on doubting. It feels almost right, but not quite. You call or fax your friends, and they give you conflicting answers, which is no help; it's still up to you. You get up and pace around, worrying the word, tugging and pulling at it. Finally the word you've been looking for jumps into your head, and you rejoice, and rush to write it down – *that's* the word!

But how do you know?

You just *do*.

Or you rush to write it down, only to discover that the word you finally remembered has some other connotation or association that makes it potentially inappropriate for this context. What do you do now? You now have two words that feel partly right and partly wrong; which do you choose? Or do you keep agonizing until you find some third word that leaves you feeling equally torn?

Welcome to the world of translation – a compromised world of half-rights and half-wrongs. (But then, what aspect of our world is that *not* true of?)

The process of remembering and vetting words and phrases, then – the semantic core of the job – is steeped in intuitive leaps. Some of those leaps are solidly grounded in long experience, others in dim memories of overheard snatches of conversation; and it is not always possible to tell the two apart. If a word jumps into your head without dragging along behind it the full history of your experience with it, an educated guess may feel very much like a calm certainty, and vice versa. A good translator will develop a rough sense of when s/he can trust these intuitive leaps and when they need to be subjected to close scrutiny and/or independent testing; but that sense is never more than a rough one, always just a little fuzzy at the crucial boundaries.

Intuitive leaps may be unavoidable, even essential, at the leading edge of the translation process; but once a rough draft has been completed, the translator steps back from her or his work, and edits it with a careful and suspicious eye. At least, that is the idea; and it is not only a good idea, it is often a successful one. Many times the translator will catch on the second or third read-through a silly mistake that s/he made at the white heat of invention. "What could I have been thinking!?"

But even editing is heavily grounded in intuitive leaps. After all, what is the source of the cool rational judgment that decides some word or phrase is wrong? The source is the exact same set of experiences that produced it in the first place – simply channeled a little differently. There are cases in which one word is right and seventeen others are wrong; but the translator, working alone, and the interpreter, working in public and without the liberty of looking things up in reference books or asking questions, doesn't always *know* which the right word is, and must rely on an intuitive sense. You make mistakes that way; the mistakes get corrected, and you learn from them, or they don't get corrected, and you make them again. And you wish that you could avoid making such mistakes, but you can't, not entirely; all you can do is try not to make the same mistakes over and over again.

Furthermore, while it is usually considered desirable for a translator to solve all the problems in a text before submitting a finished translation, this isn't always possible. Sometimes the translator will have to call the agency or client and say, "I just can't find a good equivalent for X." If X is easy and the translator should know it, s/he will lose face, and will probably lose future jobs as well; obviously, the translator should usually admit ignorance only after doing everything in her or his own power to solve a problem first.

On the other hand, a translator who admits ignorance in the face of a really difficult (perhaps even insoluble) problem actually gains face, wins the confidence of the agency or client, because it is important to recognize one's own limits; admitting ignorance of this or that difficult word indirectly casts a glow of reliability over the rest of the text, which can now be presumed to be full of things that the translator does know.

Some large translation projects are done by teams: translator A translates the first half and sends the original and translation to translator B for editing; translator B translates the second half and sends the original and translation to translator A for editing; each translator makes changes based on the other's suggestions; the "finished product" of their collaboration is further checked by an in-house person at the agency before it is shipped off to the client. Another in-house person searches databases in the World Wide Web and other Internet sources for useful terminology; both translators compile and constantly revise tentative glossaries of their terminological solutions. In this sort of collaboration, intuitive leaps are not only acceptable; they are strongly encouraged. One translator doesn't know a word, and so guesses at it; the other translator sees instantly that the guess is wrong, but the guess helps her or him to remember the correct word, or to make a better guess, or to suggest a source that may solve the problem for them. Comparing each other's tentative glossaries so as to maintain terminological consistency, they brainstorm individually and together on various problem areas, and gradually hone and polish the words chosen.

In sum, then, intuitive leaps are a necessary part of invention, subject to later editing; and they are a necessary part of editing as well, subject to discussion or negotiation among two or more translators, editors, or managers of a project. Because intuitive leaps are generally considered guesswork, they are usually kept "in-house," whether inside the translator's house and not revealed to an agency, or inside the agency and not revealed to a client; but agencies (and even some corporate clients) realize that translation is not an exact science, and are often all too willing to work together with the translator(s) to untangle knotty problems.

Finally, of course, it should be said that not all translation is scientific or technical; not all translation revolves around the one and only "correct" or "accurate" translation for a given word or phrase. In "free imitations" or "rough adaptations," such as television or film versions of novels or plays, "retellings" of literary classics for children, and international advertising campaigns, intuitive leaps are important not in order to recall the "correct" word but to come up with an interesting or striking or effective word or image or turn of phrase that may well deviate sharply from the original. Where creativity and effectiveness are prized above accuracy, the critical blockages to a good translation are typically not in the translator's memory but in the free flow of her or his imagination; intuitive or abductive leaps help to keep (or to start) things flowing.

In some cases, also, the "correct" word or phrase is desired, but proves highly problematic, as when translating from the ancient Babylonian or Sumerian – who knows what this or that word might have meant three thousand years ago? (see Roberts 1997) – or when the translator suspects that the original writer didn't quite have ahold of the word s/he wanted yet. When the Armenian-American poet Diana derHovanessian was working with an Armenian scholar to translate a collection of contemporary Armenian poetry into English, there was a word for mountain-climbing that she felt strongly was *right*, poetically "accurate" or appropriate, despite her Armenian collaborator's insistence that it had the wrong connotations for the Armenian word used by the original poet. In this situation she was translating (or trying to translate) abductively, intuitively, by the seat of her pants. Her intuitive leap was later confirmed by the original Armenian poet himself, who said that he wished he had thought to use the Armenian equivalent of the word she used; and would have done so, had he thought of it, because *it*, not the word actually printed in the poem, was the "right" one.

But these hunches are rarely so satisfactorily confirmed; they come, they insist on being heard, considered, and acted upon; the translator makes a decision, and typically the situation is gone, past, over and done with. No one even notices; no one says, "No, you're wrong," or "You were right and I was wrong." The word or words chosen become water under the bridge; new jobs await their translator.

Pattern-building (induction)

Less perhaps needs to be said in defense, let alone explanation, of the inductive process of building patterns through exposure to numerous individual cases, than about the more controversial process of abduction; it is generally recognized that induction is how translators most typically proceed with any given translation task or series of translation tasks, and thus also how translators are most effectively "trained" (or train themselves). Practice may not make perfect, but it certainly helps; the more words, phrases, and whole texts a person has translated, the better a translator that person is likely to be.

But a few comments are in order. One is that "experience" or "practice" conceived as *induction* is more than sheer mindless exposure to masses of material. It is a process of sifting mindfully through that material, constantly looking for regularities, patterns, generalities that can bring some degree of order and thus predictability and even control to the swirl of experience. To some extent this "mindfulness" can be subconscious, subliminal – but only if one has sublimated an analytical spirit, a searching contrast-and-compare mentality that never quite takes things exactly as they come but must always be asking "why?" and "why not?" and "haven't I seen something like this before?"

To put that differently, the "mindfulness" that raises experience to an inductive process is an attentiveness, a readiness to notice and reflect upon words and phrases and register shifts and all the other linguistic and nonlinguistic material to which a translator is constantly being exposed – striking or unusual words and phrases, certainly, but also ordinary ones that might have escaped earlier attention, familiar ones that might have shifted in usage or meaning, etc. You hear a word that sounds as if it might work as an equivalent for some source-language word that has bothered you in the past, and you immediately stop and ask questions: you hear someone in Spain using the word "empoderamiento" casually in conversation, for example, and you begin pestering the speaker with questions designed to establish whether that word really works as a Spanish equivalent of the English "empowerment," or whether its parallel Latin derivation is a mere misleading coincidence (making it a "false friend"). Working inductively, translators are always "collecting" words and phrases that might some day be useful, some on note cards or in computer files, others only in their heads; and that sort of collection process requires that the translator have her or his "feelers" out most or all of the time, sorting out the really interesting and potentially useful and important words and phrases from the flood of language that we hear around us every day.

It is also significant that, while the inductive process of finding patterns in large quantities of experience has the power to transform our subliminal habits, it is ultimately only effective once it is incorporated *into* those subliminal habits. In fact, the process of sublimating inductive discoveries can help explain why inductive experience is so much more useful for the practicing translator than deduction, the learning and application of general rules and theories. There is a natural movement from ongoing discoveries and insights to subliminal habit that is enhanced by induction – especially when induction is conceived as becoming conscious of something just long enough to recognize its interesting characteristics and then storing it – and can actually be hindered or blocked by deduction. But more of that in the next section.

Rules and theories (deduction)

Ideally, deductive principles – rules, models, laws, theories – of translation should arise out of the translator's own experience, the inductive testing of abductive hypotheses through a series of individual cases. In abduction the translator tries something that feels right, perhaps feels potentially right, without any clear sense of how well it will work; in induction the translator allows broad regularities to emerge from the materials s/he has been exposed to; and in deduction the translator begins to impose those regularities on new materials by way of predicting or controlling what they will entail. Lest these general principles become too rigid, however, and so block the translator's receptivity to novel experiences (and thus ability to learn and grow), deduction must constantly be fed "from below," remaining flexible in response to pressures from new abductions and inductions to rethink what s/he thought was understood.

This ideal model is not always practicable, however. Above all it is often inefficient. Learning general principles through one's own abductive and inductive experience is enormously time-consuming and labor-intensive, and frequently narrow – precisely as narrow as the translator's own experience. As a result, many translators with homegrown deductions about translation have simply reinvented the wheel: "I believe it is important to translate the meaning of the original text, not individual words." Translators who post such deductive principles on Internet discussion groups like Lantra-L have learned the hard way, through laborious effort and much concentrated reflection, what translation theorists have been telling their readers for a very long time: about sixteen centuries, if you date this theory back to Jerome's letter to Pammachius in 395:

Now I not only admit but freely announce that in translating from the Greek – except of course in the case of Holy Scripture, where even the syntax contains a mystery – I render, not word for word, but sense for sense.

(Robinson 1997b: 25)

two millennia if you date it back to Cicero in 55 before the common era:

And I did not translate them as an interpreter, but as an orator, keeping the same ideas and the forms, or as one might say, the "figures" of thought, but in language which conforms to our usage.

(Robinson 1997b: 9)

It is also what translation instructors have been telling their students for decades. Is it really necessary for individual translators to relearn this principle with so much effort? Wouldn't it make more sense for them to be told, early on in their careers, that this is the fundamental axiom of all mainstream translation in the West, and so to be spared the effort of working it out for themselves?

Yes and no. The effort is never really wasted, since we always learn things more fully, integrate them more coherently into our working habits, when we learn them in rich experiential contexts, through our own efforts. In some sense no one ever learns anything without first testing it in practice – even if that "practice" is only the experience of taking a test on material taught in class, or comparing it to one's own past experiences and seeing whether they match up. The beginning student translator who "naturally" translates one word at a time will not quite believe the teacher who says "translate the meanings of whole sentences, not individual words," until s/he has tested that principle in actual translation work and felt its experiential validity. So experience remains important even when being taught someone else's deductive principles.

But at the same time, "being told" can mean immense savings in time and effort over "figuring it out on your own." The beginning student translator told to translate the meanings of whole sentences will still have to test the principle in practice, but this experiential testing process will now be focused or channeled by the "rule" or "model," and so will move much more quickly and effectively toward its goal than it would if left to develop on its own.

This is, of course, the rationale behind translator training: given a few general principles and plenty of chances to test those principles in practice (and intelligent feedback on the success or failure of those tests), novice translators will progress much more rapidly toward professional competence than they would out in the working world on their own.

In addition, exposure to other people's deductions about translation can help broaden a translator's sense of the field. We all tend to assume that translation is pretty much the same everywhere, and everywhere pretty much the same as what we've experienced in our own narrow little niche – and this assumption can be terribly limiting. A translator who has deduced from years of experience in technical or business translation that all translators must render the meaning of the original text as accurately as possible will feel paralyzed when asked to adapt advertising copy to the requirements of a different culture, or a complex novel for children. "That's not translation!" this sort of person typically cries – because that is not the kind of translation s/he has done. Whatever lies outside each individual translator's fairly narrow experience of the field is "not translation." Exposure to other people's deductions about the field can coax translators with these ingrained assumptions past the limitations of their own experiential worlds.

And this is one rationale for translation theory: it pushes translators past narrow conceptions of the field to expanding insights into what translation has been historically (in the Middle Ages translators often wrote their own glosses or commentaries and built them *into* their translations), what it is today (radical adaptations, interpretive imitations, propagandistic refocusing), and what it might be in some imaginable future. These theoretical explorations may not be immediately applicable to the translator's practical needs; the in-house translator who only translates a certain type of technical documentation, for example, may not have a strong professional need to know how people translated in the Middle Ages, or how advertising translations often proceed in the present.

But no one ever knows what kinds of knowledge or experience will prove useful in the future. The in-house technical translator may one day be offered an advertising translation: "So-and-so's out sick today, do you think you could have a look at this full-page ad?" Does s/he really want to have to say, "I don't know anything about advertising translation, I've never thought about it, and to be quite frank I don't *want* to think about it"? A friend with an advertising agency may be looking for a translator to join the firm; does the technical translator really want not to be in a position to choose between the two jobs, simply because advertising translation (indeed anything outside her or his current narrow experience) is unthinkable?

One way of putting this is to say that the translator should be a lifelong learner, always eager to push into new territories, and at least occasionally, in accordance with his or her own learning styles (see Chapter 3), willing to let other people chart the way into those territories. No one can experience everything first hand; in fact, no one can experience more than a few dozen things even through books and courses and other first-hand descriptions. We have to rely on other people's experiences in order to continue broadening our world – even if, once we have heard those other experiences, we want to go out and have our own, to test their descriptions in practice.

It is important to remember, in these next five chapters, that abduction, induction, and deduction are all important channels of experience and learning. Each has its special and invaluable contribution to make to the learning process. Abductive guesswork without the ongoing practical trial-and-error of induction or the rules, laws, and theories of deduction would leave the translator a novice: induction and deduction are essential to professional competence. But induction without the fresh perspectives and creative leaps of abduction and the corrective "big picture" of deduction would become a rote, mechanical straitjacket. And deduction without surprises from the world of abduction or a solid grounding in professional practice would be sterile and empty.

Discussion

1   Is it enough for the translator to have profound and extensive experiences of one or more foreign languages? If so, is it enough to have been exposed to that language or those languages in books and classrooms? Or is experience of the culture or cultures in which it is natively spoken essential?

2   How important is rich experience of your mother tongue(s)? And how rich? Is it essential to be exposed to people who speak it in different regions, social classes, and professions? Or is it enough to have read in it widely and attentively?

3 Is extensive experience of a certain subject matter enough for the translator, if s/he has a rudimentary working knowledge of the foreign language a source text in that field is written in? If so, does that experience need to be hands-on practical experience of the field, experience of the objects and the people who handle them and the way those people speak about the objects? Or is it enough to have experience of books, articles, and coursework on that subject matter?

4 Could it be enough in certain cases for the translator to have fleeting and superficial experience of the foreign language and the subject matter but a rich and complex experience with dictionaries? Would it be enough for a competent professional translator from Spanish and Portuguese to have heard a little Italian and own a good Italian dictionary in order to translate a fairly easy and routine text from the Italian?

5 What role should intuition play in translation?

6 Can translation be taught? If so, can it be taught through precepts, rules, principles? Or can it only be "taught" through doing it and getting feedback?

Exercises

1 Think of the foreign culture you know best. Cast your mind back to all the times when you noticed that something, especially the way a thing was said or done, had changed in that culture. Relive the feelings you had when you noticed the change: bafflement, irritation, interest and curiosity, a desire to analyze and trace the sources of the change, etc. What did you do? How did you handle the situation?

2 Read through a source text that is new to you and mark it as follows: (a) *underline* words and phrases that are completely familiar to you, so that you don't even have to think twice about them; (b) *circle* words and phrases that are somewhat familiar to you, but that you aren't absolutely sure about, that you might want to verify in a dictionary or other source; (c) put a *box* around words and phrases that are completely unfamiliar to you. Now look back over your markings and predict the role that intuition

will play in your translation of the words and phrases in the three different categories. Finally, look up one or more circles or boxed words or phrases in a dictionary or other reference book and monitor the role that intuition actually plays in your selection, from the various alternatives listed there, of the "correct" or "accurate" or "best" equivalent for each.

3   Work in pairs with a fairly short (one-paragraph) translation task, each person translating the whole source text and then "editing" the other's translation. As you work on the other person's translation, be aware of your decision-making process: how you "decide" (or feel) that a certain word or phrasing is wrong, or off; how you settle upon a better alternative. Do you have a grammatical rule or dictionary definition to justify each "correction"? If so, is the rule or definition the first thing you think of, or do you first have a vague sense of there being a problem and then refine that sense analytically? Do you never consciously analyze, work purely from inarticulate "raw feels"? Then discuss the "problem areas" with your partner, exploring the differences in your intuitive (and experiential) processing of the text, trying to work out in each case why something seemed right or wrong to you; why it continues to seem right or wrong despite the other person's disagreement; or what it is in the other person's explanations that convinces you that you were wrong and s/he was right.

4   Work alone or in small groups to develop rules or principles out of a translation you've done – a certain word or syntactic structure should always, or usually, or in certain specified cases be translated as X. As you work on the deduction of general principles, be aware of how you do it: what processes you go through, what problems you have to solve, what obstacles you must remove, where the problems and obstacles come from, etc. To what extent do the members of your group disagree on the proper rule or law to be derived from a given passage? What does the disagreement stem from? Divergent senses of the commonality or extension of a certain pattern? Try to pinpoint the nature of each difficulty or disagreement.

Suggestions for further reading

Gorlée (1994: 42–9), Kussmaul (1995)

Chapter 6

People

- **The meaning of a word**   128
- **Experiencing people**   130
- **First impressions (abduction)**   132
- **Deeper acquaintance (induction)**   133
- **Psychology (deduction)**   138
  - **Discussion**   140
  - **Exercises**   141
  - **Suggestions for further reading**   143

T HESIS: A person-centered approach to any text, language, or culture will always be more productive and effective than a focus on abstract linguistic structures or cultural conventions.

The meaning of a word

Translation is often thought to be primarily about words and their meanings: what the words in the source text mean, and what words in the target language will best capture or convey that meaning.

While words and meanings are unquestionably important, however, they are really only important for the translator (as for most people) in the context of someone actually using them, speaking or writing them to someone else. When the Austrian philosopher Ludwig Wittgenstein quipped, famously, in his *Philosophical Investigations* (1958: para. 43), that "the meaning of a word is its use in the language," he meant that *people* using language always take precedence – or at least should take precedence – over meanings in the dictionary, semantic fields in the abstract.

Jim and Maria live together. Jim is a native speaker of North American English, Maria a native speaker of Argentinian Spanish. Maria's English is better than Jim's Spanish, so they mostly speak English together. Maria gets offended when Jim calls her "silly" – which he does frequently. Finally he says the offensive word once too often and she decides to talk about it with him. He says he means the word affectionately: in his childhood everyone in his family used "silly" as a term of endearment. It was a good thing for someone to be silly; it meant funny, humorous, genial, pleasantly childlike, a good person. Maria explained that she learned the word in school, where she was taught that it means "stupid, foolish, ridiculous." As a result of this conversation, Jim is careful to use the word "silly" in contexts where he hopes his light, playful mood and affectionate tone will make it clear to Maria that he doesn't mean to hurt her feelings with it; Maria begins to notice that the word *as Jim uses it* means something different from what she learned in school. But occasionally she hears him using it in a less loving way, as when they are having an argument and he shakes his head in disgust and snorts, in response to something she has just said, "Don't be silly!" She guesses, rightly, that for him *in that particular context* "silly" does mean more or less what she was taught: "stupid, foolish, ridiculous." But she also accepts his insistence that for him it mostly means "funny, humorous, playful."

In this example, and in ordinary day-to-day life in general, "words" and "meanings" take on their importance in intimate connection with *people*. They take on meaning through those people, arise out of those people's experiences and needs and expectations; and they tell us more about the people around us than we knew before, help us to understand them better. A dictionary could represent the two different meanings "silly" had for Jim and Maria by identifying two separate semantic fields: (1) stupid, foolish, ridiculous; (2) funny, humorous, playful. But this would only be a pale imitation of the living complexity of Jim's and Maria's shifting sense of the word in their relationship.

We almost always learn words and their meanings from people, and as a function of our complex relationships with people. The only really reliable way to learn a new word, in fact, is in context, as used by someone else in a real situation, whether spoken or written. Only then does the new word carry with it some of the human emotional charge given it by the person who used it; only then does it feel alive, real, fully human. A word learned in a dictionary or a thesaurus will most often feel stiff, stilted, awkward, even if its dictionary "meaning" is "correct"; other people who know the word will feel somewhat uncomfortable with its user.

A prime example of this is the student paper studded with words taken straight out of a dictionary or thesaurus, words that the student has never seen or heard used in a real conversation or written sentence. For the teacher who knows the words thus used, the whole paper comes to seem like gibberish, because the words are used mechanically and without attention to the nuances of actual human speech or writing.

Another example, as we saw in Chapter 5, is the "bad" translation done by someone who doesn't speak the target language fluently, and has painstakingly found all the words in a dictionary.

Experiencing people

One implication of this for the training or professional growth of a translator is that, beginning ideally in childhood and continuing throughout life, a translator should be interested in people, all kinds of people – and should take every opportunity to learn about how different people act.

Parents, obviously: every child pays close attention to how his or her parents act, because understanding your parents, at least at some level, is essential for survival. Teachers, certainly: one of the first things students try to do in any class they take is to figure out the teacher, what s/he wants, expects, likes and dislikes, etc. Other adult authority figures: should I obey or disobey them? Can I trust them or not? (Obey the ones who seem to be connected to your parents, but maybe reserve your trust for those who really seem to like and respect you; mistrust and disobey the ones who want to take you for a little ride or touch you where you don't want to be touched.) Peers: what kind of kid is X, or Y? Bossy, shy, exciting, boring?

And as children grow – especially as they grow into people who want to be translators – they continue to pay attention to the people around them, even when there is no obvious reason to do so. Friends, colleagues, relatives – that goes without saying. But also shop-keepers, salespersons, electricians and plumbers, the mail carrier, servers in restaurants, bank tellers – all the people with whom we come in contact in our everyday lives. Perfect strangers with whom we have encounters: accidental collisions, gurgling at a baby, scratch-ing a dog's ears, between floors in an elevator. Perfect strangers whom we never actually encounter, whom we overhear on a bus or watch walk across a street. We watch them; we observe them closely. We turn their words over in our ears and our mouths. We wonder what it feels like to be that person.

And what do we notice? What do we pay attention to? Manner-isms, nervous habits, posture and gestures, facial expressions, a style of walking and talking. Word choice: certain words and phrases will always provoke a vivid memory of a certain person using them in a certain situation. We will remember minute details about the situation: how hot it was that day, what so-and-so was wearing, how someone laughed, a vague feeling of unease ... With other words and phrases we will work very hard to overcome their association with a certain person or a certain situation – as when a word provoked titters in you as a child but needs to be used seriously when you are an adult; or when a word had one set of associations for you back home, in your regional dialect, but is used very differently in the metropolis where you now live.

– –

Yeah, aren't we a horrid lot? Friends and family think we want to chat about something, like modern warehouse logistics or actuators for gaseous media, they strike up a lively conversation about the subject, and all this only to find out that we were just after the _word_ for it:)
    Sometimes I happen to listen in on conversations, like in the subway, and when someone uses a word I've been searching for ages, I almost want to shake their hands. But of course, I don't.

pro verbially
Werner Richter

– –

    The more situational and personal associations you have with a word or a phrase, the more complexly and flexibly you will be able to use it yourself – and the less it will seem to you the sole "property" of a single person or group. This complexity and flexibility of use is a goal to strive for; the more complexly and flexibly you use language, the better a translator you will be. But striving for that goal does not mean *ignoring* the situational and personal associations of words and phrases. It means internalizing so many of them that they fade into your subconscious or subliminal knowing. The goal is to "store" as many vivid memories of people saying and writing things as you can, but to store them in linguistic habits where you do not need to be conscious of every memory – where those memories are "present," and work for you powerfully and effectively, but do so subliminally, beneath your conscious awareness.

    How is this done? We might think of this "storage" process in terms of Peirce's three types of reasoning: abduction, induction, and deduction. Abduction would cover the impact of first impressions; induction our ongoing process of building up patterns in the wealth of experience we face every day; and deduction the study of human psychology.

First impressions (abduction)

To experience a person "abductively" is to make a first rough attempt to understand that person based on early conflicting evidence – what we normally call "first impressions." People are hard to figure out; we can live with a person for decades and still be surprised by his or her actions several times a day. People are riddled with contradictions; even first impressions are almost always mixed, vague, uncertain. It is so rare to get a coherent or unified first impression of a person, in fact, that we tend to remember the occasions when that happened:

> "It was love at first sight."
> "I don't know, there was just something about him, something evil, he gave me the creeps."
> "We hit it off instantly, as if we'd known each other all our lives."
> "I don't know why, but I don't trust her."

(The complexities, the contradictions, the conflicts will arise later, inevitably; but for the moment it feels as if the other person's heart is laid bare before you, and it all fits together as in a jigsaw puzzle.)

Even so, despite the complex welter of different impressions that we get of a person in our first encounter, we do make judgments – perhaps by jumping to conclusions, a good description of what Peirce calls abduction. There are at least three ways of doing this:

1 *Typecasting, stereotyping.* "I know her type, she promises you the world but never follows through." "He's shy, unsure of himself, but seems very sweet." "She's the kind of person who can get the job done." "S/he's not my type." "It's a romance? Forget it, I hate romances." "Oh, it's one of *those* agencies, I know the type you mean." We make sense of complexity by reducing it to fairly simple patterns that we've built up from encounters with other people (or texts).

2 *Postponing judgment along simplified (often dualistic) lines.* "I think he could become a good friend" or "I don't think I could

ever be friends with someone like that." "She might prove useful to us somewhere down the line" or "We'll never get anything out of her." "Maybe I'll ask her/him out" or "S/he'd never go out with me." "There's something interesting in here that I want to explore, so I'll read on" or "This is so badly written it can't possibly be any good, so I'll quit now." We sense a direction our connection with this person or text might potentially take and explain that "hunch" to ourselves with simple yes/no grids: friend/not-friend, lover/not-lover, interesting/uninteresting, etc.

3   *Imitating, mimicking.* This is often misunderstood as ridicule. Some mimicking is intended to poke fun, certainly – but not all. Pretending to be a person, acting like her or him, imitating her or his voice, facial expressions, gestures, other bodily movements can be a powerful channel for coming to understand that person more fully – from the "inside," as it were. Hence the saying, "Never criticize a man till you've walked a mile in his shoes." Walking a mile in someone's shoes is usually taken to mean actually being in that person's situation, being forced to deal with some problem that s/he faces; but it applies equally well to merely imagining yourself in that person's place, or to "staging" in your own body that person's physical and verbal reactions to situations. It is astonishing how much real understanding of another person can emerge out of this kind of staging or acting – though this type of understanding can frequently not be articulated, only felt.

This "acting out" is essential training for actors, comedians, clowns, mimes – and translators and interpreters, who are also in the business of pretending to be someone they're not. What else is a legal translator doing, after all, but pretending to be a lawyer, writing as if s/he were a lawyer? What is a medical translator doing but pretending to be a doctor or a nurse? Technical translators pretend to be (and in some sense thereby become) technical writers. Verse translators pretend to be (and sometimes do actually become) poets.

Deeper acquaintance (induction)

The more experience you have of people – both individual people and people in general – the more predictable they become. Never perfectly predictable; people are too complicated for that. But increased experience with an individual person will help you understand that person's actions; increased experience with a certain type or group of people (including people from a certain culture, people who speak a certain language) will help you understand strangers from that group; increased experience of humanity in general will take some of the surprise out of odd behavior. Surprises will fall into patterns; the patterns will begin to make sense; new surprises that don't fit the patterns will force you to adjust your thinking, build more complexity into your patterns, and so on. This is the process traditionally called inductive reasoning: moving from a wealth of minute details or specific experiences to larger patterns.

The inductive process of getting to know people and coming to understand them (at least a little) is essential for all human beings, of course; but especially for those of us who work with people, and with the expressive products of people's thinking. A technician may be able to get along without much understanding of people; a technical writer is going to need to know at least enough about people to be able to imagine a reader's needs; and a technical translator is going to need to know most of all, because the list of people whom s/he will need to "understand" (or second-guess) is the longest: the agency representative who offered her or him the job, the company marketing or technical support person who wants the text translated, the technical writer who wrote the text, friends who might know this or that key word, and the eventual target-language user/reader.

And the amount of people-oriented knowledge or understanding that a successful translation of this sort requires is nothing less than staggering:

1   What do the agency hope to get out of this? What stake do they have in this particular translation? How much more than money is it? Is this a big client that they're wooing? Is there a personal connection, something other than pure business? Such things are almost never made explicit; you have to read them between the lines, hear them in the voice of the person who calls from the agency with the job.

2   Just how invested in the text is this or that in-house person at the client? Who wrote it, and why? Freelancers who work through agencies don't normally find out much about the client, but a

good deal can be read between the lines. Does it read as if it was written by a technical writer or editor, a manager, a secretary, a marketing or publicity person? Was the writer writing for print, word-processed newsletter, business correspondence (letter or fax, typed or scribbled)? Does the writer seem to have a good sense of her or his audience? Is it a supplier, a dealer, a client? Is it one person whom the writer knows, or a small group of people, or a large undefined public? Does the writer feel comfortable writing? Are there other people directly influencing the writing of the text – for example, in the form of marginal notes jotted in in several hands?

3   Who can you call or fax or e-mail to ask about unfamiliar words? How will they react to being asked to help out? Do you already owe them favors? If so, how should you phrase the request? Should you promise the friend something in return (money, dinner, help of some sort) or ask for another favor? If the friend is extremely helpful and provides words or phrases (or diagrams or drawings or other material) that almost solve your problem but not quite, how many follow-up questions will s/he put up with? This is never something that can be predicted in advance; it has to be taken as it comes, with full sensitivity to the friend's verbal and nonverbal signals.

4   Who is the target-language reader? Who are the target-language readers? Is any information available on them at all, or is it some undefined group that happens to read the translation? What do you know about people who speak the target language natively, people who grew up in the target culture, that differs in significant ways from their counterparts in the source culture? What aspects of climate, geography, geopolitical stature, cultural politics, and religious background make a target-language reader likely to respond to a text differently from a source-language reader? What proverbs, metaphors, fairy tales, Bible translations, and literary classics have shaped target-language readers along different lines from source-language readers?

It is important to stress that, while "inductive" experience of the people who have a direct impact on a translator's work is always the most useful in that work, it is not always possible to predict who those people will be in advance. Representatives of new agencies and clients call out of the blue; the people an interpreter is asked to interpret for are always changing; not all technical writers are the same, nor are medical writers, legal writers, etc. Personal differences mean stylistic differences; the better able a translator or interpreter is to recognize and understand an unexpected personality type, the better able s/he will also be to render an idiosyncratic style effectively into the target language.

And this means that it is never enough for translators to get to know certain people, or certain types of people. You never know what personalities or personality types will prove useful in a translation or interpretation job – so you need to be open to everyone, interested in everyone, ready to register or record any personal idiosyncrasy you notice in any person who comes along.

This in turn requires a certain observant frame of mind, a people-watching mentality that is always on the lookout for character quirks, unusual (not to mention usual) turns of phrase, intonations, timbres, gestures, and so on. Translators who "collect" little tidbits of information about every person they meet, every text they read, and turn them over and over in their mind long after collecting them, will be much more likely to be ready for the peculiar text than those who are completely focused on linguistic structures in the abstract.

One of the most important new developments coming out of the study of multiple intelligences and learning styles (Chapter 3) is the study of "personal intelligence," or what is now being called "emotional intelligence." Daniel Goleman (1995: 43–4) outlines five elements of emotional intelligence:

1   *Emotional self-awareness – knowing how you feel about something, and above all how you are currently feeling.* Many professional decisions are made on the basis of our reactions to people; this makes recognizing *how* we are reacting essential to successful decision-making. As Goleman (1995: 43) writes, "An inability to monitor our true feelings leaves us at their mercy." For example, if you hate your work, the sooner you recognize that and move on to something you enjoy more, the better off you will be. If you love certain parts of it and hate others, being aware of those mixed feelings will help you gravitate more toward the parts you enjoy and avoid or minimize or learn to reframe the parts you dislike. And the more astute your emotional self-awareness, the better you will also get at:

2   *Emotional self-control* – transforming and channeling your emotions in positive and productive ways. Many translators work
alone, or in large impersonal corporations, and battle loneliness,
boredom, and depression. The better able you are to change your
mood, to spice up a dull day with phone calls or e-mail chats or a
coffee break, or to "think" (visualize, breathe, soothe) yourself
out of the doldrums, the more positive and successful you will be
as a translator. Clients and agencies will do things that irritate
you; the better able you are to conceal or transform your irritation
when speaking to them on the phone or in a meeting, or even get
over the irritation before speaking to them, the more professional
you will appear to them, and the more willing they will be to give
you work. And the more effectively you are able to channel and
transform your emotions, the better you will also get at:

3   *Emotional self-motivation* – finding the drive within yourself to
accomplish professional goals. In almost every case, translators
have to be self-starters. They have to take the initiative to find
work and to get the work done once it has been given to them to
do. They have to push themselves to take that extra hour or two to
track down the really difficult terminology, rather than taking the
easy way out and putting down the first entry they find in their
dictionaries. The better able they are to channel their emotional
life toward the achievement of goals, the more they will enjoy
their work, the more efficiently they will do it, and the more
professional recognition they will receive. At the very highest
levels of self-motivation, translators experience the "flow" state
described by Mihaly Csikszentmihalyi (1990), where the rest of
the world seems to fade away and work becomes sheer delight.
And knowing and channeling your own emotions also helps you
develop powers of:

4   *Empathy* – recognizing, understanding, and responding to other
people's emotions. This is a crucial skill for professionals who
rely on social contacts for their livelihood. While many translators work alone, they also have clients whose needs they have to
second-guess and attempt to satisfy, agencies that may only hint
at the institutional complexity of a job they are trying to get done,
friends and acquaintances who know some field professionally
and may be able to help with terminology problems. Sensing how
they feel about your requests, or your responses to their requests,

will help you interact with them in a personally and professionally satisfying manner, leading both to more work and to enhanced enjoyment in your work. And of course the better able you are to empathize with others, the better you will be at:

5   *Handling relationships* – maintaining good professional and personal relationships with the people on whom your livelihood depends. Translation is a business; and while business is about money, and in this case words, phrases, and texts, it is also, as this chapter shows, about people – interpersonal relations. Successful business people are almost invariably successful socially as well as financially, because the two go hand in hand. This is perhaps clearest when money is not involved: how do you "pay" a friend for invaluable terminological help? The pay is almost always emotional, social, relational: the coin of friendship and connection. But even when a client or agency is paying you to do a job, the better able you are to handle your relationship – even, in many cases, professional friendship – with them, the happier they are going to be to pay you to do this job and future ones.

Psychology (deduction)

If deduction is the application of general principles to the solution of a problem, then the primary deductive approach to the problem of how people act is psychology. By this reasoning, the next step beyond paying close attention to people for the student translator would be to take classes in psychology.

But this may be unsatisfactory for a number of reasons.

The first and most obvious is that the psychology of translation is still undeveloped as a scholarly discipline, so that you are unlikely to find courses in it at your university, and the psychology courses you do find offered may be utterly irrelevant for a translator's needs.

Then again, what *are* a translator's needs? We just saw in discussing inductive approaches to people that it is impossible to predict exactly what kind of people-oriented knowledge will be useful in any given translation job; the same goes for deductive approaches as well. It is quite possible that extensive (or even cursory) study of psychology might provide insights into people that will help the translator translate better.

For example, the second reason why classes in psychology might be unsatisfactory to the student of translation is that psychology as a discipline is typically concerned with pathology, i.e., problems, sicknesses, neuroses and psychoses, personality disorders – and the people translators deal with in a professional capacity tend to be fairly ordinary, normal folks. But this can then be turned around into a positive suggestion: if there are courses offered at your university in the psychology of normal people, they might very well prove useful, especially if they deal with work-related topics.

PSYCHOLOGY COURSES OF POTENTIAL BENEFIT TO TRANSLATORS

Industrial psychology
The psychology of advertising
The psychology of learning
The psychology of problem-solving
Human memory and cognition
The psychology of language
Group dynamics
Intergroup behavior
Decision-making and perceived control
The social psychology of organizations
Social identity, social conflict, and information processing
Networking and social coordination
Team development
Psychology applied to business
Psychology and law
Interpersonal influence and communication
Cross-cultural training
Social-psychological approaches to international conflict

In addition, it should be remembered that psychology, psychoanalysis, psychotherapy, and psychiatry are professional fields that generate texts for translation. Translators are asked to translate psychiatric evaluations and medical records, social workers' reports, and various scholarly writings in the field (conference papers, journal articles, scholarly books); court interpreters are asked to interpret testimony from expert witnesses in psychiatry and psychology; conference interpreters at scholarly meetings in the field must obviously be well versed in how psychologists and psychiatrists think, how they see their world.

In studying psychology, in other words, one should not forget that the relevant "people" in the field are not merely the subjects of psychologists' theories and experiments. They are also the psychologists themselves. If a translator is ever asked to translate a psychological text, a class in psychology at university will provide an excellent background – not only because the translator will have some familiarity with the terms and concepts, but because s/he will have grown familiar with one real-life psychologist, the professor in the course.

Finally, there is no reason why translators should not gradually become amateur psychologists in their own right. In fact, a few weeks of reading postings on an e-mail discussion group like Lantra-L, for example, will convince the would-be translator that most of the translators writing in *are* amateur psychologists – people who have developed theories of human behavior which they will elaborate for you at great length. These theories grew out of inductive experience, which is the very best source for theories; but they have since become formulated in broad, general terms, as deductive principles, ready to explain any personal quirk or trait that comes along. The only real danger in these theories is the same danger that inheres in all deductive or theoretical thinking: that the general principles become so rigid that they no longer change in response to experience; that they become straitjackets for experience. Hence the importance of continued abductive and inductive openness to novelty, to experiences that the "theories" can't explain. Without such wrenches in the deductive works, the translator stops growing.

Discussion

If, as Ludwig Wittgenstein says, "the meaning of a word is its use in the language," and that use varies from person to person and from situation to situation, how is it ever possible to know what someone else means?

Exercises

1 Give dictionary definitions of "dog" and "cat" in your mother tongue. Think of the equivalent words in your main foreign tongue; get the equivalence fixed firmly in your imagination.

Now get comfortable in your chair; close your eyes if that helps you "daydream" better. Think of the house pets of your child-hood; visualize them, tactilize them, imagine yourself holding them in your lap or rolling around on the floor with them (what-ever you did in close contact with them); remember whether you loved them (or one particular one), hated them, were afraid of them, were indifferent to them; if you had negative feelings for them, recall in detail specific times when you felt those feelings most strongly, as when a dog snarled at you, bit you, when a cat hissed at you, scratched you.

Next reflect on the many positive and negative connotations and usages of "dog" and "cat" in English and many other languages. (In English some people call a homely woman a "dog" and a nasty woman a "cat"; "a dog's life" is an un-pleasant one; but "a dog is a man's best friend" and a sweet person is a "pussy-cat.") Which of these usages feel right to you, which feel wrong?

Discuss with the group: what connection is there between personal physical experience and our figurative use of common words like "dog" and "cat"? What similarities and differences are there between our experiences of people and our experiences of animals (especially domestic pets), and how do those simi-larities and differences affect the way we use language?

2 Think to yourself the strongest taboo word you can think of in your native language. Pay attention to your body as you say that word to yourself – how you feel, whether you feel good or bad, relaxed or tense, warm or cold, excited or anxious. Now say it very quietly out loud, and glance at your neighbors to see how they're reacting to it, all the while monitoring your body reac-tions. Now imagine saying it to your mother. Say the word 100 times – does it lose some or all of its force, its power to shock? Finally, imagine a situation, or a person, or a group of people, with whom you would feel comfortable using the word. Recall the

situations where you were taught not to use such language, who the person (or group) was in each case, how you felt when you were shamed or spanked for using it. Recall the situations where you used it with friends or siblings and felt rebellious. (If you never did, imagine such situations – imagine yourself bold enough and brave enough to break through your inhibitions and the social norms that control them and *do* it.)

Discuss with the group: how do other people's attitudes, expectations, and reactions govern the "meaning" of swear words? When we compare swear words in various languages, how can we tell which is "stronger" and which is "weaker"?

3   Think of a word or a phrase in your mother tongue that your school teachers taught you to consider "low," "substandard," "bad grammar," etc., and say it out loud to the person next to you, monitoring your body response. Does it feel good, bad, warm, uneasy, what? Next try to put yourself in a frame of mind where you can be proud of that word or phrase, where using it includes you in a warm, welcoming community. Finally, feel the conflict built into your body between the community that wants you to use words and phrases like that and the community that disapproves.

Discuss with the group: how are the boundaries between standard and nonstandard (regional, ethnic, class, gender, age) dialects policed by individuals and groups of people? How do individuals and groups resist that policing? How effective is their resistance?

4   Have a short conversation with your neighbor in some broken form of your native tongue – baby talk, foreigner talk, etc. – and try to put yourself in the speaker's body, try to feel the difficulty of expressing yourself without the calm, easy fluency that you now have in the language; also feel the conflict between your desire to speak your language "right" and this exercise's encouragement to speak it "wrong."

Discuss with the group: what other skills besides linguistic ones must you have mastered in order to speak your language fluently? Are there times when you lose those skills, at least partially – when you're wakened in the middle of the night by the phone ringing, when you have a high fever, when you've had too much to drink?

5 Playact with your neighbor a hierarchical shaming situation, without ever making it clear what the other person did wrong. Get really indignant, angry, shocked; say whatever your parents or teachers or whoever said to you when you were small: "No, that's *bad*, very *bad*, you're a *bad boy/girl*, don't *ever* do that again; what's wrong with you? whatever could you have been thinking of? how dare you? just wait till your father gets home!" Now switch roles, and monitor your body's reaction to being both the shamer and the shamed.

Discuss with the group: what lasting effects does this sort of shaming speech heard in childhood have on later language use? In what ways are foreign languages "liberating" precisely because they don't have this early-childhood power over you?

Suggestions for further reading

Bochner (1981), Fitzgerald (1993), Kim (1988), Krings (1986), Miller (1973), Robinson (1991)

Chapter 7

Working people

- **A new look at terminology**   146
- **Faking it (abduction)**   148
- **Working (induction)**   152
- **Terminology studies (deduction)**   156
  - **Discussion**   158
  - **Exercises**   159
  - **Suggestions for further reading**   160

T HESIS: It is far easier to learn and remember specialized terminology, one of the professional translator's main concerns, if one thinks of it as simply the way working people talk and write, rather than trying to memorize long lists of words taken out of context.

A new look at terminology

One of the most important aspects of the translator's job is the management of terminology: being exposed to it, evaluating its correctness or appropriateness in specific contexts, storing and retrieving it. The focal nature of terminology for translation has made terminology studies one of the key subdisciplines within the broader field of translation studies; learning specialized terminology is one of the main emphases in any course on legal, medical, commercial, or other technical translation; and "How do you say X, Y, and Z in language B?" is the most commonly asked question in on-line translator discussion groups like the Internet's Lantra-L and CompuServe's FLEFO.

But terminology studies as they are traditionally conceived are typically grounded methodologically in the neglect of one essential point: that terminology is most easily learned (i.e., stored in memory so as to facilitate later recall) in context – in actual use-situations, in which the people who use such terms in their daily lives are talking or writing to each other. Not that terminologists ignore or discount this fact; its importance is, on the contrary, widely recognized in terminology studies. But the subdiscipline's very focus on *terms* as opposed to, say, people, or highly contextualized conversations, or workplaces, reflects its fundamental assumption that terminology is a stable objective reality that exists in some systematic way "in language" and is only secondarily "used" by people – often used in confusing and contradictory ways, in fact, which is what makes the imagination of a pure or stable "primary" state so attractive.

An approach to terminology (and related linguistic phenomena such as register) from the other direction, from the interpersonal contexts of its actual use, has both advantages and disadvantages in comparison with the traditional terminology studies approach. One of its main disadvantages is that it is difficult to systematize, because it varies so widely over time and from place to place, and therefore also difficult to teach. One of its main advantages is that it is more richly grounded in social experience, and therefore, because of the way the brain works, easier to learn (to store in and recall from memory).

This unfortunate clash between ease of teaching and ease of learning creates difficulties for the contextualized "teaching" of terminology, of course, in terms of actual situational real-world usage. A systematized terminology, abstracted from use and presented to students in the organized form of the dictionary or the glossary, seems perfectly suited to the traditional teacher-centered classroom; it is easily assigned to students to be "learned" outside of class, "covered" or discussed in class, and tested. The only difficulty is that the terms learned in this way are much harder to remember than terms learned in workplace contexts. Unfortunately, workplace contexts are almost impossible to simulate in class, and are much better suited to internships.

Another difference between abstract and systematic linguistic approaches and pedagogies focusing on professional use-situations is that the former are atomistic, the latter holistic. Linguistic instruction in, say, legal or medical translation must first systematize and then teach terminologies and registers separately: the analytical processes for terminologies and registers are different; hence they are thought of as inherently different linguistic phenomena; hence they are taught in sequence, one at a time, rather than all at once.

A focus on professional use-situations, on the other hand, tends to view specialized terminologies and registers as byproducts of certain institutionally organized activities in the world, and of the personal and professional habits that are generated through participation in those activities. As such, they may exhibit various differences, even of the sort that linguists analyze. But since these linguistic phenomena are produced through and controlled by the professional activities, they are thought of as secondary to those activities; the assumption is that anyone engaging in the activities (or something like them) will naturally begin to use the terminologies and registers appropriate to them. No methodological distinction between them is therefore needed.

Depending on one's point of view, this holistic/atomistic difference can again be viewed as an advantage or a disadvantage for either approach. The holism of approaches focused on people, social situations, institutional contexts, and the like once again makes teaching harder, as it is difficult to create holistic and realistic learning experiences in class, and also to know what if anything students are getting out of those experiences. It takes a certain amount of trust to teach this way: the teacher must believe that experience is the best teacher, that students, placed in a rich learning environment, will naturally learn far more, and far more complexly and usefully and memorably, than they would in a carefully controlled lecture environment. Teaching holistically, experientially, also makes grading more difficult – even, if the holistic approach is taken far enough, impossible: how do you grade a student on an experience? Did s/he have the experience fully enough?

We know that experience is a far more powerful teacher than doctrine (in the original Latin sense of "teaching"); but our traditional pedagogies make us enormously suspicious of attempts to bring such experiential learning into the classroom, or to let it transform what we do in the classroom (giving grades, for example) in radical ways.

This chapter offers some tentative working solutions to these dilemmas.

Faking it (abduction)

Translators are fakers. Pretenders. Impostors.

Translators and interpreters make a living pretending to be (or at least to speak or write as if they were) licensed practitioners of professions that they have typically never practiced. In this sense they are like actors, "getting into character" in order to convince third parties ("audiences," the users of translations) that they are, well, not exactly real doctors and lawyers and technicians, but enough like them to warrant the willing suspension of disbelief. "Expert behaviour," as Paul Kussmaul (1995: 33) puts it, "is acquired role playing."

And how do they do it? Some translators and interpreters actually have the professional experience that they are called upon to "fake." This makes the "pretense" much easier to achieve, of course; and the more experience of this sort you have, the better. As I have mentioned before, translation has been called the profession of second choice; if your first choice was something radically different, i.e., had to do more with people or things than with words, you are in an excellent position to specialize in the translation of texts written by practitioners of your previous profession. Other people choose translation simultaneously with another profession, and may even feel guilty about their inability to choose between them; they too have an enormous advantage over other translators working in the same field, because of their "insider" command of terminology.

Most translators and interpreters, however, are not so lucky. Most of us have to pretend with little or no on-the-job experience on which to base the pretense. Some solve this problem by specializing in a given field – medical translations, legal translations, etc., some even in such narrow fields as patents, or insurance claims – and either taking coursework in that field or reading in it widely, in both languages. Interpreters hired for a weekend or a week or a month in a given field will study up on that field in advance. Gradually, over the years, these translators and interpreters become so expert at pretending to be practitioners of a profession they've never practiced that third parties ask them for medical or legal (or whatever) advice. (More on this under induction, below.)

But most of us just fake it, working on no job experience and perhaps a little reading in the field, but never quite enough. An agency calls you with a medical report translation; you've done technical translations for them before, they like and trust you, you like and trust them, they have been an excellent source of income to you in the past, and you want to help them in whatever way you can; they are desperate to have this translated as quickly as possible. You know little or nothing about medical terminology. What do you do? You accept the job, do your best to fake it, and then have the translation checked by a doctor, or by a friend who is better at faking it than you are.

Just what is involved, then, in "faking it" – in translating abductively by pretending to be a professional with very little actual experience or knowledge on which to base your pretense? The first step is imagination: what would it be like to be a doctor? What would it be like to be the doctor who wrote this? How would you see the world? How would you think and feel about yourself? What kind of person would you be? Professional habits are tied up in what the French sociologist Pierre Bourdieu (1986) calls a "habitus," a whole pattern of life-structuring activities, attitudes, and feelings. What would your "habitus" be if you were not a translator but a doctor?

And more narrowly: would you have actually written the report, or dictated it? Does the report feel dictated? What difference would it make whether it was written or dictated? If the report is concise and precise, and you imagine the doctor leaning back in a chair with a dictaphone, tired from being up all night, rubbing her or his eyes with one hand – how then does the report come out sounding so balanced, so calmly competent, even so terse? Is it because the doctor has dictated so many medical reports that they come out automatically, almost subliminally, the doctor's professional "habit" giving the specific findings of an examination a highly formulaic form that requires little or no thought? What would that feel like? How does the translator's professional "habit" resemble the doctor's? Are there enough experiential parallels or convergences between them that the translator can imagine himself or herself in that chair, dictating the medical report in the target language?

Once again, it should go without saying that the translator who is not sure how a real doctor would sound in the target language is obligated to have the product of this imaginative process checked by someone who *is* sure. This sort of abductive translation inevitably involves making mistakes. Without first-hand knowledge of the professions or workplaces from which the text has been taken, it is impossible for the translator to avoid bad choices among the various terminological alternatives in a dictionary entry.

But note two things. First, by projecting herself or himself "abductively" into a profession or a workplace, the translator gains an intuitive guide to individual word-choices. This guide is, of course, never wholly reliable – it is, after all, based on guesswork, imaginative projections, not (much) actual experience – but it is better than nothing. Some translators would dispute this, saying that no guess is better than a bad one, and if all you can do is make bad guesses you shouldn't have accepted the job at all – perhaps shouldn't even be a translator at all. But everyone has to start somewhere; no one, not even the best translator, is ever perfectly proficient on every job s/he does; all translation contains an element of guesswork. The translator who never guessed, who refused even in a first rough draft to write down anything about which s/he was not absolutely certain, would rarely finish a job. There are some texts that are so easy that no guesswork is involved; perhaps in some areas of specialization such texts even eventually become the norm. But most translators have to guess at (and later check and/or have checked) some words in almost every text they translate.

Second, it is always better to guess in a pattern, guided by a principle (even if only an imagined one), than to guess at random. The style or tone produced by a series of abductive guesses based on an imaginative projection may be wrong, but at least it will most likely be recognizable, and thus easier for a checker to fix. The translator who, like an actor or a novelist, pretends to be a practitioner in the field of the source text will probably impart to the finished translation a tonal or rhetorical coherence that will make it read more naturally – even if it is "off."

This in turn raises important questions regarding the social and/ or economic exchange between the translator and the "expert." How much work is the translator going to do before having the translation checked, and how much is s/he going to leave for the "expert" to provide? The more work the expert has to do, the less willing s/he will be to do it; the closer the translator can get the translation to the expert's notion of a "correct" or (better) "natural" text, therefore, the easier it will probably be to get help. And a translation controlled throughout by a novelistic or histrionic imagination of what it must have felt like to be the doctor (or lawyer, or engineer, or whatever) who wrote the source text is much more likely to sound "natural," even if some of the words are wrong and the tone or register or "feel" of the text is not quite right, than a collection of words and phrases chosen without a guiding principle. Even a rough "abductive" guess at professional jargon, therefore, if fully enough fleshed out through the translator's imagination, will conduce to the production of a good translation.

The rule of thumb for the abductive translation of specialized texts, therefore, might go like this: projecting yourself imaginatively into the professional activities or habitus of the source author will guide your individual choice of words, phrases, and ultimately register in a more coherent fashion than a focus on "terminology" or "register."

Working (induction)

Obviously, important as the ability to make imaginative or creative leaps and project yourself into the professional habitus of the source author is, it is even more important to gain actual work experience in a variety of jobs, or to be exposed to the textual results of that experience through books and articles, conversations with people who work in the field, etc. The more first-, second-, or third-hand experience a translator has of a given profession or workplace or job-related jargon, the better able s/he will be to translate texts in that field.

Let us imagine three separate scenarios in which such job-related experience can help the translator translate.

1   You have actually worked in the field, but it's been years, and the terminology has dimmed in your memory. (Future translators should always have the foresight to write five or ten pages of terminological notes to help jog their memories years later, when they need to remember these specialized terms for a translation. Unfortunately, few of us have such foresight.) You open the dictionary, and there, from among four or five possibilities, the right word jumps off the page and into the translation.

Or you aren't so lucky (and here is where it gets interesting): no dictionary you can find gives you even one alternative, which means that you are forced to rely on hazy memories or to jump down to scenario 2 or 3.

How do you jog your memory? Not necessarily by bearing down on the "missing" word (squinting your eyes hard, tightening your head muscles – as you may have noticed, this doesn't work) and hoping to *force* it out. A better way: you daydream about your experiences in the job where you knew that word, letting your mind roam freely over the people you worked with, the places you worked, some memorable events from that time; remember driving to and from work, etc. Forget all about needing to know a particular word; chances are, it will come to you suddenly (if not immediately, then an hour or two later).

2   You've never actually done the job before, but you have lived and worked on the peripheries of the job for years: as a legal secretary around lawyers, as a transcriptionist in a hospital, etc. Or you

have good friends who work in the field, and hear them talking about it daily. Or you habitually have lunch at a restaurant where people from that field all go for lunch, and overhear them talking shop every day. Or you are an acute observer and a good listener and draw people out whenever you talk to them, no matter who they are or what they do, so that, after a chance encounter with a pharmacist or a plumber or a postal worker you have a reasonably good sense of how they talk and how they see their world.

Or you've read about the field extensively, watched (and taped and rewatched) shows about it on television, and frequently imagined yourself as a practitioner in it. Some of the books you've read about it are biographies and autobiographies of people in the field, so that, even though you have no first-hand experience of it, your stock of second-hand information is rich and varied.

Pretending to be a practitioner in the field, therefore, is relatively easy for you, even though there are large gaps in your terminological knowledge. Creating a plausible register is no problem; when you focus on actual scenes from books and television shows, it often seems as if you know more terminology than you "actually" do – because you have been exposed to more words than you can consciously recall, and your unconscious mind produces them for you when you slip into a productive daydream state. So you stare at the dictionary, and recognize none of the words; but one unmistakably *feels* right. You know you're going to have to check it later, but for now that intuitive "rightness" is enough.

3   You have neither job experience nor an abiding interest in the field, but you know somebody who does, and so you get them on the phone, or fax or e-mail them; as you describe the words you're looking for, you listen for the note of confidence in their voices when they *know* the correct word with absolute calm and easy certainty. It's like when a foreigner is saying to you, "What's the machine called, you know, it's in the kitchen, you put bread in it and push down, and wires get hot, and – " "Oh yeah," you say easily, "a toaster." When you hear that tone of voice, you know you can trust your friend's terminological instinct. When it is obvious that your friend isn't sure, that s/he is guessing, you listen to everything s/he has to say on the subject, say thanks, and call somebody else.

Or you get onto Lantra-L or FLEFO and ask your question there – an excellent place to go for terminological help, since the subscribers to both lists are themselves translators and know the kind of detail a translator needs to have in order to decide whether the word is right or wrong. There are only two drawbacks of going to an e-mail discussion group. One is that the discussion of who uses what words how can become more interesting than the actual translation that pays the bills.

The other problem with going to a translator discussion group with a terminology question is that getting an answer may take anywhere from several hours to several days. At the end of the process you will know more than you ever wanted to know about the problematic terms (especially if you work in "major" European languages) – but the process may take longer than you can afford to delay.

One last point under "induction." Translators and interpreters are professionals too, and for credibility in the field need to *sound* like professionals in the field. In translator discussion groups like Lantra-L and FLEFO one occasionally reads postings from would-be translators who ask things like "I'd like to be a translator, but I really want

— —

One of our patrons needs to know how to translate into Spanish the word WALKER as in: Do you require a walker to get around? Usted requiere un _____ para caminar ?

Marla O'Neill

＊ ＊ ＊ ＊ ＊

>"Walker", as in a device used by the convalescent or by
>frail, elderly people to get around, is an "Andador".
>There may be additional terms, depending on the country,
>but I've never heard of anything else.

Vive la différence. I've just checked out 'artículos ortopédicos' in the Mexico City Yellow Pages and, as I thought,
all the ads talk about 'andaderas'; the same word is also
used for those things with wheels that help babies learn to
walk (and to fall down stairs when the maid leaves the stair
gates open).
  DRAE-XXI mentions "andador: utensilio . . . para enseñar
a andar a los niños," and then has a cross reference there
from "andadera". But "andador" immediately makes me
think of a narrow street, an alleyway, something like

to work at home. How can I do that?" The wry smiles that questions like this elicit on professional translators' faces are complexly motivated, of course, but they have a good deal to do with the fact that the answer seems so obvious as to be practically common knowledge: many, perhaps most, translators work at home. Shouldn't a would-be translator already know this?

The person asking the question, in other words, doesn't yet *sound* like a translator; and will probably not project enough credibility over the phone to convince an agency person to send them a job. Without that credibility, it will be virtually impossible to make a living translating at home. All this means, of course, is that the hopeful novice needs to learn to talk like a translator – a skill that may even be as important as the actual ability to translate, in terms of getting jobs. Translator discussion groups are one good place to learn this, though only in the written medium – active participation on Lantra-L or FLEFO may only help you write like a translator, not talk like one. Translator conferences and translator training programs are other excellent places for learning this crucial skill – but only if you keep your ears open and model your speech and behavior on the professionals around you.

— —

that: nada que ver con los artículos ortopédicos.

Haydn J. Rawlinson

* * * * *

>That's corredor, not andador. I've never seen andador used
>as a narrow street. Maybe you have the terms corredor/
>andador a little mixed up.

No, not at all. But that's the second message I've got suggesting confusion with "corredor". An "andador" here is most frequently a narrow street, with houses or shops on either side, closed to traffic; often a cul-de-sac, but not necessarily.

As such, it's a common element in street names. I mentioned the "Andador 16 de Septiembre" in the old quarter of Querétaro to Patricio, but now that I've thought about it, you get andadores on modern housing estates as well: a friend of mine lives on the "Andador del Puma" on the outskirts of Cuautla.

Must be a Mexican thing . . .

Haydn J. Rawlinson

Terminology studies (deduction)

If experience is the best teacher, does that mean "deductive" resources like classes in specialized terminology, dictionaries and other reference materials, and theoretical work on terminology management are useless? Not at all.

The important points to remember are: (1) everything is experience (we are never not experiencing things, even in our sleep); and (2) some experiences are richer and more memorable than others. Working in a specialized field is an experience; so is reading a highly abstract theoretical study of the terminology used in that field. The former is more likely to be memorable than the latter, because interacting with people in actual use-situations and seeing the practical applicability of the terminology to real objects and people and contexts provides more "channels" or "modes" or "handles" for the brain to process the information through; in neurological terms, abstract theorizing is relatively stimulus-poor.

But this does not mean, again, that the more abstract channels for presenting information are worthless; only that we must all work harder, teachers and students, writers and readers, to infuse abstract discourse with the rich experiential complexity of human life.

This may mean teachers offering students, or writers offering readers, hands-on exercises that facilitate the learner's exploration of an abstract model through several experiential channels – visual, tactile, kinesthetic, auditory. This is sometimes thought of as "pandering to the worst element," mainly because abstract thought is considered "higher" than holistic experience; in fact it is simply "pandering" to the way the brain actually learns best.

Or it may mean students and readers employing their own holistic techniques to work out in their own practical hands-on experience how the abstract model works. This is how the "best" (i.e., most linguistically, logically, and mathematically intelligent) students have always processed abstract thought: unconsciously they flesh it out with sights and sounds and other visceral experiences from their own lives. This is in fact the *only* way that anyone can make sense of an abstract model or system: all deduction must make a detour through induction; all theory must have some mode of access to practice; all abstraction must derive from, and be referrable back to, the concrete. Abstract theoretical thought, deduction as the highest form of logical reasoning, provides an economy of expression that the rich repetitions and circumlocutions of experiential and practice-oriented induction can never match. But for that very reason this sort of thought is difficult to apprehend without practical applications. Abstraction is a shorthand that saves enormous amounts of time – but only when one knows the language that it shortens and can refer each squiggle back to a natural word or phrase that has meaning in real-life situations.

Some suggestions:

Take classes in engineering, biology and chemistry, law, medicine, etc. – and pay attention to the professor, how s/he acts, how s/he speaks of the field. Pay attention to the best students in class, especially the ones who seem most professionally interested in the subject. What habitus are they struggling to emulate and internalize? Who or what are they trying to become? Ask questions that get the professor and various students to comment in greater detail on the real-world horizons of the field. Draw connections with your own experience. If the professor or one or more students grow impatient with questions like this, study their response: Why are they irritated? What bothers them? Speculate about the habitus of a specialist in the field that makes your questions seem irrelevant or impertinent.

When a teacher offers you an abstract model in class, explore it in other media: paint it; sketch it; draw a flowchart for it showing how one might move through it, or a "web" or "mind-map," showing what connects with what. (as in Figure 5)

Other suggestions:

Invent a kinesthetic image for the model: is it an elevator? a forklift? a weaving loom, with shuttle? a tiger slinking through the jungle? Abstract models are usually constructed to be static, which will make it very difficult in most cases to think of a kinesthetic image; but that very difficulty, the challenge of putting a static image into motion, is precisely what makes this exercise so fruitful.

Do a Freudian psychoanalysis of the model. Whether you believe in psychoanalysis or not is really irrelevant; this is primarily a heuristic, a way of getting your ideas flowing. What is the model *not* saying? What is it repressing, and why? What are its connections with sex, violence, and death; Oedipus and Electra; narcissism and melancholy; latent homosexuality?

There are more exercises along these lines below (especially exercise 3); it is not difficult to invent others. The key is to develop

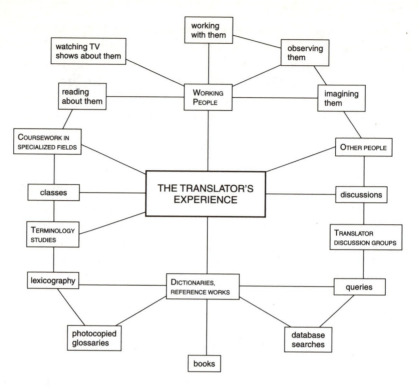

FIGURE 5 The translator's experience of terminology

techniques for dynamizing the static, enlivening the inert, humanizing the inanimate, personalizing the mechanical.

Discussion

1 Is it true that it is easier to learn things when they are grounded in complex real-world situations and experiences? Why or why not?

2 Are translators really fakers or pretenders? How else might their work be regarded?

3 Just how acceptable is it for a translator to pretend to know how to write in a given register, when in fact s/he has almost no idea? Does the answer to this question depend on how successful the translation is, or is there an ethical question involved that trans-

cends success or failure? Who decides when a translation is successful?

Exercises

1 Teacher-directed exercise. (See appendix, pp. 305–6.)

2 Perform the following actions on any source text:
   (a) Discuss it in small groups, brainstorming on useful vocabulary, etc.
   (b) Draw pictures of the activities described.
   (c) Mime the activities described, acting them out, making appropriate sound effects.
   Then translate passages in one or more of the following ways:
   (d) Make an advertising jingle for it in the target language. Use any musical style you like, including local folk songs, rock, rap, etc. Sing it to the class and explain why you chose that particular approach; describe the effect the music had on your translation process.
   (e) Make a commercial voice-over for it in the target language. Read it out loud to the class in an appropriate voice-over voice, and describe what effect thinking of the text in terms of that voice had on your translation process.

3 Bring a specialized technical dictionary (or, if one isn't available, any dictionary) to class and perform the following operations on it:
   (a) Open it at random, find a word that catches your interest, and start following the path down which it points you: looking up similar words listed along with it; looking up interesting words listed under these new entries, etc. Jot down everything of interest that you find: words, definitions, synonyms, antonyms, sample sentences. Make a mark in your notes every time you jump to a new dictionary entry. Do this for ten, fifteen, or twenty minutes, then stop at any reasonable stopping place and move on to:
   (b) Now draw a picture of the information you've gathered. The picture can be a schematic diagram of the complex interrelations between words and dictionary entries; or it can be a

complex representation of the words' referents, all fitted into a scene that seems to bring them all together (a city, a factory, a home, a forest, etc.).

4   Research a specific workplace or type of work by visiting it and talking to the people who work there. Compile a list of the fifty most common words and phrases that they use; then make a video of you (or your group) using all fifty words and phrases in natural-sounding conversation. Try to sound as much as possible like the working people you studied; if possible, make the video in the natural setting of the work. (If you don't have access to video equipment, present your "natural-sounding conversation" in front of the class.)

Suggestions for further reading

Rey (1995), Sager (1990), Snell (1983), Tommola (1992)

Chapter 8

Languages

- **Translation and linguistics**   162
- **What could that be? (abduction)**   164
- **Laying down tracks (induction)**   167
- **Teaching transfer patterns (deduction)**   172
  - **Discussion**   182
  - **Exercises**   182
  - **Suggestions for further reading**   189

T HESIS: Texts are also easiest to translate when you think of them not as syntactically structured collections of words and phrases but as channels through which people influence each other's actions, describe what they see and do, make sense of their worlds; linguistics is a useful reduction of the complexity of actual language use to a few simple stable structures; even more useful than the actual structures it offers, however, is the *process of reduction* by which the linguistic theorist moved from complexity to simplicity, actual use to ideal model, dynamic change to static structure.

Translation and linguistics

It may seem strange to hold off discussing language until this late in a book on translation. Translation is, after all, an operation performed both on and in language. In Latin translation used to be referred to as *translatio linguarum*, the translation of languages, to distinguish it from other kinds of translation, like *translatio studii*, the translation of knowledge, and *translatio imperii*, the translation of empire.

And until very recently, virtually all discussions of translation both in class and in print dealt primarily or exclusively with language. The ability to translate was thought of largely as an advanced form of the ability to understand or read a foreign language. Translation studies was thought of as a specialized branch of philology, applied linguistics, or comparative literature. Translator training revolved around the semantic transfer of words, phrases, and whole texts from one language to another. The chief issue in the history of translation theory since Cicero in the first century before our era has been linguistic segmentation: should the primary segment of translation be the individual word (producing word-for-word translation) or the phrase, clause, or sentence (producing sense-for-sense translation)? Even in our day, most of the best-known theorists of translation – J. C. Catford, Kornei Chukovskii, Valentín García Yebra, Eugene A. Nida, Jean-Paul Vinay and Jean Darbelnet, Peter Newmark, Basil Hatim and Ian Mason – are linguists who think of translation as primarily or exclusively an operation performed on language.

And it should be clear that this book is not an attempt to dismiss or diminish the importance of language for translation either. Language is an integral part of every aspect of translation that we have considered thus far. The purpose of discussing "people" or "working people," rather than, say, equivalence or terminology studies, has not been to downplay the importance of language but rather to place it in a larger social context – the context in which language takes on meaning, and in which linguistic matters are learned and unlearned.

Still, despite the omnipresence of language all through these chapters, it will be useful to devote one chapter to it as a "separate" or "autonomous" phenomenon. It never is, of course; but as linguists have shown us, it can be very useful to think of it that way.

Language, after all, seems to have a life of its own. It changes; and it stays the same. It is difficult to catch individual speakers of a language in the act of changing it, or of preventing it from changing; if anything, in fact, it changes them, and keeps them from changing. One entire school of linguistic thought from Wilhelm von Humboldt in the early nineteenth century to Edward Sapir and Benjamin Lee Whorf in the middle of the twentieth argues persuasively that language, as the shaping force of a people or a culture or a nation, molds *all* of its individual speakers in more or less uniform ways. Tell me what language you speak, and I'll tell you who you are.

And languages seem to have more or less permanent patterns, regularities, which do change with time and place, but so slowly and incrementally that at any given moment they seem somehow built in, intrinsic. We do not normally check dictionaries or grammar books when someone says something that sounds odd; we just know that people don't usually say things that way. The language "inside our heads" seems to have a shape and size and color and feel that rejects or at least resists other ways of saying things – especially when those other ways come from people outside our group, speakers of different regional dialects of our language, or of other languages. The sentence structures and idiomatic expressions of foreign languages seem not only alien but *wrong* to us, both when we are first learning a foreign language and when we speak in our language to a foreigner who doesn't speak it very well.

Hence the value of stepping back from the contexts in which language is produced and the people who produce it, and of looking at it as if it were a more or less stable "thing" in its own right. And even when it is less rather than more stable, even when language seems so volatile as to be more cataract or forest fire than structural system, it can be useful to treat it like a coherent object. Certainly simultaneous interpreters, and many other translators and interpreters as well, often seem to be riding language like a wild horse, or to be holding onto a tiger's tail; to treat these "rides" linguistically is to simplify them, to tame them; but in many cases that is the only way to talk about them at all.

What could that be? (abduction)

Understanding someone else's utterance or written message is far more complicated than we tend to think. Common sense says that if we hear or read a text in a language we know well, and the text is syntactically and semantically well formed, we will understand it. Indeed, offhand it is difficult to imagine a case in which that understanding might not immediately and automatically follow.

But there are plenty of such cases. The most common is when you expect to be addressed in one language, say, a foreign or B language, and are addressed in another, say, your native or A language: until you adjust your expectations and really "hear" the utterance as an A-language text, it may sound like B-language gibberish. This is especially true when you are in a foreign country where you do not expect anyone to speak your language; if someone does address you in your native tongue, even with perfect pronunciation and grammar, your expectations may well block understanding. Even after three or four repetitions, you may finally have to ask, "I'm sorry, what language are you speaking?" When you are told that it is your native tongue, all of a sudden the random phonemes leap into coherent order and the utterance makes sense.

This is abduction: the leap from confusing data to a reasonable hypothesis. And it happens even with utterances in our native language that should have been easy to understand. Something blocks our ability to make sense of a language, misleading expectations, distractions (as when you hear a friend or a parent or a spouse talking, you hear and register and understand all the words, but nothing makes sense because your mind is elsewhere), and all of a sudden what should have been easy becomes hard; what should have been automatic requires a logical leap, an abduction.

When the utterance or written text is not perfectly formed, this experience is even more common.

1   Your 10-month-old infant points at something on the table and says "Gah!" When you don't understand, she points again and repeats, "Gah!" more insistently. The child clearly knows what she is trying to say; she just doesn't speak your language. How do you reach a working interpretation? How do you become a competent interpreter of your infant's language? Through trial and error: you pick up every item on the table, look at the child quizzically, and say "This?" (or "Gah?"). Based on your knowledge of other languages, of course, you make certain assumptions that guide your guesswork: you assume, for instance, that "Gah" is probably a noun, referring to a specific object on the table, or a verb ("Give!"), or an imperative sentence ("Give me that thing that I want!"). Parents usually become skilled interpreters of their infants' languages quite quickly. The infant experiments constantly with new words and phrases, requiring new abductions, but repeated exposure to the old ones rapidly builds up B-language competence in the parents, and they calmly interpret for visitors who hear nothing but random sounds.

2   Fully competent native speakers of a language do not always use that language in a way that certain observers are pleased to call "rational": they do not say what they mean, they omit crucial information, they conceal their true intentions, they lie, they exaggerate, they use irony or sarcasm, they speak metaphorically. The English philosopher Paul Grice (1989: 22–40), best known as the founder of linguistic pragmatics, tried famously in a lecture entitled "Logic and Conversation" to explain precisely how we make sense of speakers who "flout" the rational rules of conversation; it wasn't enough for him that listeners make inspired guesses, or abductions: there had to be some "regimen" to follow, a series of steps that would lead interpreters to the correct interpretation of a problematic utterance. Clearly, there is something

to this; we are rarely utterly in the dark when guessing at another person's meaning. Clearly also, however, Grice overstated his case. The bare fact that we so often guess wrong suggests that understanding (or "abducing") problematic utterances has as much to do with creative imagination, intuition, and sheer luck as it does with rational regimens (see Robinson 1986).

3   Learning a foreign language obviously requires thousands of guesses or abductions.

It is my second or third week in Finland. I have learned that "no" is *ei* and "yes" is *joo* (pronounced /yoː/). To my great puzzlement, I frequently hear people saying what sounds like **ei joo*, which I translate as "no yes." This doesn't make sense, but whenever I ask anybody about it, they always insist that there is no such phrase in Finnish, no one would ever say that, it doesn't make sense, etc. And yet I hear it repeatedly. Whenever I hear my friends say it, I stop them: "You said it again!" "What?" "*Ei joo.*" "No I didn't. You can't say that in Finnish."

Finally, after about two weeks of this frustration, someone realizes what I'm talking about: *ei oo*, pronounced exactly like **ei joo*, is a colloquial form of *ei ole*, meaning "it isn't." Having explained this, he adds: "But you shouldn't say that, because it's bad Finnish." Finnish teachers, I later discover, actively discourage this colloquialism: hence "bad Finnish." As a result, even though everyone still uses it constantly, my friends repress their knowledge of it when I ask about it, and find it extremely difficult to realize what I'm referring to. It requires almost as big an abductive leap for them to understand my question as it does for me to ask it.

---

4   And, of course, translators are forever stumbling upon words they have never seen before, words that appear in no dictionary they own, words for which they must find exact target-language equivalents by tomorrow.

```
Hello Lantrans,
   Can anyone tell me the Dutch translation of ''flat fee''
and/or define what it means? My dictionary does not contain
this entry.
```

```
Context:
Your call can either be charged to your phone bill at a per
minute rate or to your credit card (Visa, Mastercard or
American Express) at a flat fee.
Thanks, best regards,

Gabor Menkes
ULTIMTEXT
```

Translation at this level is painfully slow. A translator may spend hours tracking down a difficult word: poring through dictionaries on the shelf and on-line, calling, faxing, and e-mailing friends and acquaintances who might know it, calling the agency or client and asking for help. A translator may hate or love this part of this job; but a translator who is unwilling to do it will not last long in the profession. Since translators are rarely paid by the hour, and the pay per word is the same for a word that requires hours to find as it is for "the" or "and," their financial motivation to track down the right word may be almost nil; the only reasons to continue the search despite its diminishing monetary returns are:

(a) translator ethics, the professional's determination to submit an accurate and correct translation

(b) professional pride, the translator's need to feel good about the work s/he does

(c) a pragmatic concern for repeat business: the agency or client who is pleased with the translator's work will call her or him again; and

(d) a love of language, producing a deep satisfaction in the word-hunt or the "rightness" of the right word, or both.

Laying down tracks (induction)

If the hunt for the right word is painfully slow and therefore lamentably underpaid, it can also be one of the translator's greatest professional joys. Reading in books and articles one would never ordinarily read, learning things one would never ordinarily learn, talking to people on the phone about their area of expertise: this can all be drudgery, of course, but it can also be exciting and emotionally and intellectually rewarding. The translator who takes pleasure in this underpaid hunt, it should go without saying, is less likely to burn out in the job than one who hates it and only does it out of a sense of professional ethics or duty. Unpleasant duties quickly become strait-jackets.

The other side of this process is that the hunt for the right word is usually so intense that the right word is later easy to remember: the "solution" to the translator's problem sticks easily in her or his memory and can be retrieved quickly for later use. Translation-memory software performs this same function for many translators, "remembering" not only the words the translator has used in the past but the contexts in which s/he used them; but since this software too requires a few keystrokes or mouse-clicks, most translators who use it do so mainly for backup, relying primarily on their own neural memories for most words and phrases.

In other words, the "new words" that take so long to find and seem therefore to "steal" or "waste" the translator's time and money are sublimated for later use – and when used in a later translation, the relative speed with which they are remembered begins to earn back the time and money that seemed so extravagantly spent before. Indeed the factor that contributes most to the professional translator's speed and accuracy is the internalization and sublimation not only of words but of certain linguistic "transfer patterns" – well-worn path-ways from one language to another that the translator has traveled so many times that s/he could do it while talking to a friend on the phone, or planning a menu for dinner, or worrying about a financial crisis. One glance at the source-text syntax and the translator's fingers fly across the keyboard, as if driven by a macro.

And in some sense they are. The brain doesn't work like a computer in all respects – it is far more complicated, far more elastic and flexible, far more creative, and in some things slower – but in this it does: oft-repeated activities are softwired into a neural network that works very much like a computer macro, dictating keystrokes or other steps in a more or less fixed sequence and at great speed. Thus the novice translator can take two or three hours to translate a 300-word text that would take a professional translator twenty or thirty minutes; and the discriminating reader will find twenty major errors in the novice translator's rendition and a single slightly questionable word or phrase in the professional translator's version. Practice doesn't exactly make perfect; but it brings exponential increases in speed and reliability.

But what is happening in the inductive process of internalizing these transfer patterns? What is the translator experiencing, and how can that experience be enhanced?

Linguistically speaking, the translator is experiencing a transformation of semantics and syntax – or, to put that simplistically, of words and word orders. Words and word orders appear in the source text, and have to be "carried across" (*trans-latum*) or "led across" (*trans-ductum*) into the target language. In the process they undergo a sea change, which feels at first like a metamorphosis of infinite variety, so infinite that it cannot be reduced to patterns; every word and every sequence of words must be taken on its own, thought about, reflected upon, weighed and tested, poked and prodded. The more often one makes the trip, however, the more familiar the transformations become; gradually they begin to fall into patterns; gradually translation comes to seem easier and easier.

The inductive process of wading through tens of thousands of such transfers until the patterns begin to emerge is, as Karl Weick would say, a process of "unrandomizing" what at first seems to be chaos. At first it is difficult to hold ten or fifteen foreign words in your head; then it is easy to hold those ten or fifteen words as discrete lexical items, each one having a specific meaning in your native tongue, but difficult to use them in a sentence, or even to decipher in an existing sentence. Gradually those ten or fifteen words become easy to use in a certain kind of sentence, but then they appear in another kind of sentence and once again make no sense at all.

The linguistic term for the process is overgeneralization; it is an essential if problematic step in all language learning, indeed in all attempts to formulate linguistic patterns, including the writing of grammar books (and translation textbooks). It is fundamentally the human need to impose order on chaos, to unrandomize what seems totally random. It is called *over*generalization because language, like everything else in our world, is always more complicated than any pattern we impose on it. Patterns are helpful tools in reducing the complexity of language and other phenomena, but they never entirely master that complexity.

Overgeneralization is best known to us from studies of first-language learning. The small native speaker of English discovers that you add a /d/ or /t/ sound to a word when you want to say that you did it yesterday: "I baked a cake," "I jumped off the couch," etc. And so s/he says "I maked my bed," or "I doed a bad thing." Sometimes this little speaker will be corrected by older English speakers – "It's 'I *made* my bed,' honey" – sometimes not; sometimes s/he will simply notice that other people say it differently, and gradually assimilate her or his speech to theirs.

Overgeneralization is common in second-language learning as well, except now with the added complication that the patterns are (at least) dual: influenced by the way things are said in both a primary (A) and a secondary (B) language. The beginning learner of a B language unconsciously assumes that the way s/he speaks her or his A language will provide a more or less reliable guide to speaking the B language, and is shocked to find that things are done so differently there. Even with repeated drilling by a teacher, or correction by a native speaker, the learner refuses to believe it. This cannot be! They can't possibly pronounce things so differently, use such strange words, mix up the "natural" order of words so grotesquely! The native speaker of English wants to say "The boy liked the chocolates" in Spanish – a simple enough phrase, subject–verb–object, somebody doing something to something – and balks at what s/he is told to say: *Al chico le gustaron los chocolates.* To the boy him pleased the chocolates! Surely this is a cruel joke! It would be bad enough if one person was insane enough to complicate a simple sentence like this; but hundreds of millions of people? No. It is simply not possible.

But even when the learner begins to accept certain general transfer patterns, s/he is not yet out of the woods. The Finnish learner of English notices, or is taught, or reads in a dictionary, that nouns inflected with *-na* or *-nä* are usually translated into English with prepositional phrases beginning with "as": *poikamies* is "bachelor," so *poikamiehenä is* "as a bachelor"; *poikamiehenä sanoisin, että . . .* would be "as a bachelor I would say that . . ." Especially if s/he is learning English in school, the textbook will provide lists of examples that fit this pattern, and gradually the learner will come to believe that the pattern is universal:

> *Asuin siellä lapsena.*   I lived there as a child.
> *Puhun nyt isänäsi.*   I'm speaking now as your father.

And so on. And then one day s/he comes across this inflection in another context and mistranslates, because the pattern *isn't* universal:

Mitä minuna tekisit?	*What would you do as me? (What would you do if you were me?)
Hyppäsin salamana pystyyn.	*I jumped up as a lightning. (I jumped up in a flash.)

With repeated exposure to these more complicated transfer patterns, they too come to seem not only reasonable but regular: there is a kind of fundamental "in the capacity of" semantics to the *-na* inflection, and each individual transfer of that semantics is governed by a pattern of some sort. Those patterns too will break down now and then, but the native speaker knows more or less where they break down and how to negotiate those trouble spots; and the foreigner who learns the language really well ultimately learns how to do more or less the same.

And linguistically speaking, learning to translate well is fundamentally the same process, except that the focal experience is not of one language or even two, but of the transfer from one language to another. And the transfer patterns are always unidirectional: the "feel" a translator gradually develops for the pathways from the A to the B language will not be the same for the pathways from B to A – not even the same in reverse. Before s/he can translate "between" A and B – or, as translators often write in their résumés, A < > B – the translator must (1) become fluent in the B language (2) learn to translate B > A, and (3) learn to translate A > B. B > A transfers take different linguistic pathways than A > B transfers.

Part of this difference is extralinguistic. Unless the translator has spoken both languages from birth, one is "native" and the other is "foreign." Even the most fluent near-native speaker of a language is only *near*-native. Typing is typically slower in a foreign language. It feels natural to count in the primary language of childhood, cumbersome in a language learned after adolescence. Even bilinguals from birth who are not culturally surrounded by both of their languages on a daily basis find their "foreign" language growing rusty, awkward, slow, heavy. People who live abroad for many years find their native tongues losing their freshness in much the same way. The two languages will have been learned in different contexts, from different people, and that will lend them a different feel, even for bilinguals who cannot remember ever having been monolingual: they will have learned one language from children and the other from adults; one at home and the other at school; one from mommy and the other from daddy. In a bilingual environment languages tend to become specialized in, through, and for use: one language is for everyday things, the other for business; one is for "our people," the other for "them" (outsiders, authorities, people of a different culture or race or class); one is for loving, the other for fighting. All this brings social and cultural pressures to bear on the "transfer patterns" between the two languages.

But even in a strictly linguistic sense, in terms of pure formal syntax and semantics, the transfer patterns between two languages are not simple or mechanical mirror-images of each other. This is because there are no one-to-one correspondences between any two languages. Learning to turn a passive construction in the B language into an active construction in the A language is never merely the reverse of turning an active A-language construction into a passive B-language construction. Combining two B-language sentences into a single long A-language sentence is never merely the reverse of splitting a long A-language sentence into two B-language sentences.

This is partly a result of the different expressive potentials in the two languages – the fact that reversing the order of a B-language sentence structure elicits unexpected possibilities in the A language, making the connotative and often the denotative impact of the new sentence significantly different. "The boy liked the chocolates" > *Al chico le gustaron los chocolates* will point the translator in different expressive and imaginative directions than *Al chico le gustaron los chocolates* > "The boy liked the chocolates." All transfer is loss and/ or gain – sometimes loss, sometimes gain, sometimes both at once – and the complex interplay of those losses and gains is actualized differently in every transfer.

Above all, the neural pathways for the two transfer directions are different, with the result that the subjective experience is different as well. The same is true of number sequences, where the expressive potential of language has been eliminated: the "translation" of 637281 into 182736, for example, actually proceeds down different neural pathways than the "translation" of 182736 into 637281.

Teaching transfer patterns (deduction)

The important thing to remember, as we saw in Chapter 3, is that it is always going to be easier to remember, and thus easier and faster to use, transfer patterns you have discovered and employed on your own. This should be clear from the hunt for the "right word": as we saw above, the translator who spends hours hunting for a word, discussing it on the phone with specialists in the field, comparing dictionary and encyclopedia entries with conflicting equivalents offered by other translators on-line or people actually using the word in their work, is going to remember the word better than one who simply looks it up in the dictionary and writes down what s/he finds.

The rule might be stated simplistically: induction is more effective for later subliminal use than deduction. Having the experience is a more powerful learning tool than having someone give you the answer without the experience. (Note also that this "rule" is itself deductive, and will most likely work for you only after you have tested it in practice.)

"Having the experience" is, of course, extremely time-consuming and unpredictable. This makes "giving the answer" seem a more economical teaching approach – and indeed it tends to dominate much translator training. Give students the rules; make them memorize those rules; test them on the thoroughness with which they have memorized them; then send them out into the world to put the rules into practice.

The difficulty is that, because of the way the brain functions, rules are extremely hard to memorize in effective ways. Memorized rules typically need to be recalled consciously, scanned mentally, applied systematically; exceptions and other problematic applications need to be resolved one at a time. Neurologically speaking, what is happening here is that the analytical part of the brain – the neocortex, the outermost shell of the brain, especially in the left hemisphere – is running through every tiny detail it has stored, one by one. It is laboriously recalling representational memories and subjecting them to slow and painstaking analysis. It is the equivalent, not of recognizing a friend's face, which is instantaneous (because grounded in emotional memory and processed holistically in the faster and more intuitive right hemisphere), but of describing the face of a stranger to a police officer after a crime. It is a far more articulate process – but also extremely slow and inefficient. The foreign-language learner who tries to speak a foreign language by following memorized rules can only participate in conversations in the controlled environment of the classroom, where conversational speed is kept artificially slow; in a real conversational situation, this sort of speaker is typically paralyzed. The brain simply refuses to recall rules and apply them to words and phrases fast enough to produce coherent speech in normal conversational rhythms. Speech becomes halting, awkward, broken; the speaker's eyes stare off into space, reading an imaginary page out of a textbook, rather than meeting the other person's gaze.

And as this book has been attempting to show, the same is true of learning to translate. Induction is always more effective than deduction – especially someone else's deduction. The experience of translating is always more effective than being told how to translate.

Does this mean, then, that instruction in translation is useless – or worse than useless, counterproductive?

No. As we have seen, there are many things that can be done in the classroom to make deduction experientially powerful. Deductive processes that work well in learning are in fact experientially very close to induction: you try things, some work, some don't; gradually patterns emerge out of this ongoing process of trial and error.

More, both inductive and deductive experiences need to be enhanced in the classroom: inductive processes because they are too slow, deductive processes because they are too abstract. Neither students nor teachers have the time to let inductive experience of translation accumulate gradually, naturally; the process must be accelerated (hence this textbook). By the same token, however, the deductive precepts that are usually offered students as accelerations of that process are in and of themselves difficult to internalize, memorize, and apply in practice, and every effort should be made to bring them into the experiential realm of induction.

Let us explore the intertwined operation of induction and deduction in linguistic theories of translation through a close look at two passages from a popular linguistic overview of the field, Basil Hatim and Ian Mason's *Discourse and the Translator* (1990). They are critical, for example, of J. C. Catford's (1965) linguistic approach to translation, which seems to have more to do with the desire to draw up abstract formulae than it does with the translator's actual experience of translating:

> Yet much of the discussion [in Catford] is about structural contrasts between language systems rather than about communication across cultural barriers and about individual,

de-contextualised sentences instead of real texts. Thus, translation theory becomes a branch of contrastive linguistics, and
translation problems become a matter of the non-correspon-
dence of certain formal categories in different languages. For
Catford (1965: 32):

> A formal correspondent is any TL category which may be
> said to occupy, as nearly as possible, the "same" place in
> the economy of the TL as the given SL category occupies
> in the SL.

The assumption that "formal correspondence" thus defined is of
any relevance to translation studies leads naturally to an investigation of "equivalence probability" – an attempt to arrive at a
statistical calculation of the degree of probability that a given
SL category will, in any given text, be rendered by an equivalent TL category. Thus, the probability that French *dans* will be
rendered by English *in* is calculated, in the case of a particular
pair of texts, at 73 per cent. It is then hoped that statistical
analysis of a large sample of texts might lead to the formulation
of "translation rules". Manifestly, however, any such extrapo-
lation can lead only to statements about language systems, not
about the communicative factors surrounding the production
and reception of texts. The notion of equivalence probabilities
between such categories as prepositions may be relevant to
certain elementary errors in raw MT output . . . But it is of
no concern to the human translator, for whom translation of *en
quoi consiste la logique mathématique* as *what mathematical
logic consists of* is not a problem.

(Hatim and Mason 1990: 26–7)

In the terms used in this book, Hatim and Mason are here
arguing that Catford's approach is a series of *deductions* that are
largely useless for the practical matter of translating specific words
and phrases; in their book they are going to be moving toward a
linguistic formulation of specific translator *inductions* that, even
when restated in deductive or "rule" form, will prove more useful
for the translator.

This critique of Catford is one articulation of a complaint that
is frequently lodged by practitioners about theory: it has no practical
value; it doesn't help me translate better; it's sheer abstract

intellectual game-playing; I shouldn't have to waste my time with such fancy frills. The translator or translation student who likes to play with abstract concepts regardless of their practical applications may find enjoyment in linguistic theories of this sort; but not for very long, and in any case it's not for everyone.

The question is, what is the practically minded translator or translation student to *do* with such theories? Many would say "ignore them"; but students are often not in a position to ignore what a teacher requires them to read and learn. Besides, even a skeptical reading of Catford's book will yield a stubborn sense that there is *something* interesting and potentially useful here, if only the static furniture of Catford's specific analytical models could be cleared away. Is there another approach to a book like Catford's that might enable the reader to get more practical value out of it?

One answer to this question might begin with Hatim and Mason's blanket statement that Catford's large-scale patterns of equivalence "are of no concern to the human translator, for whom translation of *en quoi consiste la logique mathématique* as *what mathematical logic consists of* is not a problem." Is this really true? For the experienced French–English translator, it most certainly is; faced with *en quoi consiste la logique mathématique*, this translator effortlessly and indeed unconsciously summons up a well-worn transfer pattern and rapidly types *what mathematical logic consists of*. For a beginning translator, however, that particular transfer may pose something of a problem – especially in deciding whether to dangle the preposition *of*. A more literal (Catford would say "rank-bound") translation, "in what mathematical logic consists," would be considered "better English" by some grammatical purists who insist that one should never end a clause with a preposition. And how does one decide between these two renderings? What is the deciding factor? What pressures, what deductions does the beginning translator bring to bear on the decision?

Hatim and Mason's objection to Catford's linguistic theories of translation is that they are too static, too much oriented toward a comparison of finished products (source text and target text) rather than toward the dynamic process of translation, in which the translator has to make a series of complex decisions. And they are largely right about Catford. But even a static product-oriented theory can be salvaged for practical profit through an exploration of the dynamic processes by which the theorist originally formulated the static categories. We could ask, for example, how it is ever possible to know or "say" that a given target-language category occupies, "as nearly as possible, the 'same' place in the economy of the TL as the given SL category occupies in the SL." What is the "economy" of a language? How does one recognize a "place" or other structure in that economy? What mental processes (comparing, contrasting, sorting, spatializing, etc.) must one employ to see the complex dynamic of language use as an "economy" or other static system?

Given a series of sentences with *dans* in them, for example, the French > English or French > language-X translator could seek to construct a process model for narrowing words and phrases down to "same places": in which sentences does *in* or some other obvious TL equivalent seem closer to *dans*, in which do they seem farther apart? How would you justify that particular intuition about "closeness" and "distance" to a third party? What larger patterns would you summon in support of your intuition? Semantic, syntactic, contextual, social? What is the next step in discovering or inventing or defending a pattern?

This sort of approach to an older linguistic theory of translation, one based on static patterns of equivalence, is primarily directed at exploring how Catford *derived* his static categories – and secondarily, but more importantly, at generalizing from the processes thus discovered to the translator's own processes of reduction, deduction, pattern-forming. How does an individual like Catford, how does the student himself or herself, build a sense of the "economy" of an entire language, and then "place" a given "category" in that economy? How do words, phrases, linguistic events become "categories" in the first place? Catford is attempting to reduce the complexity of language to patterns that will make it easier for him to talk about translation. And since we all reduce complex fields to simple patterns all the time, since that is one of the critical functions of the human brain, we can use the processes by which he achieved his particular reductions as helpful guides to our own simplifications – even if we want to avoid the specific *directions* he took. How do we get from hundreds and hundreds of experiential regularities to the formulation of a tentative "rule" such as "it's more idiomatic in English to dangle prepositions"?

As we've seen in previous chapters, a powerful tool for breaking static rules and categories down into fluid processes is the full range of visualizing and dramatizing; and the exercises at the end of this chapter will encourage you to apply these techniques to a series of linguistic theories of translation. In Catford's case, a helpful visual tool might be a flowchart mapping the process of freezing words and phrases as "categories" (*dans/in* as instances of one category, *en quoi/what . . . of* as instances of another, and so on) and of freezing a whole collection of experiences of a language as linguistic "economies," as in Figure 6.

Hatim and Mason work very hard to avoid the specific pitfalls of linguistic approaches similar to Catford's, those based on the *results* of a movement from induction to deduction "rules" ("cat-

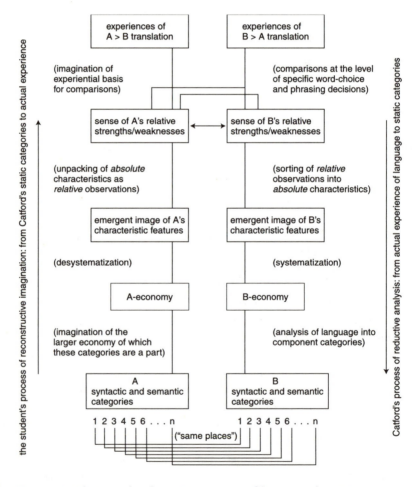

Figure 6 Charting the dynamic progress of linguistic theorizing

egories") rather than on the movement itself ("experiences"). But even their theories harden into rigidly general patterns that leave little or no room for the translator's situational flexibility; indeed in some sense they must do. That is the nature of the movement: from flux to stability, from complexity to simplicity, from flexibility to rigidity. When this happens, therefore, much the same sort of visual unpacking of the induction-to-deduction movement that worked with Catford might be fruitfully applied to Hatim and Mason as well. For example, with a passage like this:

> In tracing an intertextual signal to its pre-text, the semiotic area being traversed is what we have called the **intertextual space**. It is here that text users assess the semiotic status of the intertextual reference. We suggest that answers to the following questions might form the basis of an inter-semiotic translation of intertextual reference:
>
> 1. What is the informational status of a given reference in the communicative transaction (features of field, mode, tenor, time, place, etc.)?
>
> 2. What is the intentional status of the reference in question as action?
>
> 3. What is the semiotic status of the reference as a sign "interacting" with other signs?
>
> The three questions may be put differently. Question 1 relates to the "form" of the intertextual signal; question 2 relates to the "function" of the signal; and question 3 assesses the priority of one over the other in the production of the sign. It is on the sign entity as a semiotic construct, however, that the ultimate decision bears: should the translator relay form, content or both, and in what proportions?
>
> In other words, the principal aim is to evaluate which aspects of the sign are to be retained and which aspects must be jettisoned in the act of transferring that sign into another language. A hierarchy of preferences is developed which, in practice, seems to reverse the order of the three questions posed above: a translator's first responsibility is to the intertextual reference as a semiotic construct, which by definition involves intentionality. Bottom of the list of priorities would then be the

> informational, denotative status . . . And, as we argued above,
> intention may be perceived adequately only within overall inter-
> action.
>
> (Hatim and Mason 1190: 134–5)

This passage purports to describe the translation process from inside the translator's head – any translator, presumably including the reader. Hatim and Mason are arguing that the translator needs to ask these questions about a text while translating it: what is it trying to say, what is it trying to accomplish by saying it, and how does that social action fit in the larger realm of purposive social activity? This is already, you will note, a reduction of the translator's options; there are hundreds, perhaps thousands, of questions that one might ask about a text while translating it, and these are only three fairly important ones – fairly important, one might add, in certain translation contexts. (When translating a passage from Virgil in Latin class to demonstrate that you have fully appreciated the complexities of the Latin grammar, you may not need to ask a single one of the three questions Hatim and Mason say "the translator" "will" always ask.)

Still, their approach is clearly process-oriented, geared to the actual decision-making processes translators undergo in actually doing a translation; and they are well aware that the actual answers translators get to the questions they are supposed to ask will vary widely. Again, however, their movement from the complexity of inductive experience (which will always generate hundreds of counterexamples to any rule anyone cares to formulate) to deductive laws effectively ties the translator's hands. At first they write that "answers to the following questions *might* form the basis of an inter-semiotic translation of intertextual reference" – in other words, here is *one possible* deductive model, one way of structuring or patterning your complex experience of linguistic transfer. Not too many lines down, this possible model has turned into the "ultimate" one: "It is on the sign entity as a semiotic construct, however, that the *ultimate* decision bears: should the translator relay form, content or both, and in what proportions?" And a few lines below that the possible model is hardening into a hierarchy of priorities, so that "the translator" (an ideal translator, now, not any random real one) not only asks these three questions but asks them in a given order: "A hierarchy of preferences is developed which, in practice, seems to reverse the order of the three questions posed above: a translator's first responsibility is to the intertextual reference as a semiotic construct, which by definition involves intentionality." The "preferences" are no longer Hatim and Mason's preferences, and the "hierarchy of preferences" is no longer a model which "might" be usefully imposed on translation decisions; the "hierarchy of preferences" simply *is*, it "is developed," in some abstract normative realm beyond the translator's power to choose the questions s/he will ask or the order s/he will ask them in.

Various visualization and dramatization exercises might once again be employed to explore and strategically reverse this "hardening" movement from inductive experience to normative deductive laws. A flowchart might again be drawn up, tracing the imaginative steps by which Hatim and Mason moved from "we think these are the questions translators *should* ask" to "we think these are the questions translators *tend to* ask" to "we (prefer to) think this is the order translators ask them in" to "a hierarchy of preferences is developed." The social or interpersonal issues of authority and submission might be explored through a dramatization of that process, with one student or group of students playing Hatim and Mason and pushing toward higher and higher levels of deductive certainty and another student or group of students resisting that move, so that the Hatim and Mason group must invent increasingly inventive justifications for their specific deductions.

One way of putting the methodological shift we've been exploring here is that it displaces the focus from *theory*, and specifically the static form and content of specific theories, which students are asked to "learn" (memorize for tests and supposedly remember forever), to *theorizing*, specifically the complex processes by which a person organizes a group of loosely related insights into a pattern or regularity and ultimately into a rule. As long as the focus in class (or in the reading of a book or article) is on the static form and content of a theory, students (or readers) are faced with a choice between the acceptance or rejection of the theory in whole or in part – and if it seems irrelevant to their needs, they will almost certainly reject it, even if they are required to memorize it for a test. If the focus is shifted to the process of theorizing, however, even an apparently useless or irrelevant or "wrong" theory can become a useful mirror for students' and readers' own theorizing processes, which are, after all, far more useful to them in their professional *and* private lives as translators than any specific rules will ever be. The ability to move flexibly and creatively from a loose collection of observations to a tentative pattern or "rule," and to revise that "rule" in response to new experiences that conflict with it, is the experiential form of deduction that makes good translators into good thinkers – indeed, that makes people translate better by thinking better.

Discussion

1 How realistic is it to discuss language in the abstract, structurally, systematically – linguistically? Does language ever exist in a stable form that can be reduced to unchanging structures? If not, what value do linguistic analyses and descriptions have for the study of translation?

2 "Overgeneralization" is a term that linguists use to describe the mental processes involved in learning one's first language as a child; it is not generally applied to the work linguists do in their attempts to reduce the complexity of natural language to the simplicity of formal systems. Some linguists, in fact, might be offended to hear their work described as involving overgeneralization. Just how "insulting" is the insistence that linguists too overgeneralize? What is at stake in this terminological debate?

Exercises

1 Read the following extract from Eugene Nida and Charles Taber, *The Theory and Practice of Translation* (1969: 12–13):

> The best translation does not sound like a translation. Quite naturally one cannot and should not make the Bible sound as if it happened in the next town ten years ago, for the historical context of the Scriptures is important, and one cannot remake the Pharisees and Sadducees into present-day religious parties, nor does one want to, for one respects too much the historical setting of the incarnation. In other words, a good translation of the Bible must not be a "cultural translation." Rather, it is a "linguistic translation." Nevertheless, this does not mean that it should exhibit in its grammatical and stylistic forms any trace of awkward-

ness or strangeness. That is to say, it should studiously avoid "translationese" – formal fidelity, with resulting unfaithfulness to the content and the impact of the message.

(a) Work in groups to describe the "one" in this passage who "cannot and should not make the Bible sound as if it happened in the next town ten years ago," and who "respects too much the historical setting of the incarnation" to want to attempt such a thing. How old is this person? Male or female? Race, social class? What level of education? Just how devout a Christian (and what kind of Christian) does s/he have to be? Or could s/he be an atheist?

Now imagine another kind of "one," who does want to modernize the Bible in radical ways and knows that it can be done. What kind of person is this? (Age, sex, race, class, education level, religious affiliation, etc.) Does s/he know and believe that "one" "should not" do this? If so, does s/he feel guilty about trying it? If so, why is s/he doing it anyway? If not, or if s/he doesn't even know that this is "bad translation," what motivates her or him to undertake such a project?

Finally, describe the "Nida" and/or "Taber" who wrote this paragraph, exploring motivations for portraying the translator as "one" who has these specific features. Imagine "Nida" or "Taber" imagining this "one," and consider the *felt* differences and overlaps between saying that one *cannot* translate this way (is it really impossible? should it be?), one *shouldn't* translate this way (what are they guarding against? what is the worst-case scenario here? what would happen if translators began doing what they *shouldn't* do?), and one *doesn't want to* translate this way (is this like telling a child "you don't want more ice cream"? or what?).

(b) Based on the above description, discuss the difference between a "cultural translation" and a "linguistic translation" and their relationship to "sounding like a translation." Does "cultural" here mean "loose" or "free" or "adaptative" and "linguistic" mean "strict" or "faithful"? Or are there "free" and "strict" cultural translations and "free" and "strict" linguistic translations? And do "free" translations always sound less (or more?) like translations than "strict" ones?

Draw a diagram of Nida and Taber's argument in this paragraph: a tree diagram, a flowchart, a three-dimensional image, or however you like.

2 Study the following composite passage from Mona Baker, *In Other Words* (1992: 144–5, 149, 151):

The distinction between theme and rheme is speaker-oriented. It is based on what the speaker wants to announce as his/her starting point and what s/he goes on to say about it. A further distinction can be drawn between what is given and what is new in a message. This is a hearer-oriented distinction, based on what part of the message is known to the hearer and what part is new. Here again, a message is divided into two segments: one segment conveys information which the speaker regards as already known to the hearer. The other segment conveys the new information that the speaker wishes to convey to the hearer. Given information represents the common ground between speaker and hearer and gives the latter a reference point to which s/he can relate new information.

Like thematic structure, information structure is a feature of the context rather than of the language system as such. One can only decide what part of a message is new and what part is given within a linguistic or situational context. For example, the same message may be segmented differently in response to different questions:

What's happening tomorrow?	We're climbing Ben Nevis
	New
What are we doing tomorrow?	We're climbing Ben Nevis.
	Given New
What are we climbing tomorrow?	We're climbing Ben Nevis.
	Given New

The organization of the message into information units of given and new reflects the speaker's sensitivity to the hearer's state of knowledge in the process of communication. At any point of the communication process, there will have already been established a certain linguistic and non-linguistic environment. This the speaker can draw on in order to relate new information that s/he wants to convey to elements that are already established in the context. The normal, unmarked order is for the speaker to place the given element before the new one. This order has been found to contribute to ease of comprehension and recall and some composition specialists therefore explicitly recommend it to writers. . . .

Failure to appreciate the functions of specific syntactic structures in signalling given and new information can result in unnecessary shifts in translation. . . .

The above discussion suggests that, when needed, clear signals of information status can be employed in written language. Different languages use different devices for signalling information structure and translators must develop a sensitivity to the various signalling systems available in the languages they work with. This is, of course, easier said than done because, unfortunately, not much has been achieved so far in the way of identifying signals of information status in various languages.

(a)

(i) Work alone or in small groups to analyze and discuss the "actors" or "agents" in this passage. Who does what to whom? Theme/rheme is a "speaker-oriented" distinction, suggesting that the speaker herself or himself makes it; given/new information is a "hearer-oriented distinction, based on what part of the message is known to the hearer and what part is new," suggesting that the hearer makes it. But a few lines down Baker calls new information the segment that "the speaker wishes to convey to the hearer." When she says that "a message is divided into two segments," who does the dividing? The speaker? The hearer? The translator? The scholar? All four? How do their perspectives differ? Should the translator *be* a scholar, or strive to inhabit the scholar's perspective from "above" the dialogue between speaker and hearer? Who is the "one" in "One can only decide what part of a message is new and what part is given within a linguistic or situational context"? Who is the "segmenter" in the passive construction "For example, the same message may be segmented differently in response to different questions"?

(ii) These early paragraphs make it sound as if every decision about information status must be made by real people, speakers and hearers (and possibly translators and scholars), in real-life contexts, based on speakers' knowledge of what hearers know, or on hearers' surmises as to what they think speakers think hearers know, or on translators' or scholars' surmises about speaker-knowledge in relation to hearer-knowledge. Put this way, the task of judging the information status of any given sentence, and thus of building an effective target-language word order, seems hopelessly complicated.

In later paragraphs, however, Baker seems to suggest that the "dividing" and "segmenting" is done less by speakers and/or hearers as autonomous subjects than by the "signalling system" of the language itself; and that translators (and presumably linguists also) must simply develop an appreciation for or "sensitivity to the various signalling systems available in the languages they work with." This assumption allows the translator or linguist to analyze words rather than having to guess at real people's unspoken intentions or surmises. But how does this work? What does the signalling system include? Does it actually control real speakers' and hearers' decisions? Or does it control them only insofar as they too "appreciate" or are "sensitive to" the signalling system their language provides for information status?

(iii) In the sentence, "The above discussion suggests that, when needed, clear signals of information status can be employed in written language," what are some cases in which these clear signals are needed? When aren't such signals needed? Does the speaker/writer decide when such signals are needed, and then employ them? If such signals are not present, does that mean that the speaker/writer has decided that they aren't needed, and has not employed them? Or does it mean that the speaker/writer is simply unaware that they are needed? In other words, is Baker encouraging us to imagine ourselves as the speaker/writer and to make cogent decisions about when to employ clear signals regarding information status? If so, does the same encouragement apply to the translator as well? Should the translator, faced for example with a text in which clear information status signals have not been employed, employ such signals herself or himself in the target text? Or is Baker really talking about something other than the contextual "need" for such signals? Could the sentence be construed to mean something like "The above discussion suggests that, when faced with the infinite variability of actual real-life contextualized language use, the linguist can detect clear signals of information status in written language"? Is this sentence Baker's way of constructing an argumentative transition from real-life contextual variability, which tends to make linguistic analysis difficult or impossible, to the kind of controlled linguistic environment where rational analytical decisions can and must be made?

(iv) When Baker writes, "This is, of course, easier said than done because, unfortunately, not much has been achieved so far in the way of identifying signals of information status in various languages," who are the "actors" or "agents" behind the passive verbs "said," "done," and "achieved"? Are they the same person? Are they the same type of person? Does she expect the translator, for example, to inhabit all three positions, "saying" that translators should read information-status signalling systems competently, "doing" it, and "achieving" success in the identification of those systems in different languages? Or is the "sayer" the translation theorist, the "doer" the translator, and the "achiever" the linguist? If so, does this imply that the translator is complexly dependent on the translation theorist (who "says" what must be "done") and on the linguist, whose analytical "achievements" make it possible for translators to understand linguistic structures? Or is it possible for translators to develop a sensitivity to these signalling systems without having them analyzed first by a linguist, without even being aware of them? If so, could the reading of information-status signalling systems even be easier "done" than "said" (let alone "achieved") in practice?

(b) Take the last quoted paragraph of Baker's text as your source text (the one beginning "The above discussion"), and, alone or in small groups, translate it into your target language, three times:

(i) Without paying attention to the information status of the various sentences (how much you presume Baker knows about how much your prospective readers know about information status and translation) or the signalling systems of English and your target language.

(ii) Assuming target-language readers who are totally ignorant of linguistics and need to have everything spelled out clearly.

(iii) Assuming target-language readers who not only know all of this already but can be expected to be somewhat impatient with it ("yes, yes, we know all this"). Let this assumption transform your translation in radical ways; move things around, rearrange sentences and even the whole paragraph if need be, omit and add, etc. For example, Baker's paragraph repeats the conceptual cluster "information status signals" four times; do you really want to reproduce that repetition for your impatient knowledgeable reader? If you read the first sentence as actually an argumentative transition from extralinguistic variability to linguistic control rather than as a statement about when signals are needed in written language, how are you going to translate that for your impatient readers? (The ability to read a textual segment as only apparently about what it seems to be about is part of that "sensitivity to signalling systems" that Baker calls for; how does that ability transform your translation when aimed at a knowledgeable reader?) If you assume that your reader is a professional translator who is already highly sensitive to the signalling systems in his or her languages, who gained that sensitivity not by reading linguistic analyses of those systems but through long immersion in the two languages and twenty years of professional translating, and who is easily irritated at the suggestion that translators must rely on linguists for such sensitivity, how would that assumption guide your translation of the last sentence (the "easier said than done" one implying that greater linguistic achievements would make it easier to do)?

Suggestions for further reading

Austin (1962/1976), Baker (1992), Catford (1965), Chomsky (1965), Chukovskii (1984), Felman (1983), García Yebra (1989a, 1989b, 1994), Grice (1989), Hymes (1972), Nida and Taber (1969), Vinay and Darbelnet (1977)

Chapter 9

Social networks

- **The translator as social being**   192
- **Pretending (abduction)**   194
- Pretending to be a translator   194
- Pretending to be a source-language reader and target-language writer   197
- Pretending to belong to a language-use community   198
- **Learning to be a translator (induction)**   202
- **Teaching and theorizing translation as a social activity (deduction)**   204
  - **Discussion**   212
  - **Exercises**   213
  - **Suggestions for further reading**   219

T HESIS: Translation involves far more than finding target-language equivalents for source-language words and phrases; it also involves dealing with clients, agencies, employers; networking, research, use of technology; and generally an awareness of the roles translation plays in society and society plays in translation.

The translator as social being

It should go without saying: not only are translators social beings just by virtue of being human; their social existence is crucial to their professional lives. Without a social network they would never have learned any language at all, let alone one or two or three or more. Without a social network they would never have kept up with the changes in the languages they speak. Without a social network they would never get jobs, would find it difficult to research those jobs, would have no idea of what readers might be looking for in a translation, would have no place to send the finished translation, and could not get paid for it.

All this is so obvious as to seem to require no elaboration. Everyone knows that translators are social beings, and depend for their livelihood on their social connections with other human beings.

What is strange, however, is that the significance of this fact for the theory and practice of translation was recognized so very recently by translation scholars. Until the late 1970s, with the rise of poly-systems theory, the mid-1980s, with the rise of *skopos/Handlung* theory, and the late 1980s and early 1990s, with the rise of postco-lonial theory, virtually no one thought of translation as essentially a social activity. Translation was a linguistic activity performed on texts. The significant factors controlling translation were abstract structures of equivalence, defined syntactically and semantically – not the social network of people, authors, translation commissioners, terminology experts, readers, and others on whose real or presumed input or influence the translator relied to get the job done. The only real issue was accuracy, and accuracy was defined both narrowly, in terms of linguistic equivalence, and universally, with no attention to the differing needs and demands and expectations of real people in real-world situations. If a client wanted a summary or an expansion, so that it was difficult to establish neat linguistic equivalence between a source text and a shorter or longer target text, that simply wasn't translation. Medieval or more recent translations that blurred the distinction between translation and commentary, so that target texts contained material not found in the source texts, were not translations. If it could not be discussed in the abstract structural terms of linguistic equivalence, it was not translation, and generally wasn't discussed at all. A translation either *was* accurate, in the sense of truly conveying the informational content (and, for some theorists, as much of the style and syntax as possible) of the source text – and accurate in the abstract, purely in terms of linguistic analysis, without any attention at all to who commissioned it and for what purpose, in what historical circumstances – or it was not a translation and thus of no interest to translators or translation scholars.

These attitudes have changed drastically since the late 1970s; this book is one reflection of those changes. However, old habits die hard. The intellectual tradition on which the abstract linguistic conception of translation was based is very old; it runs back to the beginnings of Western civilization in the origins of the medieval church and indeed of Greek rationalism (see Robinson 1991 and 1996). The inclination to ignore the social construction, maintenance, and distribution of knowledge is an ancient Western tradition, and its legacy is still very much a part of our thought today, despite massive philosophical assaults on it all through this century. As a result, it still seems "intuitively right" today, despite a growing awareness of the impact society has on translation, to judge the success of a translation in terms of pure linguistic equivalence. We know better; but at some deep level of our intellectual being, we can't help ourselves.

As a result of these inner conflicts, you may find much of the material in this book simultaneously (1) perfectly obvious, so obvious as not to need saying at all, and (2) irrelevant to the study of translation, so irrelevant as to seem almost absurd. It does "go without saying" that translators are social beings, that social networks control or channel or influence the activity of translation in significant ways, that there are many more factors determining the "success" or "goodness" of a translation than pure linguistic equivalence – but at the same time those factors seem somehow secondary, peripheral, less important than the bare fact of whether the translator conveyed the whole meaning of the source text.

Pretending (abduction)

Pretending to be a translator

What is a translator? Who is a translator? Many of us who have been calling ourselves translators for years originally had no plans to enter that particular profession, and may even have done numerous translations for pay before beginning to describe ourselves as translators. Is there a significant difference between "translating" and "being a translator"? How does one *become* a translator?

```
Hi there!!
   My name is Volker, I am 30 years old, German, living in the
Netherlands and a starting free-lance translator.
   As I have never worked as free-lance-translator before, I
have some questions about this way of working. Do you know
any organization in the Netherlands or in Germany, which I
could turn to?
   Amongst other questions, I have no idea, how a free-lance-
translator   calculates   the   tariffs/fees/payments.   Are
there any rules or standards?
   Can you help me?
   Thanks anyway for your time!!

Volker
```

This is a question often asked in on-line translator discussion groups such as Lantra-L and FLEFO: how do I become a translator? Usually the asker possesses significant foreign-language skills, has lived (or is living) abroad, and has heard that translating might be a potential job opportunity. Sometimes the asker has even done a translation or two, enjoyed the work, and is now thinking that s/he might like to make a living doing it. But it is amply clear both to the asker and to the other listserve subscribers that this person is *not* yet a translator. What is the difference?

The easiest answer is: experience. A translator has professional experience; a novice doesn't. As a result, a translator talks like a translator; a novice doesn't. A translator has certain professional assumptions about how the work is done that infuse everything s/he says; because a novice doesn't yet have those assumptions, s/he often says things that sound silly to translators, like "I can't afford to buy my own computer, but I have a friend who'll let me work on hers any time I want." (In the middle of the night? When she's throwing a party? Does she have a recent version of major word-processing software, a late-model fax/modem, and an e-mail account?)

And this answer would be almost entirely true. Translators sound like translators because they have experience in the job. The problem with the answer is that it doesn't allow for the novice-to-translator transition: to get translation experience, you have to sound credible enough (professional enough) on the phone for an agency or client to entrust a job to you. How do you do that without translation experience?

One solution: enter a translator training program. One of the greatest offerings that such programs provide students is a sense of what it means to be a professional. Unfortunately, this is not always taught in class, and has to be picked up by osmosis – by paying attention to how the teachers talk about the profession, how they present themselves as professionals. Some programs offer internships that smooth the transition into the profession.

Even then, however, the individual translator-novice has to make the transition in his or her own head, own speech, own life. Even with guidance from teachers and/or working professionals in the field, at some point the student/intern must begin to present himself or herself as a professional – and that *always* involves a certain amount of pretense:

"Can you modem it to our BBS by Friday?"
"Yes, sure, no problem. Maybe even by Thursday."

You've never used a modem before, you don't know what BBS stands for (bulletin board system) or how one works, but you've got until Friday to find out. Today, Tuesday, you don't say "I don't have a modem" or "What's a BBS?" You promise to modem the translation to their BBS, and immediately rush out to find someone to teach you how to do it.

"What's your rate?"
"It depends on the difficulty of the text. Could you fax it to me first, so I can look it over? I'll call you right back."

It's your first real job and you suddenly realize you have no idea how much people charge for this work. You've got a half hour or so before the agency or client begins growing impatient, waiting for your phone call; you wait for the fax to arrive and then get on the phone and call a translator you know to ask about rates. When you call back, you sound professional.

Of course, this scenario requires that you know that it is standard practice to fax source texts to translators, and for translators to have a chance to look them over before agreeing to do the job. If you don't know that, you have no way of stalling for time, and have to say, "Uh, well, I don't know. What do you usually pay?" This isn't necessarily a disastrous thing to say; agencies depend on freelancers for their livelihood, and part of that job involves helping new translators get started. Especially if you can translate in a relatively exotic language combination in which it is difficult to find topnotch professionals, the agency may be quite patient with your inexperience. And most agencies – even direct clients – are ethical enough not to quote you some absurdly low rate and thus take advantage of your ignorance. But if your language combination is one of the most common, and they've only called you because their six regular freelancers in that combination are all busy, this is your chance to break in; and sounding like a rank beginner is not an effective way to do that.

So you pretend to be an experienced translator. To put it somewhat simplistically, you become a translator by pretending to be one already. As we saw Paul Kussmaul (1995: 33) noting in Chapter 7, "Expert behaviour is acquired role playing." It should be obvious that the more knowledge you have about how the profession works, the easier it will be to pretend successfully; hence the importance of studying the profession, researching it, whether in classrooms or by reading books and articles or by asking working professionals what they do. And every time you pretend successfully, that very success will give you increased knowledge that will make the "pretense" or abductive leap easier the next time.

Note, however, that the need to "pretend" to be a translator in some sense never really goes away. Even the most experienced translators frequently have to make snap decisions based on inadequate knowledge; no one *ever* knows enough to act with full professional competence in every situation.

Hallo, all Lantrans!
I have just got my first contract as a freelance translator, and I would like to hear from more experienced people:
how do you go about taxes when you work for a client in a
country different from your own? Do you pay taxes in the
other country, in yours, or in both? Is it any different
when you are working full-time with a normal contract and
do the translation work at evenings?

Thank you in advance for your help.
Ana Cuesta

The main difference between an experienced translator and a
novice may ultimately be, in fact, that the experienced translator has a
better sense of when it is all right to admit ignorance – when saying
"I don't know, let me check into that," or even "I don't know, what
do you think?", is not only acceptable without loss of face, but a sign
of professionalism.

Pretending to be a source-language reader and target-language writer

Another important aspect of abductive "pretense" in the translator's
work is the process of pretending to be first a source-language reader,
understanding the source text as a reader for whom it was intended,
and then a target-language writer, addressing a target-language readership in some effective way that accords with the expectations of the
translation commissioner.

How do you know what the source text means, or how it is
supposed to work? You rely on your skill in the language; you check
dictionaries and other reference books; you ask experts; you contact
the agency and/or client; if the author is available, you ask her or him
what s/he meant by this or that word or phrase. But the results of this
research are often inconclusive or unsatisfactory; and at some point
you have to decide to proceed as if you already had all the information you need to do a professional job. In other words, you pretend to
be a competent source-language reader. It is only a partial pretense; it
is not exactly an "imposture." You are in fact a pretty good source-
language reader. But you know that there are problems with your
understanding of this particular text; you know that you don't know
quite enough; so you do your best, making educated guesses

(abductions) regarding words or phrases that no one has been able to help you with, and present your translation as a finished, competent, successful translation.

How do you know who your target-language readers will be, what they expect, or how to satisfy their expectations? In some (relatively rare) cases, translators do know exactly who their target-language readers will be; more common, but still by no means the rule, are situations in which translators are told to translate for a certain class or group or type of readers, such as "EU officials," or "the German end-user," or "an international conference for immunologists." Conference, court, community, medical, and other interpreters typically see their audience and may even interact with them, so that the recipients' assumptions and expectations become increasingly clear throughout the course of an interpretation. But no writer ever has fully adequate information about his or her readers, no speaker about his or her listeners; this is as true of translators and interpreters as it is of people who write and speak without a "source text" in another language. At some point translators or interpreters too will have to make certain assumptions about the people they are addressing – certain abductive leaps regarding the most appropriate style or register to use, whether in any given case to use this or that word or phrase. Once again, translators or interpreters will be forced to pretend to know more than they could ever humanly know – simply in order to go on, to proceed, to do their job as professionally as possible.

Pretending to belong to a language-use community

Anthony Pym (1992a: 121–5) makes a persuasive argument against the widespread assumption that "specialist" texts are typically more difficult than "general" texts, and that students in translation programs should therefore first be given "general" texts to practice on, in order to work up the more difficult "specialist" texts later in their training. As Pym sets up his argument, it revolves around what he calls the sociocultural "embeddedness" or "belonging" of a text, meaning the social networks in which its various words, phrases, styles, registers, and so on are typically used. He shows that the more "embedded" a text is in broad social networks of the source culture, the harder it will be to translate, because (1) it will be harder for the translator to have or gain reliable information about how the various people in those networks understand the words or phrases or styles (etc.), (2) the chances are greater that no similar social networks exist in the target culture, and (3) it will be harder for the translator to judge how target-language readers will respond to whatever equivalent s/he invents.

> Jean Delisle, for example, openly recommends the use of such ["general"] texts in the teaching of translators, since "initial training in the use of language is made unnecessarily complicated by specialised terminology" . . . This sounds quite reasonable. But in saying this, Delisle falsely assumes that "general texts" are automatically free of terminology problems, as if magazine articles, publicity material and public speeches were not the genres most susceptible to embeddedness, textually bringing together numerous socially continuous and overlapping contexts in their creation of complex belonging. A specialised text may well present terminological problems – the translator might have to use dictionaries or talk with specialists before confidently transcoding the English "tomography" as French "tomographie" or Spanish "tomografía" –, but this is surely far less difficult than going through the context analysis by which Delisle himself takes seven pages or so to explain why, in a newspaper report on breast removal, the expression "sense of loss" – superbly embedded in English – cannot be translated (for whom? why?) as "sentiment de perte" . . . No truly technical terms are as complex as this most vaguely "general" of examples! The extreme difficulty of such texts involves negotiation of the nuances collected from the numerous situations in which an expression like "sense of loss" can be used and which, for reasons which escape purely linguistic logic, have never assumed the same contiguity with respect to "sentiment de perte".
>
> (Pym 1992a: 123)

Pym argues that highly specialized technical texts are typically embedded in an international community of scientists, engineers, physicians, lawyers, and the like, who attend international conferences and read books in other languages and so have usually eliminated from their discourse the kind of contextual vagueness that is hardest to translate. As Pym's "tomography" example shows, too, international precision tends to be maintained in specialist groups through the use of Greek, Latin, French, and English terms that change only slightly as they move from one phonetic system to another. "General" texts, on the other hand, are grounded in less closely regulated everyday usage, the way people talk in a wide variety of ordinary contexts, which requires far more *social* knowledge than specialized texts – far more knowledge of how people talk to each other in their different social groupings, at home, at work, at the store, etc. Even slang and jargon, Pym would say, are easier to translate than this "general" discourse – all you have to do to translate slang or jargon is find an expert in it and ask your questions. (What makes that type of translation difficult is that experts are sometimes hard to find.) With a "general" text, everybody's an expert – but all the experts disagree, because they've used the words or phrases in different situations, different contexts, and can never quite sort out in their own minds just what it means with this or that group.

But Pym's take on "specialized" texts, and specialist groups, is in some cases a bit simplistic. The key to successful "specialized" translation is not just knowing that "tomography" is *tomographie* in French and *tomografía* in Spanish – i.e., not just finding equivalents for the words – but first reading and then writing like a member of the social groups that write and talk that way. To understand a medical text in one language one must read like a doctor or a nurse or a hospital administrator (or whatever) in that language; to translate it effectively into another language one must *write* like a doctor (or whatever) in that other language. And however "international" these specialists typically are, they are also real people who interact with their peers in intensely local and socially embedded ways as well. The meanings of words and phrases may be more carefully defined in specialist discourse; but the specific way in which those words and phrases are strung together to make a specialized text will vary significantly with the group using them; and the effective professional translator will have to "pretend" to be a member of that group in order to render them plausibly into the target language.

Two examples. I was asked to translate a list of eighty chemical terms from English into Finnish – no context, no sentences, just eighty words. All of them were Latinate, precisely the sort of term that Pym quite rightly says is quite easy to translate, since it usually requires little more than adjusting spellings to the other language's phonetic system: tomography, *tomographie, tomografía*. And it was, as Pym predicts, a very easy job; but because I was translating into Finnish, which is not my native language, I faxed my translation to a friend in Finland who has a Ph.D. in chemistry. She made a few corrections and sent it back. Reading through her return fax, I noticed that she had introduced some inconsistencies into the translation of -ethylene. In some compounds, it was translated *-etyleeni*; in others, *-eteeni*. Concerned about this, I called her and asked; she said that usage in that area is currently in transition in the Finnish chemist community, and the inconsistencies reflect that transition. My guess is, in fact, that another member of that community might have construed the transition differently, and given me a slightly different version of the inconsistencies, using both *-etyleeni* and *-eteeni* but in different compounds. No matter how international the social network, usage will always be shaped by the local community.

And more recently: I was asked to translate some instructions for a pharmaceutical product from English into Finnish, and couldn't find or think of a Finnish translation for "flip-off seal," so I got on-line and asked three or four translators I know in Finland who do a lot of medical texts. They gave me three substantially different answers, all three duly checked with doctor friends. The most interesting variation was in the terms they offered for "seal": *suoja* "protection, cover," *hattu* "hat," and *sinetti* "seal." I would not have thought that *sinetti*, which does mean most kinds of seal (but not the animal), would have been used for a medicine vial's tamper protection; but a doctor friend assured my translator friend that it was. *Hattu* "hat" is clearly colloquial; Finns use the word in casual conversation to describe anything that vaguely resembles a hat when they don't know the correct term, or when the correct term would sound too technical. This is a good reminder that even specialists belong to more than one community; and even within the specialist community they often maintain two or more registers, one technical and "official," one or more slangy and informal. *Suoja* "protection, cover" is the most neutral of the three; it is in fact the one I ended up using, partly because my own (foreign) intuition was opposed to *sinetti* – but mainly because the *suoja* reply was the only one that came in before my deadline.

Lesson 1: the more social networks or communities or groups you're grounded in, and the more grounded in each you are, the better able you will be to "pretend" to be a reader-member of the source-text community and a writer-member of the target-text community.

Lesson 2: the less grounded you are in the communities themselves, the more important it is to be grounded in the translator community, or to have other friends who either know what you need to know or can connect you with people who do. Even so, to "pretend" to be a doctor or an engineer when you have never been either you must be able to sort out conflicting "expert" advice and pick the rendition that seems to fit your context best – which in turn requires *some* grounding in the social networks where the terms are "natively" used.

Lesson 3: in the professional world of deadlines, the translator's goal can never be the perfect translation, or even the best possible translation; it can only be the best possible translation *at this point in time.* If a translator friend talks to a doctor friend and provides you with a plausible-sounding term or phrase before your deadline, you don't wait around hoping that a better alternative might arrive some time in the next few days. You deliver your translation on time and feel pleased that it's done. Of course, if another friend sends you an alternative after the deadline and you suddenly realize that *this* is the right way to say it and you and your other friend were totally wrong before, you phone the agency or client and, if it is still possible, have them make the change.

Learning to be a translator (induction)

In this light, learning to be a translator entails more than just learning lots of words and phrases in two or more languages and transfer patterns between them; more than just what hardware and software to own and what to charge. It entails also, and perhaps most importantly, grounding yourself in several key communities or social networks, in fact in as many as you can manage – and as thoroughly as you can manage in each.

Above all, perhaps, in the translator community. Translators know how languages and cultures interact. Translators know how the marketplace for intercultural communication works (hardware and software, rates, contracts, etc.). Translators will get you jobs: if they can't take a job and want to suggest someone else for an agency or client to call, and they know you from a conference or a local or regional translator organization, they'll dig out your card and suggest you; or if they've enjoyed your postings in an on-line discussion group, they'll give the agency or client your e-mail address. Translators have to be grounded in many social networks, and will almost always know someone to call or fax or e-mail to get an answer to a difficult terminological problem – so that being grounded in the translator community gives you invaluable links to many other communities as well. Hence the importance of belonging to and getting involved in translator organizations, attending translator conferences, and subscribing to translator discussion groups on the Internet or CompuServe.

But you should also, of course, be grounded in as many other communities as you can: people who use specific specialized discourses and people who don't; specialists at work, at professional conferences, and at the bar; people who read and/or write for professional journals, or for "general" periodicals for news, science, and culture, and/or for various popular magazines and tabloids; people who tell stories, things they saw on or read in the news, things that happened to them or their friends, jokes they've heard recently, things they've made up. Translating is, in fact, very much akin to other forms of reading and writing, telling and listening; it is a form of communication, a channel for the circulation of ideas and opinions, information and influence. And translators have a great deal in common with people who use other channels for circulating those things both within and between cultures. It is essential for translators to ground themselves in the communities that use these channels in at least two language communities, of course – this is the major difference between translators and most other communicators – but it helps translators to think *and* act globally to imagine their job as one of building communicative connections with dozens, perhaps hundreds, of different social networks all over the world. The professional translator should be like a neuron, with dendrites reaching out to vast communicative networks, and always able to shunt information or requests (as well as various regulatory impulses – in neurological terms "inhibitory" or "excitatory" impulses – such as "here's what you ought to do" or "I think that would be unethical") to this or that network at will.

Eugene Nida (1985) has written an article entitled "Translating Means Translating Meaning." The implication is that the translator burrows into the source text in quest of meaning, extracts it, and renders it into the target language – the traditional view of the profession. A more interculturally and socially aware perspective on translation would paraphrase that to read: "Translating Means Channeling Meaning – and Influence, and Connectedness – Through Vast Global Communicative Networks." Or, more aphoristically:

translation is transmission
translators are links in the communicative chain
translation is synaptic action in the global brain.

Teaching and theorizing translation as a social activity (deduction)

In a later chapter of *Translation and Text Transfer* (1992a: 152–3), Anthony Pym comments on the historical invisibility of translators as monolingual rulers' servants – "controlled nobodies" – and raises the very political question of loyalty or fidelity, especially the knotty problem of *proving* one's loyalty to a ruler who cannot do what the translator does:

> It is not particularly scandalous that few translators have been kings, princes or priests. There is even a certain pride to be taken in the fact that political and moral authorities have had to trust the knowledge conveyed by their translating servants. But how might the prince know that a particular translator is worthy of trust? It would be foolish to suggest that all translators are equally competent, that their fidelity corresponds automatically to what they are paid, or that their loyalty is beyond doubt. Some kind of extra-textual support is ultimately necessary. Perhaps the prince's confidence is based on a diploma from a specialised translation institute, references from previous employers, comparisons with other translators, or even on what the individual translator is able to say about the practice of translating, since theorisation is itself a mode of professional self-defence.

This conception of translation theory as a necessary part of the translator's defensive armor against attacks from the uncomprehending is at once age-old – it was, after all, Jerome's fundamental motivation for theorizing translation in his letter to Pammachius in

395, and Martin Luther's likewise in his circular letter on translation in 1530 – and also relatively new. The official and dominant reason for theorizing translation for over two thousand years, after all, has almost invariably been to control the translators' actions, not (as for Jerome, Luther, and Pym) to help them justify those actions after the fact: to make translators absolutely subject to the ruler's command (be faithful, not free!), not to give them defenses against the ruler's incomprehension.

This is once again the distinction between internal and external knowledge, raised in Chapter 1: from the "ruler's" or user's external point of view, the only possible reason for translation theory to exist is to develop and enforce normative standards for accurate and faithful translation – to make sure that translators are translating in conformity with collectively imposed standards and not, say, becoming the "traitors" they are always halfway suspected of becoming (*traduttore traditore*). From the translator's internal point of view, however, translation theory exists largely in order to help them to solve problems that arise and to defend their solutions when criticized, and thus to grow professionally in skills, knowledge, disposition, demeanor, and credibility.

Note, however, that both of these conceptions of the reasons for theorizing translation are explicitly social: they derive justifications for translation theory not from "pure knowledge" or "value-free science," but from the necessity of living and working in the social world, of getting along with other people (in this case the people who pay us to do the work). And while it is by no means new to theorize translation for these social reasons, it is only since the late 1970s – beginning with the functional/action-oriented/translation-oriented/ *skopos*/*Handlung* school in Germany (Katharina Reiß, Hans J. Vermeer, Justa Holz-Mänttäri, Christiane Nord, others) and the polysystems/translation studies/manipulation school in the Benelux countries and Israel (Itamar Even-Zohar, Gideon Toury, André Lefevere, James S. Holmes, Theo Hermans, others) – that translation theorists have been explicitly theorizing the *theorizing* of translation in these social terms. Translation, all of these theorists have been insisting, is controlled by social networks, social interactions, people saying to one another "do this," "I'll give you X amount of money if you do this," "could you help me with this," etc. – and translation theory is an inescapable part of that. In fact, if theory isn't a part of such social interactions, these theorists believe, it is useless – a mere academic game, a way to get published, to build a reputation, to be promoted, and so forth.

Since what is variously known as the polysystems or "descriptive translation studies" (DTS) or "manipulation" school is typically more interested in large cultural systems than in local social networks, we will be returning to the work of that group of theorists in Chapter 10; here our concern will be with the German school variously called functional translation theory, action/*Handlung*-oriented translation theory, translation-oriented text analysis, or *skopos* theory.

This group has worked to stress the importance of the social functions and interactions of translation for primarily *realistic* purposes. It is more realistic, they believe, to study translation in terms of what really happens when people translate, what social forces really control translation, than in the traditional abstract universal terms of text-based equivalence (translate sense-for-sense, not word-for-word). Since their claim is that translation has always *been* social but is just now being *perceived* in terms of its true social nature, this approach is fundamentally corrective: it seeks to undermine traditional approaches that lay down general laws without regard for the vast situational variety that is translation practice.

In this sense the functional/action-oriented/*skopos* theorists develop their correctives to traditional text-oriented theories by moving a few steps closer to what Peirce calls induction: they explore their own inductive experiences of translating in the social/professional world, observe what they and their colleagues actually do, what actually happens in and around the act of translating, and build new theories or "deductions" from those observations. This dedication to the "practical" experiences of real translators in real professional contexts has made this approach extremely attractive to many practitioners and students of translation. Like all theorists, functional translation theorists do simplify the social field of translation in order to theorize it; they move from the mind-numbing complexity of the real world to the relative stability of reductive idealizations and abstractions, of diagrams that pretend to be all-inclusive, and sometimes of jargon that seems to come from Mars. But because they are themselves professional translators whose theories arise out of their own practical/inductive experiences, they also retain a loyalty to the complexity of practice, so that even while formulating grand schemas that will explain just how the social networks surrounding translators function, they keep reminding their readers that things are never quite this simple – that this or that theoretical component is sometimes different.

A good illustration of the theoretical method behind this approach might be gleaned from Christiane Nord's book *Text Analysis in Translation* (1991), her own English translation of her earlier German book *Textanalyse und Übersetzen* (1988). Nord usefully and accessibly summarizes the main points of the functional or action-oriented approach in her first chapter, in analyses and diagrams and examples as well as in pithy summary statements printed in a larger bold font and enclosed in boxes; let us use those statements to introduce a functional approach here:

Being culture-bound linguistic signs, both the source text and the target text are determined by the communicative situation in which they serve to convey a message.

(1991: 7)

Implication: all texts, not just translations, are determined by the communicative *situation*, not abstract universal rules governing writing or speaking. It is impossible, therefore, to say that text-based "equivalence" is or should be the defining criterion of a good translation, or that a single type of equivalence is the only acceptable one for all translation. These things are determined by and in the communicative situation – by people, acting and interacting in a social context.

The initiator starts the process of intercultural communication because he wants a particular communicative instrument: the target text.

(1991: 8)

This group of theorists was the first to begin speaking and writing of "initiators" or "commissioners" who need a target text and ask someone to create one. That such people exist, and that their impact on the process and nature of translation is enormous, should have been obvious. But no one paid it significant theoretical attention. The only significant "persons" in traditional theories were the source-text author, the translator, and the target-text reader; the source-text author and target-text reader were imagined to exert some sort of magical influence over the translator without the mediation of the actual real-world people who in fact channel that influence through phone calls, faxes, e-mail messages, and payments.

The function of the target text is not arrived at automatically from an analysis of the source text, but is pragmatically defined by the purpose of the intercultural communication.

(1991: 9)

Implications: (1) that translations are intended to serve some social function or functions; (2) that these functions are not textual abstractions like "the rhetorical function" or "the informative function," but extratextual actions designed to shape how people behave in a social context; (3) that these functions cannot be determined in stable or permanent ways but must be renegotiated "pragmatically" in every new communicative context; and (4) that the guiding factor in these negotiations is the purpose (*skopos*) of the intercultural communication, what the various people hope to achieve in and through it.

The translator's reception (i.e. the way he receives the text) is determined by the communicative needs of the initiator or the TT [target-text] recipient.

(1991: 10)

Implication: the translator reads the text, the interpreter hears the text, neither in absolute submission to some transcendental "spirit" of the text nor in pure anarchistic idiosyncrasy, but as guided by the wishes of the people who need the translation and ask for it.

The translator is not the sender of the ST [source-text] message but a text producer in the target culture who adopts somebody else's intention in order to produce a communicative instrument for the target culture, or a target-culture document of a source-culture communication.

(1991: 11)

Implications: (1) that the translator is the instrument not of the original author, as is often assumed in older theories, but of the target culture; (2) that there are social forces – namely, people working together – in the target culture who organize that culture's communicative needs and present the translator with a specific task in the satisfaction of those needs; and thus (3) that the source-text message always comes to the translator mediated and shaped, to some extent "pre-interpreted," by complex target-cultural arrangements.

A text is a communicative action which can be realized by a combination of verbal and non-verbal means.

(1991: 15)

A text is not, that is, a static object that can be studied in "laboratory conditions" and described in reliable objective ways. It is a social action, and partakes of the situational variety of all such actions. It takes on its actional force not only through its words but through tone of voice (as spoken or read aloud), gestures and expressions, "illustrations, layout, a company logo, etc." (1991: 14). By the same token, a source text found by the translator in a book or a dentist's office will be significantly different from one faxed or e-mailed to the translator by a client or agency – even if the words are identical. The nonverbal action of sending a text to be translated by electronic means actually changes the communicative action.

The reception of a text depends on the individual expectations of the recipient, which are determined by the situation in which he receives the text as well as by his social background, his world knowledge, and/ or his communicative needs.

(1991: 16)

209

Or as Nord (1991: 16) glosses this, "The sender's intention and the recipient's expectation may be identical, but they need not necessarily coincide nor even be compatible." More: not all translation users (initiators, commissioners, recipients) even *expect* them to coincide or be compatible. Some do; but this is far from the absolute ideal requirement for all translation that more traditional theories have made it out to be.

By means of a comprehensive model of text analysis which takes into account intratextual as well as extratextual factors the translator can establish the "function-in-culture" of a source text. He then compares this with the (prospective) function-in-culture of the target text required by the initiator, identifying and isolating those ST elements which have to be preserved or adapted in translation.

(1991: 21)

The translator mediates, in other words, between two textual actions, the source text as an action functioning in the source culture and the (desired) target text which the initiator wants to function in a certain way in the target culture. In the end, the initiator's requirements will determine the nature of the target text, but those requirements must be filtered through what the translator has determined as the "function-in-culture" of the source text. Ethical considerations come into play when the translator (or some other person) feels that there is too great a discrepancy between the two textual actions.

Functional equivalence between source and target text is not the "normal" skopos [purpose] of a translation, but an exceptional case in which the factor "change of functions" is assigned zero.

(1991: 23)

Since the target text will serve different cultural and social functions in the target culture from those served by the source text in the source culture, it is exceedingly rare for a translation to be "functionally equivalent" to its original. Functional *change* is the normal skopos;

the usual question is "How will the skopos or purpose of this textual action change in the target culture?" Hence Nord's functional definition of translation:

Translation is the production of a functional target text maintaining a relationship with a given source text that is specified according to the intended or demanded function of the target text (translation skopos). Translation allows a communicative act to take place which because of existing linguistic and cultural barriers would not have been possible without it.

(1991: 28)

A relationship: not a single stable relationship, to be determined in advance for all times and all places; just a relationship, which will vary with the social interactions that determine it.

This conception of translation as governed by social function in real social interactions has obvious implications for the theorizing and teaching of translation as well.

First, it is clear that translation theorists and teachers, far from standing above or beyond or outside these social networks, are very much caught up in them as well. Theorists attempt to make sense of the social networks controlling translation not for "pure science" reasons but to teach others (especially translators) to understand the social processes better, so as to play a responsible and ethical role in them. Being "responsible" means responding, making active and informed and ethical decisions about how to react to the pressures placed on one to act in a certain way in a certain situation; the function of translation theory and translation instruction must be to enhance translators' ability to make such decisions.

And second, just as translators generate theory in their attempts to understand their work better – for example, to respond more complexly to criticism, to distinguish true problem areas from areas where the critic is simply misinformed, to improve the former and defend the latter, and to renegotiate borderline cases – so too must translation theorists and teachers build their theoretical and pedagogical models at the cusp where deductive principles begin to arise out of inductive experience, and always remember the practical complexity out of which those principles arose. That complexity is not only an explosively fertile source of new ideas, new insights, new understanding; it is the only place in which theories, rules, and precepts can be grasped and applied in action. Students learning, teachers teaching, and theorists theorizing, like translators translating, are social animals engaged in a highly social activity controlled by the interactive communicative needs of real people in real social contexts.

Discussion

1 What certainties, stabilities, sureties are lost in a shift from text-based theories of translation to social action-based theories? How important are those certainties? Can we afford to do without them?

2 The idea of pretending to be a professional translator causes some students anxiety; in others it generates a pleasant sense of anticipation. How do you feel about it? And how can talking about how you feel about it help you do it?

3 In what ways are you currently grounded in a translator community? What kinds of professional help do you get from other members of that community? What aspects of your groundedness in that community remain undeveloped? How could you develop those aspects in professionally useful ways?

4 Try to list all the social communities to which you belong. Discuss how you can tell where one community ends and another one begins. Explore some ways in which your personality, behavior, speech patterns, and so on change when you move from one community to another (students, language professionals, family, neighbors, the garage where your car is fixed, etc.). What communities are a peripheral part of your life? Why?

5 In what ways do the translation theories you know serve the translator? How effective are those forms of "service"? How could translation theory be made to serve translators better?

Exercises

1   Read this passage from Katharina Reiß and Hans J. Vermeer, *Grundlegung einer allgemeinen Translationstheorie* ("Foundations for a General Theory of Translation," 1984: 98–9), in the German original and/or English translation (by DR) (with permission):

> Normen schreiben vor, daß und wie gehandelt wird. Sie lassen aber einen gewissen Spielraum für die Art der Handlung zu. Die Hauptsache ist, daß auf eine Situation so reagiert wird, daß die Reaktion als sinnvoll erklärt werden kann. (Wir lassen noch offen, daß die Erklärung vom Handelnden und vom Interaktionspartner je getrennt gefordert wird . . .) Es ist weniger wichtig, wie eine Norm erfüllt wird, als daß versucht wird, sie zu erfüllen. Relevant ist die Funktion der Handlung.
>
> Eykman . . . zeigt auf, daß Bilder durch andere Bilder, Formulierungen durch andere Formulierungen ersetzt werden können, ohne daß sich die Textfunktion ändert. Eykman spricht von "Abwandlung" (gegenüber Variation). – Für Translation heißt das: (1) Abwandlung ist unter gegebenen Bedingungen legitim. (2) Die Bedingungen liegen im Kulturspezifischen, z. B. im gleichen Grad des Üblichen als Adäquatheitsbedingung.
>
> Was man tut, ist sekundär im Hinblick auf den Zweck des Tuns und seine Erreichung.
>
> Eine Handlung ist dann "geglückt", wenn sie als situationsadäquat (sinnvoll) erklärt werden kann. Die Erklärung wird, wie angedeutet, zunächst vom Handelnden (Produzenten) selbst verlangt: Er muß angeben, welches seine "Intention" war. Wie wurde bereits darauf hingewiesen, daß eine Handlung nicht unbedingt einer Intention (optimal) entspricht. (Man schlägt sich auf den Finger, ehe man den Nagel dann doch trifft.) – Andererseits versucht auch der Interaktionspartner des Handelnden (der Rezipient) eine Erklärung ("Interpretation") für das Verhalten des Produzenten. Die "Erklärung" des Rezipienten kann von der des Produzenten abweichen. Beide versuchen, die gegenseitigen Erklärungen vorwegnehmend einzuschätzen und in ihrem Handeln zu berücksichtigen ("reflexive Ko-Orientierung").

(Zur Überindividualität von Interpretationen vgl. Schnelle
. . .) – "Glücken" ist also eine Feststellung, die von
Produzent und Rezipient getrennt getroffen wird und für
beide (und evtl. dritte) getrennt gilt.

Norms determine that and how someone acts. They do
however leave a certain room for play in the *type* of action
undertaken. The main thing is that one respond situationally
in such a way that one's response can be construed as
meaningful. (Let us leave it open for now whether such
construals can ever be demanded separately of both participants in an interaction, the "producer" and the "recipient"
. . .) It is less important *how* a norm is satisfied than that an
attempt is made to satisfy it. What is relevant is the action's
function.

As Eykman . . . has shown, images can be replaced with
other images, formulations with other formulations, without
altering the function of a text. Eykman speaks not of "variation" but of "adapation" (*Abwandlung*). For translation
this means (1) that adaptation under specific conditions is
legitimate, and (2) that these conditions are culture-specific;
for example, a condition of adequacy may require that the
same degree of "usualness" or ordinariness be maintained.

What one does is secondary to the purpose of that doing
and its attainment.

An action "succeeds," then, when it can be construed as
situationally adequate (meaningful). As has been suggested,
a construal of this adequacy is first demanded of the actant
(producer) himself: he must tell us what he intended. We
just saw how an action does not always correspond opti-
mally to its intention. (You hammer your finger before
connecting with the nail.) On the other hand, the actant's
interaction partner (the recipient) also seeks to construe
("interpret") the producer's behavior, and the recipient's
construal may well diverge from that of the producer.
Both attempt to anticipate these mutual construals and
take them into consideration in their actions ("reflexive
coorientation"). (For the supraindividuality of interpretations, cf. Schnelle . . .) The "success" of an action is
thus an assessment made separately by its producer and

recipient, and it retains a separate validity for each – eventually also for a third.

(a) Take a common metaphorical phrase in English or some other source language and come up with a series of possible translations for it, including literal renditions, paraphrases, etc. For example, "It ain't over till the fat lady sings" might be translated into Spanish as *No se acaba hasta que cante la gorda* ("It isn't over till the fat lady sings"), *No se acaba hasta que se acaba* ("It isn't over till it's over"), *Siempre hay esperanza* ("There's always hope"), etc. Collect as many substantially different translations as you can – at least three or four.

(Another Spanish–English example: the title of Laura Esquivel's novel, *Como agua para chocolate*, translated into English as *Like Water for Chocolate*. But these examples are easy to multiply: once in a blue moon, have egg all over your face, at sixes and sevens, shape up or ship out, read someone the riot act, etc. The main thing is, once you have chosen a phrase, to come up with realistic scenarios in which the various possibilities might seriously be considered.)

Now pair off and create social interactions such as Reiß and Vermeer discuss, with one person as "producer" and the other person as "recipient," with the idea of discussing, defending and/or attacking, the "success" of a specific translation of the phrase in a specific context. Flesh out that context in detail first: an advertising agency coordinating a fourteen-country advertising campaign for audio tapes, working with a freelancer; the acquisitions editor for a major trade press that is publishing the memoirs of an opera diva in translation, working with a translator who is also a professor of musicology; an in-house translator and her boss discussing how to translate this phrase used humorously in a technical document; a reader of the diva's memoirs writing a letter to the editor or op-ed piece protesting the translation of the title, in imaginary dialogue with the translator or a potential "third" person (such as the acquisitions editor or original author).

Argue over what would constitute a "successful" translation from your "character's" particular point of view. If you are able to reach an agreement, spend a few minutes afterwards exploring how comfortable or uncomfortable you are with that compromise.

(b) Now try to imagine a "general" framework for evaluating "successful" or "good" translations. Is it even possible? If so, do you have to compromise with the radical social relativism of Reiß and Vermeer's model? How? What is gained and/or lost by doing this? Try to diagram the framework, or to represent it in some other visual way.

2   Study the diagram of the *Basissituation für translatorisches Handeln* "basic situation for translatorial activity" (Figure 7) from Justa Holz-Mänttäri's book *Translatorisches Handeln*, along with its English translation and expanded commentary (by DR):

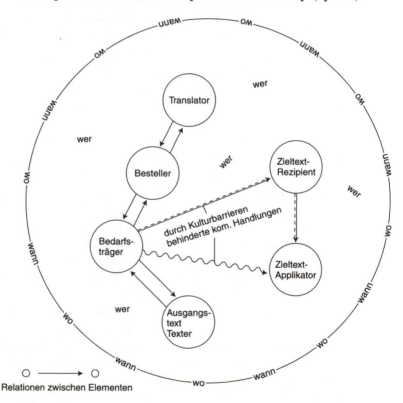

FIGURE 7 The "basic situation for translatorial activity"
Source: Holz-Mänttärri 1984: 106 (with permission)

Bedarfsträger (**[target-text] "need-bearer"**: the person who needs a translation and so initates the process of obtaining one; also called the "translation initiator")

Besteller (**commissioner**: the person who asks a translator to produce a functionally appropriate target text for a specific use situation)

Ausgangstext-Texter (**source-text texter**: original writer or speaker)

Translator (**translator/interpreter**: German scholars use the Latin word *translator* to mean the producer of either written or spoken texts, who are normally called *der Übersetzer* and *der Dolmetscher*, respectively)

Zieltext-Applikator (**target-text applier**: person who gives the target text its practical applications, works with it in the social world, for example publishes it, uses it as advertising copy, sends it as a business letter, assigns it to students, etc.)

Zieltext-Rezipient (**target-text recipient**: the person for whom a message is "texted" or produced in textual form)

durch Kulturbarrieren behinderte kom. Handlungen: **communicative activities hindered by cultural barriers**

wann: **when**

wo: **where**

wer: **who**

Relationen zwischen Elementen: **relations between elements**

(a) Work in groups to develop a plausible story for the diagram as Holz-Mänttäri presents it. Identify the "translation initiator" or "need-bearer," the "commissioner," the "source-text texter," the translator/interpreter, the "target-text applier," and the "target-text recipient," by name and profession. Set the stage in terms of "who," "where," and "when." Start with the "need-bearer" or translation-initiator on the left side of the diagram and move either to the source-text texter or the commissioner next (or possibly both at once); then to the translator/interpreter; and finally to the target-text applier/ recipient loop. What kind of translation "need" is this? Does the source text exist at the beginning of the process, or does the "need-bearer" go to the source-text texter to have one produced? Who is the commissioner and what part does s/he play in this process? How does the commissioner find the translator/interpreter? How is the target text to be "applied" in practice? Who is the intended recipient (or recipient-group), and how does the target-text applier get it to that recipient or recipient-group? Be as detailed as you can; tell the story like a newspaper article, or a short story, but with an omniscient third-person narrator who knows everything.

(b) Now redraw and rethink the diagram to fit the following scenarios:

- The translation-initiator is also the translator and the target-text recipient; she is reading a novel and finds a sentence in a foreign language that she can just barely make out, so she translates it for herself in order to follow the plot properly (is there a commissioner? a target-text applier?).

- Samuel Beckett writes *En attendant Godot* in French, then translates it himself into English as *Waiting for Godot* (why? for whom? is the translation commissioned? does Beckett's editor or agent or producer or director or some other person serve as target-text applier?).

- A German tourist is picking up a package at the post office in Salvador, Brazil, and is told by the postal clerk that he owes duties on it; he speaks no Portuguese, and the clerk speaks no German; the next person in line offers to interpret between them, and the transaction is satisfactorily completed.

- The source-text texter is a Bulgarian physics professor who has been invited to speak at an international conference in English; she writes the paper in Bulgarian and gets a grant from her dean to pay a native English-speaker in Sofia (whom she finds by calling the English department of her university) to translate it into English; she sends it to the conference organizers, who send her some suggestions for changes before it is included in the published conference proceedings; she has her translator check the changes and sends it back; she also pays the translator to help her with some pronunciations so that the conference participants will understand her as she reads.

(c) Now rethink and redraw the diagram to account for a role not indicated on Holz-Mänttäri's original diagram: the research consultant.

- The translator asks the client for previous translations of similar texts to help with terminology; he calls the client and asks to talk with technical writers, engineers, technicians, marketing people, etc. (would these research consultants be counted as part of the commissioner? part of the source-text texter?).
- The translator sends out an e-mail query over Lantra-L or FLEFO, asking for help with specific words or phrases; she faxes or e-mails friends in the source-text and/or target-text culture who might be able to help; and has her husband, who is a native speaker of the target language, edit the target text for fluency.
- A community interpreter is interpreting a conversation between a poor Texan Chicana accused of child abuse and the Anglo social worker sent by the county to investigate the charges; she stops the conversation many times to ask one of the speakers for clarification on this or that vague word or phrase, so that both speakers serve at various times as source-text texter, target-text recipient, and research consultant.

(d) Finally, retell any one of the stories in (a)–(c) from a first-person point of view, adopting at least two different roles in succession. Rethink and redraw the diagram to accommodate this new point of view.

Suggestions for further reading

Even-Zohar (1981), Holz-Mänttäri (1984), Nida (1985), Nord (1991), Pym (1992a, 1992b), Reiß (1976), Reiß and Vermeer (1984), Vermeer (1989)

Chapter 10

Cultures

- **Cultural knowledge**   222
- **Self-projection into the foreign (abduction)**   225
- **Immersion in cultures (induction)**   228
- **Intercultural awareness (deduction)**   231
  - **Discussion**   238
  - **Exercises**   239
  - **Suggestions for further reading**   244

T HESIS: Cultures, and the intercultural competence and awareness that arise out of experience of cultures, are far more
complex phenomena than it may seem to the translator who needs
to know how to say "wrap-around text" in German, and the more
aware the translator can become of these complexities, including
power differentials between cultures and genders, the better a translator s/he will be.

Cultural knowledge

It is probably safe to say that there has never been a time when the
community of translators was unaware of cultural differences and
their significance for translation. Translation theorists have been
cognizant of the problems attendant upon cultural knowledge and
cultural difference at least since ancient Rome, and translators almost
certainly knew all about those problems long before theorists articulated them. Some Renaissance proponents of sense-for-sense translation were inclined to accuse medieval literal translators of being
ignorant of cultural differences; but an impressive body of historical
research on medieval translation (see Copeland 1991, Ellis 1989,
1991, 1996, Ellis and Evans 1994) is beginning to show conclusively
that such was not the case. Medieval literalists were not ignorant of
cultural or linguistic difference; due to the hermeneutical traditions in
which they worked and the audiences for whom they translated, they
were simply determined to bracket that difference, set it aside, and
proceed as if it did not exist.

Unlike the social networks that we explored in Chapter 12,
therefore, cultural knowledge and cultural difference have been a
major focus of translator training and translation theory for as long
as either has been in existence. The main concern has traditionally
been with so-called *realia*, words and phrases that are so heavily and

exclusively grounded in one culture that they are almost impossible to translate into the terms – verbal or otherwise – of another. Long debates have been held over when to paraphrase (Japanese *wabi* as "the flawed detail that creates an elegant whole"), when to use the nearest local equivalent (German *gemütlich* becomes "cozy, comfortable, homey," Italian *attaccabottoni* becomes "bore"), when to coin a new word by translating literally (German *Gedankenexperiment* becomes "thought experiment," *Weltanschauung* becomes "world view," Russian *ostranenie* becomes "defamiliarization"), and when to transcribe (French *épater les bourgeois, savoir faire,* German

---

Braniff Airlines had a slogan, "Fly in Leather," giving the impression that flying Braniff meant flying in luxury. The Spanish translation gave a slightly different impression: "Fly Naked."

The Coors slogan, "Turn It Loose," got translated into Spanish as something like "Suffer From Diarrhea."

Vicks Cough Drops were a tough sell in Germany, where people pronounced the V as an F, turning the company name into a popular colloquial word for the sex act.

Puffs Tissues had similar problems in Germany, where the company name means a whorehouse.

Pepsi's slogan "Pepsi Adds Life" met some resistance in China, where the translation promised: "Pepsi Brings Your Ancestors Back from the Grave." Marketers quickly launched a new translation, "Baishi Kele," literally meaning "One Hundred Things to be Happy About."

Coca-Cola had similar problems in China. Since "Coca-Cola" doesn't really mean anything, they decided not to translate it but to create a new Chinese word with similar-sounding syllables. Unfortunately, the characters they chose meant "Bite the Wax Tadpole." So they put their thinking caps back on and came up with another string of similar-sounding syllables, "Kekou Kele," literally meaning "Palatable and Happy" or "Happiness in the Mouth."

Zeitgeist, Angst, Sanskrit *maya, mantra,* Yiddish *schlemiel, tsuris,* Greek *kudos,* Finnish *sauna,* Arabic *alcohol,* Chinese *tao*). And these "untranslatable" culture-bound words and phrases continue to fascinate translators and translation theorists (for a compendium of such words, see Rheingold 1988; for a history of early theoretical thought on the subject, see Rener 1989).

What has changed in recent translation scholarship on culture is an increasing emphasis on the collective control or shaping of cultural knowledge: the role played by ideology, or what Antonio Gramsci (1971) called "hegemony," in constructing and maintaining cultural knowledge and policing transfers across cultural barriers. Beginning in the late 1970s, several groups of scholars in the Benelux countries and Israel began to explore the impact of cultural systems on translation – notably the impact of the target-culture system on what gets translated, and why, and how, and how the translation is used. And beginning in the late 1980s, other groups of scholars around the world began to explore the ongoing impact of colonization on translation – especially the surviving power differentials between "first-world" and "third-world" countries and how they control the economics and ideology and thus also the practice of translation. We will be looking at these theories below, under the heading "Intercultural Awareness."

Another important question is, as Anthony Pym (1992a: 25) puts it, "what then is a culture?" Noting that "Those who travel on foot or have read the diachronic part of Saussure know that there are no natural frontiers between languages" (1992a: 25), he goes on:

> How might one define the points where one culture stops and another begins? The borders are no easier to draw than those between languages or communities. One could perhaps turn to a geometry of fuzzy sets or maybe even deny the possibility of real contact altogether, but neither mathematics nor ideological relativism are able to elucidate the specific importance of translation as an active relation between cultures.
>
> Although questions like the definition of a culture are commonly thought to be beyond the scope of translation theory, their solution could become one of translation studies' main contributions to the social sciences. Instead of looking for differentiated or distilled cultural essences, it could be fruitful

to look at translations themselves in order to see what they have to say about cultural frontiers. It is enough to define the limits of a culture as *the points where transferred texts have had to be (intralingually or interlingually) translated*. That is, if a text can adequately be transferred [moved in space and/or time] without translation, there is cultural continuity. And if a text has been translated, it represents distance between at least two cultures.

(1992a: 25–6)

Texts move in space (are carried, mailed, faxed, e-mailed) or in time (are physically preserved for later generations, who may use the language in which they were written in significantly different ways). Cultural difference is largely a function of the distance they move, the distance from the place or time in which they are written to the place or time in which they are read; and it can be marked by the act or fact of translation: native speakers of English today read Charles Dickens without substantial changes (though American readers may read "jail" for "gaol"), but they read William Shakespeare in "modernized English," Geoffrey Chaucer in "modern translation," and *Beowulf* in "translation." Watching *The Benny Hill Show* on Finnish television in the late 1970s I often had no idea what was being said in rapid-fire culture-bound British English slang and had to read the Finnish subtitles to understand even the gist of a sketch. As we approach cultural boundaries, transferred texts become increasingly difficult to understand, until we give up and demand a translation – and it is at that point, Pym suggests, that we *know* we have moved from one culture to another.

Self-projection into the foreign (abduction)

One of the problems with this formulation, however, as postcolonial theorists of translation have shown, is that we often *think* we understand a text from a quite different culture, simply because it is written in a language we understand. Do modern English-speakers really share a culture with Shakespeare? Or do the various modernizations of his works conceal radical cultural differences, and so constitute translations? If a native speaker of American English is often puzzled by colloquial British English, how much more by Scottish English, Irish English, and then, another quantum leap, by Indian English,

South African English? Do native speakers of British, American, Australian, and Indian English all share a culture? We might surmise that such was the design of the British colonizers: impose a common language on the colonies, and through language a common culture. But did it work? What cultural allusions, historical references, puns, inside jokes, and the like do we miss in thousands of texts that do not seem to require translation?

Do men and women of the "same" culture understand each other? Deborah Tannen (1990) says no, and has coined the term "genderlect" to describe the differences. Do adults and children of the "same" culture (even the same family) understand each other? Do members of different social classes, or majority and minority groups, understand each other? Yes and no. Sometimes we think we understand more than we actually do, because we gloss over the differences, the areas of significant misunderstanding; sometimes we think we understand less than we actually do, because ancient cultural hostilities and suspicions (between men and women, adults and children, upper and lower classes, straights and gays, majority and minority members, first-world and third-world speakers of the "same" language) make us exaggerate the differences between us.

One of the lessons feminist and postcolonial theorists of translation have taught us since the mid-1980s is that we should be very careful about trusting our intuitions or "abductions" about cultural knowledge and cultural difference. Cultural boundaries exist in the midst of what used to seem like unified and harmonious cultures. As silenced and peripheralized populations all over the world find a voice, and begin to tell their stories so that the hegemonic cultures that had silenced and peripheralized them can hear, it becomes increasingly clear that misunderstanding is far more common than many people in relatively privileged positions have wanted to believe. The happy universalism of liberal humanist thought, according to which people are basically the same everywhere, everybody wants and knows basically the same things and uses language in roughly similar ways, so that anything that can be said in one language can be said in another, has come under heavy attack. That universalism is increasingly seen as an illusion projected outward by hegemonic cultures (patriarchy, colonialism, capitalism) in an attempt to force subjected cultures to conform to centralized norms: be like us and you will be civilized, modern, cultured, rational, intelligent; be like us and you will be seen as "truly human," part of the great "brotherhood of man."

The effect of this consciousness-raising has been to build suspicion into cultural intution – into "abductive" leaps about what this or that word or phrase or text means. "A first-world translator should *never* assume his or her intutions are right about the meaning of a third-world text": a dictum for our times, overheard at a translators' conference. By the same token, a male translator should never assume his intuitions are right about the meaning of a text written by a woman; a white translator about a text written by a person of color, and so on.

Recent battles over "political correctness" on Lantra-L and FLEFO make it clear that many translators, especially in Europe, are angered and baffled by this new suspicion of old assumptions and intuitions, and are inclined to associate it narrowly with US academics, who are portrayed as trendy left-wingers on a rampage of righteousness. US and Canadian academic and professional translators, for their part, astonished at the gross insensitivity of many of their European colleagues, wonder whether it might not be just some New World fad after all – except for their strong sense that this new suspicion of first-world intuitions *came* from the third world, especially perhaps from India and Africa, in the form of a series of increasingly vocal and persuasive challenges to first-world control of "universal" or "human" linguistic intuitions.

The intensity with which this debate rages is a good indication of just how attached we all grow to our linguistic and cultural habits, and to the pathways down which those habits channel our intuitions and experiences. It is not only time-consuming labor to retrain our intuitions; it is emotionally unsettling, especially when the state to which we are called to retrain them is one of uncertainty and self-doubt. What language professional who relies on her intuitions to earn a living wants to retrain herself to think, systematically, "If you think you understand this, you're probably wrong"? No one.

And yet this state of uncertainty and self-doubt is really little different from the state in which professional translators entered the profession. In fact, it is little different from the state in which we encounter difficult texts every day. The text is problematic; the sense it seems at first glance to make can't possibly be right, but we can't think of any other sense it might make; we sit there staring at the problem passage, feeling frustrated, on edge, a little disgusted with the writer for making our job so difficult, a little disgusted with ourselves for not knowing more, not being more creative, etc. This feeling is an all-too-common one for translators.

In this light, then, anger at "political correctness" may just be more of the same irritation: why do I have to make my job even harder than it already is?

There are at least two answers to this question. One is that, if the professional community expects you to make your job even harder than it already is, then to do your job well you had better go ahead and make it harder. The other is that, if you are sensitive to the feelings of other people and other groups, you will not deliberately use language that offends them, or blithely impose your assumptions of what they *must* mean on their words; again, therefore, to do your job well you will go ahead and make it harder.

The big "if" in this question, of course, is whether "the professional community" does in fact expect translators to be sensitive to issues of discriminatory usage, hate speech, and so on – or rather, *which* professional community expects that, or what part of the professional community expects it. Is it just North America? How much sensitivity is required? How much change? How much self-doubt and uncertainty? There are no easy answers. In this matter as in so many others, professional translators must be willing to proceed without clear signposts, working as ethically and as responsibly as they know how but never quite knowing where the boundaries of ethical and responsible action lie.

Immersion in cultures (induction)

The important thing to remember is, we do go on. Trained to become ever more suspicious of our "immediate" or "intuitive" understanding of a text to be translated, we doggedly go on believing in our ability eventually to work through to a correct interpretation. Thwarted over and over in our attempts to find a target-language equivalent for a culture-bound and therefore apparently untranslatable word or phrase, we keep sending mental probes out through our own and the Internet's neural pathways, hoping to turn a corner and stumble upon the perfect translation. It almost never happens. We almost always settle for far less than the best. But we go on questing. It is perhaps our least reasonable, but also most professional, feature.

And no matter what else we do, we continue to immerse ourselves in cultures. Local cultures, regional cultures, national cultures, international cultures. Foreign cultures. Border cultures. School cultures, work cultures, leisure cultures; family cultures, neighborhood cultures. We read voraciously. We learn new foreign languages and spend weeks, months, years in the countries where those languages are natively spoken. We nose out difference: wherever things are done a little differently, a word or phrase is pronounced differently or given a slightly unexpected twist, people walk differently, dress differently, gesture differently, we pay attention. Perhaps here is a cultural boundary that needs to be crossed. Why do we want to cross it? Because it's there. Because that is what we do, cross boundaries.

And maybe in some ultimate sense it's an illusion. Maybe cultural boundaries cannot be crossed. Maybe we are all locked into our groups, our enclaves, even our own skins. Maybe you have to be a man to understand men, and a woman to understand women; maybe you have to have light skin to understand people with light skin, and dark skin to understand people with dark skin. Maybe no one from the first world can ever understand someone from the third, and vice versa. Maybe all first-world "understanding" of the third world, male "understanding" of women, majority "understanding" of minorities is the mere projection of hegemonic power, a late form of colonialism. Maybe no one ever understands anyone else; maybe understanding is an illusion projected and policed by superior force.

Still, we go on trying to understand, to bridge the communicative gaps between individuals and groups. It's what we do.

And we do it specifically by immersing ourselves in cultural otherness, in the way other people talk and act. We do it in the belief that paying close attention to how people use language and move their bodies in space and time will yield us valuable knowledge about the "other side" – whoever and whatever lies beyond whatever cultural boundary we find or sense or imagine before us. Somehow beliefs, values, ideas, images, experiences will travel across those boundaries from their heads and bodies into ours, through language, through expression and gesture, through the contagion of somatic response. (A laughing person makes us happy, a crying person makes us sad; a yawning person makes us sleepy, and a frightened or anxious person awakens our fear and unease; see Robinson 1991: 5ff.)

The more of this cultural "data" we gather, the more we know about how cultures work; and what we mainly learn is how different they are, how difficult it is to cross over into another cultural realm and truly understand what is meant by a word or a raised eyebrow. The more "culturally literate" we become, the more *and* the less at-home we feel in foreign cultures. More, because we accept our difference, our alienness, our lack of belonging, and learn to live with it, even to cherish it, to love the extra freedom it gives us to break the rules and be a little more idiosyncratic than the natives. Less, because that freedom is alienation; that idiosyncrasy means not belonging.

If it's hard to be a stranger, it is even more so to stop being one. "Exile is neither psychological nor ontological", wrote Maurice Blanchot: "The exile cannot accommodate himself to his condition, nor to renouncing it, nor to turning exile into a mode of residence. The immigrant is tempted to naturalize himself, through marriage for example, but he continues to be migrant." The one named "stranger" will never really fit in, so it is said, joyfully. To be named and classified is to gain better acceptance, even when it is question of fitting in a no-fit-in category. The feeling of imprisonment denotes here a mere subjection to strangeness as confinement. But the Home, as it is repeatedly reminded, is not a jail. It is a place where one is compelled to find stability and happiness. One is made to understand that if one has been temporarily kept within specific boundaries, it is mainly for one's own good. Foreignness is acceptable once I no longer draw the line between myself and the others. First assimilate, then be different within permitted boundaries. "When you no longer feel like a stranger, then there will be no problem in becoming a stranger again." As you come to love your new home, it is thus implied, you will immediately be sent back to your old home (the authorized and pre-marked ethnic, gender or sexual identity) where you are bound to undergo again another form of estrangement. Or else, if such a statement is to be read in its enabling potential, then, unlearning strangeness as confinement becomes a way of assuming anew the predicament of deterritorialization: it is both I and It that travel; the home is here, there, wherever one is led to in one's movement.

(Minh-Ha 1994: 13)

Intercultural awareness (deduction)

There is a field of study within communication departments called intercultural communication (ICC). One might think that translation studies would be an integral part of that field, or that the two fields would be closely linked. Unfortunately, neither is the case. ICC scholars study the problems of communicating across cultural boundaries, both intra- and interlingually – but apparently translation is not seen as a problematic form of cross-cultural communication, perhaps because the professional translator already knows how to get along in foreign cultures. (For early exceptions to this rule, see Sechrest *et al.* 1972 and Brislin 1972.)

ICC scholars are fond, for example, of tracing the steps by which a member of one culture adapts to, or becomes acculturated into, another:

> *denial* (isolation, separation) >
> *defense* (denigration, superiority, reversal) >
> *minimization* (physical universalism, transcendent universalism) >
> *acceptance* (respect for behavioral difference, respect for value difference) >
> *adaptation* (empathy, pluralism) >
> *integration* (contextual evaluation, constructive marginality)
> (Bennett 1993: 29)

The first three stages, denial, defense, and minimization, Bennett identifies as "ethnocentric"; the second three, acceptance, adaptation, and integration, as "ethnorelative." (See also Padilla 1980, Hoopes 1981, Gudykunst and Kim 1992: 214–15.)

These models might usefully be expanded to include translation and interpretation, which, though certainly a less traumatic and intimidating form of cross-cultural communication than, say, a monolingual's first trip abroad or an encounter with someone from a very different subculture, are no less problematic. For example:

1 *Ethnocentrism*: the refusal to communicate across cultural boundaries; rejection of the foreign or strange; universalization of one's own local habits and assumptions (the anti-ideal that ICC was developed to combat)

2 *Cross-cultural tolerance*: monolinguals communicating with foreigners who speak their language; members of different

subcultures within a single national culture coming into contact
and discovering and learning to appreciate and accept their differences; problems of foreign-language learning (unnoticed cultural differences, prosodic and paralinguistic features) and
growing tolerance for cultural and linguistic relativism (the
main area of ICC concern)

3   *Integration*: fluency in a foreign language and culture; the ability
to adapt and acculturate and feel at home in a foreign culture,
speaking its language(s) without strain, acting and feeling (more
or less) like a native to that culture (the ICC ideal)

4   *Translation/interpretation*: the ability to mediate between cultures, to explain one to another; mixed loyalties; the pushes and
pulls of the source and target cultures.

ICC aims to train monoculturals to get along better in intercultural situations; translation/interpretation studies begins where
ICC leaves off, at fluent integration. The ultimate goal of ICC is
the base line of translator/interpreter training.

	ICC competence NO	*ICC competence* YES
ICC mediation NO	ethnocentrism	integration
ICC mediation YES	tolerance	translation/interpretation

This does not mean, of course, that translators and interpreters are
somehow "above" all the complex problems that plague ICC at lower
levels of cross-cultural competence and mediation. In fact, the same
problems carry over into the high levels at which translators and
interpreters work. These problems are the focus of a good deal of
recent research in translation.

The first group of scholars to begin to move the cultural study of
translation out of the realm of *realia* and into the realm of large-scale
political and social systems have been variously identified as the
polysystems, translation studies, descriptive translation studies, or
manipulation school (see Gentzler 1993). Beginning in the late
1970s, they – people like James Holmes (1975), Itamar Even-Zohar
(1979, 1981), Gideon Toury (1995), André Lefevere (1992), Susan
Bassnett (1991), Mary Snell-Hornby (1995), Dirk Delabastita and
Lieven d'Hulst (1993), Theo Hermans (1985) – explored the cultural
systems that controlled translation and their impact on the norms and

practices of actual translation work. One of their main assumptions was, and remains today, that translation is always controlled by the target culture; rather than arguing over the correct type of equivalence to strive for and how to achieve it, they insisted that the belief structures, value systems, literary and linguistic conventions, moral norms, and political expediencies of the target culture always shape translations in powerful ways, in the process shaping translators' notions of "equivalence" as well. (An example of this is given in exercise 1, below, from André Lefevere's (1992) book *Translation, Rewriting, and the Manipulation of Literary Fame*.) This "relativistic" view is typical of the cultural turn translation studies has taken over the past two decades or so: away from universal forms and norms to culturally contingent ones; away from prescriptions designed to control *all* translators, to descriptions of the ways in which target cultures control specific ones.

In the late 1980s and 1990s several new trends in culturally oriented translation theory have expanded upon and to some extent displaced descriptive translation studies. In particular, feminist and postcolonial approaches to translation have had a major impact on the field. The innovations they have brought have been many, but methodologically their focal differences from descriptive translation studies are two:

1   Where the descriptivists were neutral, dispassionate, striving for scientific objectivity, the feminists and postcolonialists are politically committed to the overthrow of patriarchy, colonialism, and capitalism, and determined to play an activist role in that process. As a result, their writing styles are more "passionately engaged" (if seen from within) or "politically correct" (if seen from without). They are also even more tolerant of propagandistic and other highly contested forms of translation than the descriptivists. Their sympathies are always with oppressed minority cultures.

2   The feminists and postcolonialists have also leveled serious criticism at the descriptivist notion that the target culture always controls translation. Especially in a postcolonialist perspective, this idea seems bizarre: the history of colonialism is full of cases in which an imperial source culture like England or France or Spain initiated and controlled a process of translating the Bible and other source texts into the "primitive" "local" target

languages of the colonies. This usually involved sending a missionary from the source culture into the target culture to learn the target language (which often meant reshaping it to fit source-linguistic norms – see Rafael 1988/1993, Cheyfitz 1991, Niranjana 1992), invent an orthography for it, and translate the Bible, catechism, and imperial laws into it. Rafael and others have also shown how the colonial target cultures resisted this control in complex ways; but primary control of the translation process was clearly in the hands of the source culture, not the target.

The most succinct and accessible introduction to postcolonial translation studies is offered by Richard Jacquemond (1992; see also Robinson 1997a). Jacquemond is specifically concerned with translation between France and Egypt, but is also interested generally in the power differentials between cultures, in particular between "hegemonic" or dominant or more powerful cultures (usually former colonizers) and "dominated" or less powerful cultures (usually former colonies). The translator from a hegemonic culture into a dominated one, he says, serves the hegemonic culture in its desire to integrate its cultural products into the dominated culture – this is the classic case where the source culture controls translation. Even when the target culture desires, or seems to desire, the translation, that desire is manufactured and controlled by the source culture. Going the other way, the translator from a dominated culture into a hegemonic again serves the hegemonic culture, but this time not servilely, rather as the "authoritative mediator" (Jacquemond 1992: 156) who helps to convert the dominated culture into something easy for the hegemonic culture to recognize as "other" and inferior.

He covers four broad areas of comparison:

1   A dominated culture will invariably translate far more of a hegemonic culture than the latter will of the former. Only 1–2 percent of works translated into Western/Northern languages are from Eastern/Southern cultures; 98–99 percent of works translated into Eastern/Southern languages are from Western/Northern cultures. Even within the West/North – Europe and the United States in particular – there is a striking imbalance: less than one-twentieth of total book production in the UK and the US comprises translations; in continental Europe it ranges from one-third to one-half. Far more books are translated out of English into

other languages – languages perceived as "less international," less well known, less economically viable – than out of those languages into English.

2   When a hegemonic culture does translate works produced by the dominated culture, those works will be perceived and presented as difficult, mysterious, inscrutable, esoteric, and in need of a small cadre of intellectuals to interpret them, while a dominated culture will translate a hegemonic culture's works accessibly for the masses. Asia, Africa, and South America translate a broad spectrum of European and North American works, and they achieve broad-based popularity; Europe and North America translate a tiny segment of Asian, African, and South American works, and they are published in minuscule quantities for a specialist audience by small presses and academic publishing houses.

3   A hegemonic culture will only translate those works by authors in a dominated culture that fit the former's preconceived notions of the latter. Japan, for example, in Western eyes is a place of mysticism, martial arts, and ruthless business dealings, and Japanese books selected for translation into Western languages will tend to confirm those stereotypes. Slangy urban youth novels like those written by Banana Yoshimoto will be perceived as "un-Japanese" and will be more difficult to publish in translation.

4   Authors in a dominated culture who dream of reaching a "large audience" will tend to write for translation into a hegemonic language, and this will require conforming to some extent to stereotypes.

Interestingly, while postcolonial approaches to translation have tended to analyze the power structures controlling translation and call for more resistance to those structures, feminist approaches have been more oriented toward resistance than to analysis. One of the strongest formulations of a feminist approach to translation, Lori Chamberlain's (1988) article on the metaphorics of translation, does offer a powerful analysis of patriarchal ideology and the sway it has held over thinking about translation for centuries (see exercise 2, below); but by far the bulk of feminist work on translation has been written in a strong activist mode, embodying and modeling resistance to the patriarchy through translation. Three main strands of feminist translation theory can be traced:

1 Recovering the lost or neglected history of women as translators and translation theorists (Krontiris 1992, Robinson 1995, Simon 1995)

2 Articulating the patriarchal ideologies undergirding mainstream Western translation theory (Chamberlain 1988)

3 Formulating a coherent and effective feminist practice of translation: Should feminist translators translate male writers at all, and if so, how? Should male writers and nonfeminist female writers be translated propagandistically? If so, should the feminist translator attempt to highlight the writer's sexism or other traditional value system, or should she convert it to a more progressive view? When translating feminist writers who work to create a new feminist language out of bits and pieces of the source language, how and to what extent should the target language be reshaped as well? (Maier 1980, 1984, 1989, Lotbinière-Harwood 1991, Godard 1989, Simon 1995, Levine 1992, Díaz-Diocaretz 1985, von Flotow 1997, Anderson 1995).

Because of their willingness to undertake and defend unashamedly propagandistic translation projects against the patriarchy, feminist translators and translation scholars have come under serious fire from conservatives who insist that there is *never* any real justification for distorting the meaning or import of the source text. It is, however, a critical part of the cultural turn of recent translation studies to question all such *nevers* – to explore the ways in which the various requirements and prohibitions placed on translators are not universals, to be obeyed in all circumstances, but culturally channeled lines of force, often intensely local in their impact.

In fact, the cultural turn might best be highlighted by imagining two scenarios:

In the first scenario, God created heaven and earth and everything on it, including translation. To everything He gave a stable form, appearance, and name. To the act of restating in a second language what someone has expressed in a first He gave the name translation; its appearance was to be lowly, humble, subservient; its form fidelity or equivalence, as exact a correspondence as possible between the meaning of the source and target texts. These properties He decreed for all times and all places. This and only this was translation. Anyone who deviated from the form and appearance of translation did not deserve the name of "translator," and the product of such deviation could certainly not be named a "translation."

In the second scenario, translation arose organically out of attempts to communicate with people who spoke another language; its origins lay in commerce and trade, politics and war. Translators and interpreters were trained and hired by people with money and power who wanted to make sure that their messages were conveyed faithfully to the other side of a negotiation, and that they understood exactly what the other side was saying to them. Eventually, when these people grew powerful enough to control huge geographical segments of the world (the Catholic Church, the West), these power affiliations were dressed up in the vestments of universality – whence the first scenario. But translation remained a contested ground, fought over by conflicting power interests: you bring your translator, I'll bring mine, and we'll see who imposes what interpretation on the events that transpire. Today as well, professional translators must in most cases conform to the expectations of the people who pay them to translate. If a client says edit, the translator edits; if the client says don't edit, the translator doesn't edit. If the client says do a literal translation, and then a literal back-translation to prove you've followed my orders, that is exactly what the translator does. Translators can refuse to do a job that they find morally repugnant, or professionally unethical, or practically impossible; they can also resist and attempt to reshape the orders they get from the people with the money. But the whats and the hows and the whys of translation are by and large controlled by publishers, clients, and agencies – *not* by universal norms.

And in this second scenario, which is obviously the one advanced by the cultural turn in translation studies, the "propagandistic" nature of much feminist translating is nothing to be shocked about. A feminist editor at a feminist press hires a feminist translator to translate a book for a feminist readership; the otherwise admirably feminist book has a disturbingly sexist chapter in it. Should the translator ignore the mandate of the editor, the press, and the readership to produce a feminist text, in order to adhere to some translator-ideal conceived a thousand years ago by a blatantly patriarchal church whose other tenets are not accepted blindly by *any* of the

principals in the process? What possible motivation would the translator have to render the sexist portions of the book "faithfully"? The
only motivation to keep sexism sexist would be an imagined fidelity
not to the press (which was paying her fee), nor to the readers (whose
book purchases keep the press afloat), but to some other authority,
medieval, ecclesiastical, long-dead, with only vestigial ideological
power over contemporary translators – and a most suspect ideology
and power at that!

Surely, many readers will say, something valuable is lost in this.
Translation is no longer handmaiden to genius, to the motions of the
muse; it is a petty mercantile operation, subject to the whims of the
marketplace. What a low, sordid affair, to translate for the highest
bidder, and to do the job any way that bidder bids! How crass! How
far has translation fallen!

Perhaps. For the advocates of the cultural turn, however, it has
been a fortunate fall. The "exalted" state of the translator in more
traditional ideologies was not only extremely narrow and confining –
indeed anything but exalted – it was also utterly unrealistic. It had
nothing to do with the real world of translation. The picture painted of
professional translation by the new scholars in the field may not be as
glorious as the old humanistic myths; but it has the advantage of
leaving the translator's feet more firmly on the ground.

Discussion

1 How attached are you to the notion that anything that can be
thought can be said, and anything that can be said can be understood, and anything that can be thought and said in one culture or
language can be said and understood in another? How important
is it for you to believe this? Can you imagine being a translator
without believing it? If so, how do you think translation is possible? If not, how does talk of radical cultural relativism make
you feel?

2 "A first-world translator should *never* assume his or her intuitions
are right about the meaning of a third-world text" – or a male
translator about a text written by a women, etc. What is your
"take" on this statement? How far do you agree, how far do you

disagree? How easy or hard is it *not* to assume your intuitions are right about a text? How much does it depend on the text?

3 Political correctness: serious social reform or liberal silliness?

4 Of the two scenarios on pp. 236–7, which do you find more attractive? Why?

Exercises

1 Study the following passage from André Lefevere, *Translation, Rewriting, and the Manipulation of Literary Fame* (1992: 44–5):

> Since Aristophanic comedy is rather radical in attacking certain ideologies and defending others, most of the translators whose "Lysistratas" have been published over the past century and a half have felt the need to state their own ideology. Most of the the translators whose work was published during the first half of that century and a half would agree with A. S. Way's statement: "the indecency of Attic comedy, which is all-pervading, which crops up in every play, and in the most unexpected places, is a sad stumbling-block to the reader, and a grievous embarrassment to the translator" (xix). While most of these translators fervently disagreed with an ideology that condoned this indecency, few went as far as the first translator of Aristophanes during the past century and a half, C. A. Wheelwright, who stated in his introduction that "The *Lysistrata* bears so evil a character that we must make but fugitive mention of it, like persons passing over hot embers" (62). In his translation he simply omits the very crux of the play: the oath the women take at the formal start of their sex strike. Furthermore, he simply ends his translation at line 827 of the original, refusing to translate lines 828 to 1215, one quarter of the play, not because he had suddenly forgotten all his Greek, but because his ideology was incompatible with the one expressed in Greek by Aristophanes.

Most other translators have tried to make *Lysistrata* fit their ideology by using all kinds of manipulative techniques. All of their strategies have been adequately described by Jack Lindsay in the introduction to his translation. Their "effort," he points out, "is always to show that the parts considered offensive are not the actual expression of the poet, that they are dictated externally" (15). Thus J. P. Maine states in his 1909 introduction that "Athens was now under an oligarchy, and no references to politics was [sic] possible, so Aristophanes tries to make up indecency [sic]" (1: x–xi). In his introduction written in 1820 and reprinted in 1909, in the second volume edited by Maine, John Hookham Frere states that "Aristophanes, it must be recollected, was often under the necessity of addressing himself exclusively to the lower class" (2: xxvi). Both Maine and Hookham Frere blame patronage for Aristophanes' woes, but each blames a completely different type of patronage. Two years later Benjamin Bickley Rogers writes that "in truth this very coarseness, so repulsive to ourselves, so amusing to an Athenian audience, was introduced, it is impossible to doubt, for the express purpose of counterbalancing the extreme gravity and earnestness of the play" (x). In this case Aristophanes is portrayed not as the sovereign author, but as the conscientious craftsman who has no other choice than to bow to the demands of his craft, and nothing will prevent (some) readers from wanting to feel that Aristophanes the man would not have done what Aristophanes the craftsman had to do.

It was left to A. S. Way, twenty-three years later, to express the translator's dilemma in the most delicately wordy manner:

> The *traduttore*, then, who would not willingly be a *traditore*, may not exscind or alter, but he may well so translate, where possible, that, while the (incorruptible) scholar has the stern satisfaction of finding that nothing has been shirked, the reader who does not know the Greek may pass unsuspectingly over not a few unsavoury spots – not that his utmost

endeavours can make his author suitable for reading (aloud) in a ladies' school. (xx)

The translator is caught between his adherence to an ideology that is not that of Aristophanes, indeed views sexual matters in a quite different manner, and his status as a professional who most be able to convince other professionals that he is worthy of that title, while at the same time not producing a text that runs counter to his ideology.

(a) Discuss the ideology prevailing in your culture with regard to overt references to sexual acts in literature and especially on stage, and consider how that might affect Aristophanes translations into your target language.

(b) Go to the library and find as many Aristophanes translations into that target language as you can, and compare them both with each other and with your own assumptions about the ideology controlling them, as formulated in (a). How do the actual translations confirm or complicate your expectations?

(c) Do variations on the translations you found. Pick a scene describing overt sexuality and experiment with different versions: do one that uses the most vulgar terms you know; another that uses more clinical, scientific terms; a more euphemistic one; a moralizing one that shows open disapproval of the acts being described. As you do each variation, pay special attention to how you feel about each: where your own ideological resistances are, to vulgarity, to clinical distance, to euphemism, to moralism, or to several or all of them in different ways. Discuss these ideological resistances with others in the class; alone or in groups, write brief descriptions of them.

(d) Now study the Lefevere passage for the author's resistances to what he is describing. He is working hard to appear neutral and nonjudgmental; does he succeed? Does he favor some of the translators (say, Jack Lindsay) over others? Does he disapprove of the radically altered translations of Aristophanes: Wheelwright "simply omits the very crux of the play," other translators have used "all kinds of manipulative techniques," etc.?

(e) Reread the last paragraph, about translators being caught between their own ideology and that of the author, while being judged by readers on how well they extricate themselves from that trap. Is that a fair assessment of the translator's dilemma? Does it seem to apply to your professional situation, or the situation into which you imagine yourself entering in a very short time? Is it true of all translated texts, or only some? If the latter, which texts? Are there ways out of or around the problem?

2 Study the following passage from Lori Chamberlain, "Gender and the Metaphorics of Translation" (1988: 455–6):

The sexualization of translation appears perhaps most familiarly in the tag *les belles infidéles* – like women, the adage goes, translations should be either beautiful or faithful. The tag is made possible both by the rhyme in French and by the fact that the word *traduction* is a feminine one, thus making *les beaux infidéles* impossible. This tag owes its longevity – it was coined in the seventeenth century – to more than phonetic similarity: what gives it the appearance of truth is that it has captured a cultural complicityi between the issues of fidelity in translation and in marriage. For *les belles infidéles*, fidelity is defined by an implicit contract between translation (as woman) and original (as husband, father, or author). However, the infamous "double standard" operates here as it might have in traditional marriages: the "unfaithful" wife/translation is publicly tried for crimes the husband/original is by law incapable of committing. This contract, in short, makes it impossible for the original to be guilty of infidelity. Such an attitude betrays real anxiety about the problem of paternity and translation; it mimics the patrilineal kinship system where paternity – not maternity – legitimizes an offspring.

Another way of expanding the famous Gilles Ménage adage about *les belles infidéles* is not that translations *should* be either beautiful or faithful but rather that the more beautiful they are, the less likely they are to be faithful, and the more faithful they are, the less likely they are to be beautiful.

(a)   How true do *you* believe this is about women? Are beautiful women really more likely to cheat on their partners than less beautiful ones? Whether you say yes or no, does your experience bear your opinion out, or is mainly something you agree with because people generally believe it? What other stereotypes do you (or your culture) have about beautiful women? Are they respected, scorned, worshipped, loved, feared, hated? What other qualities in a woman will contribute to her being either faithful or unfaithful?

(b)   Does the adage work the same way when applied to men? Are good-looking men more or less likely to be faithful to their partners than less-good-looking men? Or do looks have nothing to do with it? What other stereotypes do you (or your culture) have about handsome men? Are they ambitious, narcissistic, superficial, controlling, passive, gay, successful, rich? What other qualities in a man will contribute to his being either faithful or unfaithful?

(c)   Put yourself in the position of someone who is worried about his or her partner (husband or wife or lover) being unfaithful. How do you react? Are you jealous? What emotions fuel your jealousy? Are you possessive? Do you want to control the other person? Do you try to be openminded and tolerant? How does that feel?

(d)   Now shift all this to translation. Does it make sense to think of translation along similar lines? Which parts of the emotional reactions to (in)fidelity in relationships work when applied to translation, which don't? How do cultural stereotypes of women fit "fidelity" theories of translation? What happens if you think of a translation as a faithful or unfaithful man, or as a handsome or ugly man? What roles do emotions like jealousy and possessiveness or openminded tolerance play in cultural thinking about translation?

(e)   Chamberlain's reading of the gender metaphorics of translation is based on the notion that the translation theorist comparing a translation to a woman – beautiful and unfaithful or faithful and ugly – sides with the source author or "father/husband." This would be an "external" perspective on translation (see Chapter 1). How would an "internal" or translator-oriented perspective see these gender metaphorics? Does the translator have to identify with the translation? If so, does a female translator have to accept the negative image of women *and* translation implied by the adage? Does a male translator have to submerge his patriarchal desire to control in order to identify with a woman, become a woman, accept subordination and disapproval? Is the only alternative to this the scenario Chamberlain traces, in which the translator identifies with the father/husband/original and so becomes a prescriptive theorist? Are these gender metaphors purely harmful for translators, or is it possible to transform the gender politics in ways that create new possibilities for translators' practical work and professional self-image (open marriage? bisexuality?)?

Suggestions for further reading

Anderson (1995), Bassnett (1991), Bennett (1993), Chamberlain (1988), Cheyfitz (1991), Copeland (1991), Delabastita and d'Hulst (1993), Díaz-Diocaretz (1985), Ellis (1989, 1991, 1996), Ellis and Evans (1994), Even-Zohar (1979), Gentzler (1993), Godard (1989), Gudykunst and Kim (1992), Hermans (1985), Holmes (1975), Hoopes (1981), Jacquemond (1992), Krontiris (1992), Lefevere (1992), Levine (1992), Lotbinière-Harwood (1991), Maier (1980, 1984, 1989), Minh-Ha (1994), Niranjana (1992), Padilla (1980), Pym (1992a), Rafael (1988/1993), Robinson (1995, 1997a), Simon (1995), Snell-Hornby (1995), Toury (1995), von Flotow (1997)

Chapter 11

When habit fails

- **The importance of analysis**   246

- **The reticular activation system: alarm bells**   249

- **Checking the rules (deduction)**   253

- **Checking synonyms, alternatives (induction)**   259

- **Picking the rendition that feels right (abduction)**   260

  - **Discussion**   262

  - **Exercise**   262

  - **Suggestions for further reading**   262

THESIS: Translators can never rely entirely on even the highly complex and well-informed habits they have built up over the years to take them through every job reliably; in fact, one of the "habits" that professional translators must develop is that of building into their "subliminal" functioning alarm bells that go off whenever a familiar or unfamiliar problem area arises, calling the translator out of the subliminal state that makes rapid translation possible, slows the process down, and initiates a careful analysis of the problem(s).

The importance of analysis

It probably goes without saying: the ability to analyze a source text linguistically, culturally, even philosophically or politically is of paramount importance to the translator.

In fact, of the many claims made in this book, the importance of analysis probably goes *most* without saying. Wherever translation is taught, the importance of analysis is taught:

- Never assume you understand the source text perfectly.
- Never assume your understanding of the source text is detailed enough to enable you to translate it adequately.
- Always analyze for text type, genre, register, rhetorical function, etc.
- Always analyze the source text's syntax and semantics, making sure you know in detail what it is saying, what it is not saying, and what it is implying.
- Always analyze the syntactic, semantic, and pragmatic relationship between the source language (especially as it appears in this particular source text) and the target language, so that you know what each language is capable and incapable of doing and saying, and can make all necessary adjustments.

246

● Always pay close attention to the translation commission (what you are asked to do, by whom, for whom, and why), and consider the special nature and needs of your target audience; if you aren't given enough information about that audience, ask; if the commissioner doesn't know, use your professional judgment to project an audience.

These analytical principles are taught because they do not come naturally. A novice translator attempting his or her first translation is not likely to realize all the pitfalls lurking in the task, and will make silly mistakes as a result. When translating from a language that we know well, it is natural to assume that we understand the text; that the words on the page are a fairly easy and unproblematic guide to what is being said and done in the text. It is also natural to assume that languages are structurally not all that different, so that roughly following the source-text word order in the target language will produce a reasonably good translation.

Natural as these assumptions are, they are wrong, and experienced translators learn to be wary of them – which inevitably means some form of analysis. Because this analytical wariness does not come naturally, it must be taught – by experience, or by a translation instructor.

The "accelerated" approach developed in this book also assumes that experienced professional translators will gradually move "beyond" analysis in much of their work, precisely by internalizing or sublimating it. It will seem to professional translators as if they rarely analyze a text or cultural assumptions, because they do it so unconsciously, and thus so rapidly. The analytical procedures taught in most translator training programs are not consciously used by professional translators in most of their work, because they have become second nature. And this is the desideratum of professional training: to help students first to learn the analytical procedures, then to sublimate them, make them so unconscious, so automatic, so fast, that translation at professional speeds becomes possible.

At the same time, however, the importance of *conscious* analysis must never be lost. Rapid subliminal analysis is both possible and desirable when (1) the source text and transfer context are unproblematic and (2) the translator possesses the necessary professional knowledge and skills. It is not possible when the source text and transfer context are problematic; and it is not desirable when the translator's knowledge base and skills are inadequate to the task at hand. In these latter cases it is essential for the translator to shift into the conscious analytical mode taught in schools.

In the ideal model elaborated in Chapter 4, professional translation proceeds subliminally, at the unconscious level of habit (which comes to feel like instinct), as long as the problems faced are covered by the translators' range of internalized experience. As long as the problems that arise are ones they have faced before, or close enough in nature to ones they have faced before that analogical solutions are quick and easy to develop, the wheel of experience turns rapidly and unconsciously; translation is relatively fast and easy. When the problems are new, or strikingly difficult, alarm bells go off in the translators' heads, and they shift out of "autopilot" and into "manual," into full conscious analytical awareness. This will involve a search for a solution to the problem or problems by circling *consciously* back around the wheel of experience, running through rules and precepts and theories (deduction), mentally listing synonyms and parallel syntactic and pragmatic patterns (induction), and finally choosing the solution that "intuitively" or "instinctively" *feels* best (abduction).

This is, of course, an *ideal* model, which means that it doesn't always correspond to reality:

- The less experience translators have, the more they will have to work in the conscious analytical mode – and the more slowly they will have to translate.
- Even in the most experienced translators' heads the alarm bells don't always go off when they should, and they make careless mistakes (which they should ideally catch later, in the editing stage – but this doesn't always happen either).
- Sometimes experienced translators slow the process down even without alarm bells, thinking consciously about the analytical contours of the source text and transfer context without an overt "problem" to be solved, because they're tired of translating rapidly, or because the source text is so wonderfully written that they want to savor it (especially but not exclusively with literary texts).

In those first two scenarios, the translator's real-life "deviation" from the ideal model developed here is a deficiency to be remedied by more work, more practice, more experience; in the third, it is a personal preference that needs no remedy. Ideal models are helpful tools in structuring our thinking about a process, and thus also in guiding the work we do in order to perform that process more effectively. But they are also simplifications of reality that should never become straitjackets.

The reticular activation system: alarm bells

Our nervous systems are constructed so that oft-repeated actions become "robotized." Compare how conscious you were of driving when you were first learning with how conscious you are of it now – especially, say, how conscious you are of driving a route you know well, like your way to or from work. For that, our bodies no longer need our conscious "guidance" at all. No route-planning is required; our nervous system recognizes all the intersections where we always turn, keeps the car between the lane lines, maintains a safe distance from the car in front; all the complex analyses involved, what those brake lights and yellow flashing lights mean, how hard to push on the accelerator, when to push on the brake and how hard, when to upshift or downshift, are unconscious.

But let the highway department block off one lane of traffic for repairs, or send you on a detour down less familiar streets; let a child run out into the street from between parked cars, or an accident happen just ahead – *anything* unusual – and you instantly snap out of your reverie and become painfully alert, preternaturally aware of your surroundings, on edge, ready to sift and sort and analyze all incoming data so as to decide on the proper course of action.

This is a brain function called reticular activation. It is what is often called "alarm bells going off" – the sudden quantum leap in conscious awareness and noradrenalin levels whenever something changes drastically enough to make a rote or robotic, habitual or subliminal state potentially dangerous. The change in your experience can be outward, as when a child runs into the street in front of your car, or a family member screams in pain from the next room, or you find your pleasant nocturnal stroll interrupted by four young men with knifes; or it can be inward, as when you suddenly realize that you have forgotten something (an appointment, your passport), or that you have unthinkingly done something stupid or dangerous or potentially embarrassing. When the change comes from the outside, there are usually physical outlets for the sudden burst of energy you get from noradrenalin (which works like an amphetamine) pumping through your body; when you suddenly realize that you have just done something utterly humiliating there may be no immediate action you can take, but your body responds the same way, producing enough noradrenalin to turn you into a world-class sprinter.

Our brains are built to regulate the degree to which we are active or passive, alert or sluggish, awake or asleep, etc. Brain scientists usually refer to the state of alert consciousness as "arousal," and it is controlled by a nerve bundle at the core of the brain stem (the oldest and most primitive part of our brains, which controls the fight-or-flight reflex), called the *reticular formation.* When the reticular formation is activated by axons bringing information of threat, concern, or anything else requiring alertness and activity, it arouses the cerebral cortex with noradrenalin, both directly and through the thalamus, the major way-station for information traveling to the "higher thought" or analytical centers of the cerebral cortex. The result is increased environmental vigilance (a monitoring of external stimuli) and a shift into highly conscious reflective and analytical processes.

The translator's reticular activation is generally not as spectacular, physiologically speaking, as some of the cases mentioned above. There is no sudden rush of fear, shock, or embarrassment; the noradrenalin surge is small enough that it doesn't generate the frantic need for physical activity, or the feeling of being about to explode, of those more drastic examples. Still, many translators do react to reticular activation with increased physical activity: they stand up and pace about restlessly; they walk to their bookshelves, pull reference books off and flip through them, tapping their feet impatiently (a good argument against getting those reference books on CD-ROM, or finding on-line versions on the World Wide Web: it's good to have an excuse to walk around the room!); they rock back violently in their chairs, drumming their fingers on the armrests and staring intently out the window as if expecting the solution to come flying in by that route. Many feel a good deal of frustration at their own inability to solve a problem, and will remain restless and unable to sink fully back into the rapid subliminal state until the problem is solved: it's the middle of the night and the client's tech writer isn't at work; the friends and family members who might have been able to help aren't home, or don't know; dictionaries and encyclopedias are no help

("Why didn't I go ahead and *pay* that ludicrous price for a bigger and newer and more specialized dictionary?!"); every minute that passes without a response from Lantra-L or FLEFO seems like an eternity.

When the solution finally comes, *if* it feels really right, the translator heaves a big sigh of relief and relaxes; soon s/he is translating away again, happily oblivious to the outside world. More often, some nagging doubt remains, and the translator works hard to put the problem on hold until a better answer can be sought, but keeps nervously returning to it as to a chipped tooth, prodding at it gently, hoping to find a remedy as if by accident.

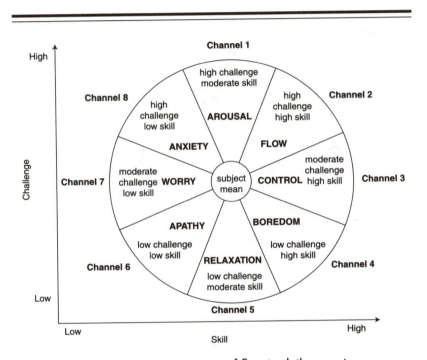

FIGURE 8 The systematic assessment of flow in daily experience (*Source*: Fausto Massimini and Massimo Carli, "The Systematic Assessment of Flow in Daily Experience" [1995: 270] (with permission from the Cambridge University Press))

On this diagram, channels 1 and 2 are the optimal states for translators and interpreters; channels 3–8, because they involve varying degrees of mismatch between challenge and skill, are less desirable (though quite common). Channels 3–5 are found in competent translators whose work isn't challenging or varied enough; channels 6–8 are found in translators of various competence levels in overly demanding working conditions (impossible deadlines, badly written source texts, angry and demanding initiators, inadequate support).

The channels might also be used to describe translator and interpreter training programs: the best programs will shuttle between 1 and 2; those that are too easy will bore students in channels 3–5, and those that fail to maintain the proper balance between challenge and student skills (fail, that is, to keep the former just slightly higher than the latter) will demoralize students in channels 6–8.

Channel 1, Arousal: full conscious analytical awareness, activated by the reticular formation. When the challenge posed by a translation task exceeds the translator's skills by a small but significant amount, when a problem cannot be solved in the flow state, s/he must move into full arousal or conscious awareness. The subject of this chapter.

Channel 2, Flow: the subliminal state in which translating is fastest, most reliable, and most enjoyable – so enjoyable that it can become addictive, like painting, novel-writing, or other forms of creative expression. The ideal state explored by most of this book.

Channel 3, Control: a state of calm competence that is mildly satisfying, but can become mechanical and repetitive if unenhanced by more challenging jobs. Common in corporate translators after a year or two in the same workplace. New variety and new challenges are needed for continued or increased job satisfaction.

Channel 4, Boredom: the state that develops in translators who rarely or never work anywhere close to their capacity levels.

Channel 5, Relaxation: a state of calm enjoyment at the ease of a translation job, especially as a break from overwhelmingly difficult or otherwise stressful jobs. The key to the pleasantness of this channel is its shortlivedness: too much "relaxation," insufficient challenges over a long period of time, generate boredom.

Channel 6, Apathy: a state of indifference that is rare in translators at any level – except, perhaps, in undermotivated beginning foreign-language students asked to translate from a textbook twenty sentences with a single grammatical structure that is easy even for them.

Channel 7, Worry: a state of concern that arises in inexperienced translators when faced with even mildly difficult problems that they feel they lack the necessary skills to solve.

Channel 8, Anxiety: a high-stress state that arises in any translator when the workload is too heavy, the texts are consistently far too difficult, deadlines are too short, and the emotional climate of the workplace (including the family situation at home) is insufficiently supportive.

Checking the rules (deduction)

Until fairly recently, virtually everything written for translators consisted of rules to be followed, either in specific textual circumstances or, more commonly, in a more general professional sense:

King Duarte of Portugal (1391–1438, reigned 1433–1438) writes in *The Loyal Counselor* (1430s) that the translator must (1) understand the meaning of the original and render it in its entirety without change, (2) use the idiomatic vernacular of the target language, not borrowing from the source language, (3) use target-language words that are direct and appropriate, (4) avoid offensive words, and (5) conform to rules for all writing, such as clarity, accessibility, interest, and wholesomeness.

Etienne Dolet (1509–46) similarly writes in *The Best Way of Translating from One Language to Another* (1540) that the translator must (1) understand the original meaning, (2) command both the source and the target language perfectly, (3) avoid literal translations, (4) use idiomatic forms of the target language, and (5) produce the appropriate tone through a careful selection and arrangement of words.

Alexander Fraser Tytler, Lord Woodhouselee (1747–1813), writes in his *Essay on the Principles of Translation* (1791) that the translation should "give a complete transcript of the ideas of the original work," "be of the same character with that of the original," and "have all the ease of original composition."

For centuries, "translation theory" was explicitly normative: its primary aim was to tell translators how to translate. Other types of translation theory were written as well, of course – from the four-teenth through the sixteenth century in England, for example, a focal topic for translation theory was *whether* (not how) the Bible should be translated into the vernacular – and even the most prescriptive writers on translation addressed other issues in passing. But at least since the Renaissance, and to some extent still today, the sole justi-fication for translation theory has most typically been thought to be the formulation of rules for translators to follow.

As we saw Karl Weick suggesting in Chapter 4, there are certain problems with this overriding focus on the rule. The main one is that rules tend to oversimplify a field so as to bring some sort of reassur-ing order to it. Rules thus tend to help people who find themselves in precisely those "ordinary" or "typical" circumstances for which they were designed, but to be worse than useless for people whose circum-stances force them outside the rules as narrowly defined.

The most common such situation in the field of translation is when the translator, who has been taught that the only correct way to translate is to render faithfully exactly what the source author wrote, neither adding nor subtracting or altering anything, finds a blatant error or confusion in the source text. Common sense suggests that the source author – and most likely the target reader as well – would prefer a corrected text to a blithely erroneous one; but the ancient "rule" says not to change anything. What is the translator to do?

Most professional translators today would favor a broader and more flexible version of that rule, going something like: "Alter nothing *except* if you find gross errors or confusions, and make changes then only after consulting with the agency or client or author." There are, however, translators today who balk at this sort of advice, and are quick to insist that, while it is true that translators must occasionally don the editor's hat and make changes in consulta-tion with the client, this is emphatically *not* translation. Translation is transferring the meaning of a text *exactly* from language to language, without alteration; any changes are made by the translator in his or her capacity as editor, not translator.

It was not clear in the original what was meant. That is, I could have "translated" the French, but it alone didn't satisfy the logic of the situation. So I asked the author, and the "additional" English is what he gave me. I guess my point is, we sometimes have to go above and beyond the source text, when logic requires, and with the assistance of the necessary resources, to provide clear meaning in the target text.

Josh Wallace

* * * * *

Couldn't agree with you more. There are indeed situations where the original does not suffice and the translator has to don his Editorial hat and contact the client. But it is editorial work, not translational. The translator is bound to the original, while the editor can, and does, change the text to suit the actual physical world. I've encountered several incidents where the original contradicted itself, or wasn't specific or clear enough. But as I've said, this is professional editing and not translation.

All the best,
Avi Bidani

— —

Still, despite the many problems attendant upon normative translation theory, translation theory as rules for the translator, it should be clear that there are rules that all professional translators are expected to know and follow, and therefore that they need to be codified and made available to translators, in books or pamphlets or university courses. Some of these rules are textual and linguistic:

— —

By the same token, I tend to leave ''commune'', ''canton'' and words like that in French. But somehow ''département'' rubs me up the wrong way. What do you think?
   I usually translate ''la Communauté Urbaine de Bordeaux'' by ''the Bordeaux Urban Community'' (a local authority responsible for managing the city and suburbs). Do you agree with me there?

Alex Rychlewski

* * * * *

Département is the typically French administrative unit that has become known in the English-speaking world. You're more likely to lose readers by translating it. Of course its similarity to the English faux-ami ''department'' is a drawback: make sure English-language typesetters put in the accent-aigu and the extra e in the French word.
   How about something on the lines of ''the Greater Bordeaux Council''? Community sounds more like the people, not the government.

Tony Crawford

* * * * *

In Quebec, we say "Communauté urbaine de Montréal" and "Montreal Urban Community".

As for "département", I would say "department of Martinique", just as I would say "state of Hawaii" or "province of Ontario". This is the usage found in the Geographical Names section of the Merriam-Webster's Collegiate Dictionary. That dictionary defines "department" as "a major territorial administrative subdivision". Furthermore, the words "commune" and "canton" are also English words. The first means the smallest administrative district in many European countries and the second means, according to the context, (1) a small territorial division of a country, (2) one of the states of the Swiss confederation or (3) a division of a French arrondissement. The last term is also an English word and means either an administrative district in some large French cities or the largest division of a French department.

None of these terms should be italicised or otherwise marked as foreign words in an English text, unless some special effect is being sought.

Regards,
K.-Benoit Evans

Should *faux amis* like *département*/department be used in translation just because in some areas (like Quebec) they have become standard? (Indeed, *are* they *faux* amis? Is their "friendship" or semantic kinship false?) Or should the nearest acceptable equivalent be used instead? It is a knotty problem, especially since different end-users in different times and places and circumstances will want or need or demand different solutions – and all rules in this area are attempts to codify those needs in general and universal ways, something that can never be done to everyone's satisfaction. Still, translators facing a word like *département* in French and recognizing how problematic it is (or could be) need to know what to do with it. Should they just do whatever they think best? In many cases, yes. But when? Should they call the client or agency and check? Clients and agencies will get very tired of translators who call every day with a dozen such queries; but clearly there are times when it is essential to call. What are those times? How do you know? On-line translator discussion groups are an excellent source of help, but as we see, the sort of help they can mostly provide is a *range* of answers, the sorts of rules other professional translators have either set up for themselves or been taught or told in the past, with lots of room for disagreement. Still, for the translator wondering how to proceed, even that can be very useful indeed.

Most translators do not, perhaps, consult translation "rule-books" very often. Indeed most do not possess such things – compilations of the laws governing translation in their country, or publications of their translator organizations or unions detailing the ethical principles governing the profession, or theoretical books listing specific translation problems between two specific languages and how to handle them, like Vinay and Darbelnet (1977) or Newmark (1987). Most pick up a rather general sense of the laws and ethical principles and preferred methods of translation from other people, in practice, and when faced with a gray area must frequently ask what to do. This is the "alarm bell" or reticular activation phenomenon: you suddenly stop, realizing that there is something that you need to know to proceed, but don't.

There are many deductive "authorities" that the translator may need to consult.

THE TRANSLATOR'S AUTHORITIES

1 *Legislation governing translation*
Lawmakers' conception of how translators should translate; typically represents the practical and professional interests of end-users rather than translators; because it has the force of law, however, these *become* the practical and professional interests of translators as well.

2 *Ethical principles published by translator organizations/unions*
Other translators' conception of how translators should translate and otherwise comport themselves professionally; typically represents the profession's idealized self-image, the face a committee of highly respected translators in your country would like all of their colleagues to present to the outside world; may not cover all cases, or provide enough detail to help every translator navigate through every ethical dilemma.

3 *Theoretical statements of the general ethical/professional principles governing translation*
One or two translation scholars' conception of how translators should translate and otherwise comport themselves professionally; like (2), typically represents the profession's idealized self-image,

but filtered now not through a committee of practicing translators but through a single scholar's (a) personal sense of the practical and theoretical field and (b) need to win promotion and tenure in his or her university department; may be more useful for scholarly or pedagogical purposes than day-to-day professional decision-making.

4   *Theoretical studies of specific translation problems in specific language combinations; comparative grammars*
One or two translation scholars' conception of the linguistic similarities and differences and transfer patterns between two languages; may lean more toward the comparative-linguistic, systematic, and abstract, or more toward the translational, practical, and anecdotal, and at best will mix elements from both extremes; like (3), may be more useful for scholarly or pedagogical purposes than for practical decision-making in the working world, but at best will articulate a practicing professional translator's highly refined sense of the transfer dynamics between two languages.

5   *Single-language grammars*
One or two linguists' conception of the logical structure governing a given language; typically, given the rich illogicality of natural language, a reduction or simplification of language as it is actually used to tidy logical categories; best thought of not as the "true" structure of a language but rather as an idealization that, because it was written by an expert, a linguist, may carry considerable weight among clients and/or end-users.

6   *Dictionaries, glossaries, terminological databases (Termium, Eurodicautom)*
A scholar's or committee's conception of the logical structure governing the semantic fields of the words that s/he or they consider the most important in the language or (in a bilingual dictionary or database) language pair; given the vast complexity of language, always a best guess based on limited knowledge and an interpretation based on limited experience and perspective; always by definition incomplete, almost always by necessity at least slightly out of date; with those provisos, undeniably valuable, a translator's best friend.

7   *Previous translations and other materials obtained from the client, agency, database, library*
Other translators' and tech writers' conception of the specialized discourse that the translator will be attempting to imitate; typically

an extremely useful but potentially unreliable source of words and phrases; when obtained from the client, this material carries authoritative weight even when the translator feels that it is inaccurate or misleading (and even when the client wants the translator to reinvent the target-language terminology), as it reflects the target-language discourse that the client has been using.

8   *Expert advice and information from people who have worked in the field or have some other reliable knowledge about it*
A conception of the field formed, and shared with the translator, by people who use the relevant discourse every day in their jobs, as front-line practitioners or as translators; typically obtained by the translator by phone, fax, or on-line inquiry, from a circle of experts that the translator knows personally or picks out of the telephone directory (need a legal term, call a lawyer or legal secretary), or that subscribe to the same on-line translator discussion group.

Checking synonyms, alternatives (induction)

There is not much to say about reticular activation in either the inductive or the abductive mode: both are so common, so ordinary, as to be barely perceptible to the translator who relies heavily on them every day. The most typical form of an inductive approach to a problem that arises is the mental listing of synonyms: the "right" word doesn't come to mind immediately, so the translator runs quickly down through a mental list of likely possibilities. As has been noted throughout this book, translators tend to collect such lists; they are the people who can not only give you a definition for words like "deleterious" or "synergistic" or "fulgurated," but can quickly and casually rattle off a handful of rough synonyms for each. The translator knows, perhaps better than anyone, that there are never perfect synonyms in a single language, let alone between two different languages; hence the importance of gathering as many different *rough* synonyms for every semantic field that ever comes up, and keeping them somewhere close to the surface of memory, ready to be called up and compared at a moment's notice. Translators go through life alert to language, always looking to fill in gaps in their lists, or to add to already overflowing lists, knowing that some day they might need every word they have ever stored.

These mental lists, sometimes methodically stored in personal or corporate databases for rapid and reliable access, constitute one essential inductive process of accumulating semantic experiences that translators use when habit fails – when the autopilot shuts down and they must go to "manual." But there are many others as well: mental lists of ethical principles ("Should I correct this?" "Should I notify the agency about this?"), good business practices ("I can't finish this by the deadline, what should I do?" "I really need to charge extra for this, but how much, and how do I present it?"), moral beliefs ("Do I really want to do a translation for an arms manufacturer, a tobacco company, a neo-Nazi group?"), and so on. In each case, the problem translators face is too complicated to deal with by rote, subliminally, uncritically; so they shift into a conscious analytical mode and begin sifting back through the inductive layers of their experience, exploring patterns, comparing and contrasting, articulating to themselves – in some cases for the first time – the principles that seem to emerge from the regularities.

Picking the rendition that feels right (abduction)

And at last, of course, they have to make a decision. Language is an infinitely fascinating subject for translators, and many of them could go on worrying a problem area for days, weeks – perhaps even forever. Fortunately or unfortunately, clients and agencies are rarely willing to wait that long, and at some point translators must put a stop to the analytical process and say "that's good enough" (see Pym 1993: 113–16).

Just when that point is, when translators will feel comfortable enough with a solution to move on, is impossible to predict – even for the translators themselves. The feeling of being satisfied with a solution, and of knowing that you are satisfied *enough* to move on, is rarely subject to rational analysis. It comes abductively, as an intuitive leap; the swirl of certainties and uncertainties, the mixture of conviction ("this seems like a good word, maybe even the right word") and doubt ("but I *know* there's a better one"), eventually filter out into a sudden moment of clarity in which a decision is made. Not necessarily a perfect or ultimate decision; the translator may have to go back and change it later. But a decision nonetheless. A decision to move on.

And in the end it does come down to this: with all the professional expertise and craftsmanship in the world, with decades of experience and a fine, even perfectionist, attention to detail, every translator does finally translate by the seat of his or her pants, picking the rendition that *feels* right. This may not be the ultimate arbiter in the translation process as a whole – the translator's work will almost certainly be edited by others – but it is the ultimate arbiter for the translator as a trained professional, working alone. The translator's "feeling" of "rightness" draws on the full range of his or her professionial knowledge and skill; but it is in the end nevertheless a feeling, a hunch, an intuitive sense. The translation *feels right* – or it feels right enough to send off. It is made up of thousands of decisions based ultimately on this same criterion, most made quickly, subliminally, without analytical reflection; some made painstakingly, with full conscious awareness, checking of authorities, and logical reasoning; but all relying finally on the translator's abductive seal of approval: okay, that'll do.

The difference between a good translator and a mediocre one is not, in other words, that the former translates carefully, consciously, analytically, and the latter relies too heavily upon intuition and raw feels. Both the good translator and the mediocre translator rely heavily on analysis and intuition, on conscious and subliminal processing. The difference is that the good translator has *trained* his or her intuitions more thoroughly than the mediocre one, and in relying on those intuitions is actually relying on years of internalized experience and intelligent reflection.

On the other hand, no one's intuitions are ever fully trained. Good translators are lifelong learners, always looking for more cultural knowledge, more words and phrases, more experience of different text types, more transfer patterns, more solutions to complex problems. Translation is intelligent activity requiring constant growth, learning, self-expansion.

In that sense we are all, always, becoming translators.

Discussion

1   Just how rule-governed should a translator's work be? Is the translator's creativity ever hampered or diminished by adherence to the rules of the marketplace? If so, what should the translator who feels hampered do about it? In aspects of translation where the marketplace does not impose specific rules on the translator, to what extent should the translator impose those rules on himself or herself?

2   Just how conscious should a translator's analytical processes be? Should translators slow down their translations in order to be more analytically thorough and cautious? Should the initial translating work be rapid and more or less subliminal, and the editing process be conscious and slow and analytical? Should even the editing proceed more or less subliminally, unless a problem arises?

Exercise

Translate the following text into your target language. Let yourself sink into a reverie state while you translate: relax, breathe rhythmically, listen to music, let your mind wander to the shirts you've put on in your life.

> Buttoning a shirt: take the two sides of the shirt front in your two hands and line them up, starting from the bottom. Move your fingers on one hand up the shirt to the bottom button, and the fingers on the other hand up the shirt to the bottom buttonhole. Push the button through the buttonhole. Slide your fingers up to the next button and buttonhole, and the button it through the hole. Keep moving up the shirt, one button and one buttonhole at a time, until you read the ladder but on and button the top button. Or, if you like, leave the top button undone.

What happened when you reached the problem area ". . . until you read the ladder but on"? What did you do? Could you feel yourself coming out of your reverie state and starting to analyze? Did the two mental states feel qualitatively different?

Suggestions for further reading

Fuller (1973), Picken (1989), Wilss (1996)

Appendix for teachers

This book offers an alternative approach to both translating and the training of translators – one that seeks to bridge the traditional gaps between the two, bringing translator training closer to the experiential processes of professional translators so as to help teachers teach student translators to translate faster, more reliably, and more enjoyably.

The book is structured to achieve that goal in several ways.

First, it approaches translation from an "internal" or translator-based perspective, seeking to understand translation as professional translators do. The differences between this internal and a user-oriented "external" perspective are outlined in Chapters 1 and 2. Briefly, this internal perspective means seeing the translator less as the producer of a certain kind of text – the traditional approach to translator training – and more as a learner who must enjoy the work to continue doing it. This book offers exercises that work on text-production as well, but in general text-production is seen as the by-product of being a certain kind of person: a lover of language and culture, a lover of linguistic and cultural mediation, a lover of learning.

Second, it draws on recent pedagogical research on brain-compatible teaching and learning, seeking to develop new strategies for translator training that are strongly based in professional translators' neural/intellectual/imaginative processes. Since the primary research in this latter area has not been done, the book's pedagogical techniques have been developed by the modification of innovative holistic methods from foreign-language and other related classrooms – especially Georgi Lozanov's (1971/1992) suggesto-pedia, or accelerated learning. The book is not suggestopedic in any technical sense, nor does it require any special training in suggesto-pedic or other methodologies; in the interests of making the exercises accessible to as many different teachers and students as possible, suggestopedic and other accelerated teaching methods have been adapted to the ordinary classroom. These pedagogical approaches entail "multimodal" experience, eyes-ears-and-hands-on exercises that encourage the learner to use as many information-processing channels as possible: visual, auditory, and kinesthetic; drawing, storytelling, acting and miming; imaging, discussing, moving.

And third, it integrates the theory and practice of translation in experiential ways, seeking to build bridges between exciting new developments in translation theory and the rich and relatively unre-searched practical world of professional translation. Chapters 6–10 offer a series of integrated views of different theoretical approaches to translation: psychological in Chapter 6, terminological in Chapter 7, linguistic in Chapter 8, sociological in Chapter 9, and cultural in Chapter 10. The reigning idea throughout is that there is not a single "correct" or "useful" theoretical approach to translation; rather, each learner can learn to take whatever s/he finds useful from the full range of theoretical approaches, which is presented somewhat schemati-cally but nevertheless fully and fairly here. The model on which the integration between practice and theory is based is presented in Chapter 4; briefly, it borrows some concepts from the American philosopher Charles Sanders Peirce to see the translator as converting new experience into habit or "second nature." This new experience is "abductive" or based on guesswork and creative, intuitive leaps; "inductive" or based on well-established working patterns; and "deductive" or based on rules, precepts, laws, theories. The key to integrating all three "ductive" processes is the understanding that all three are forms of *experience*: translators use all of them, guesses, practice, and rules, to deal with novel situations, and also to convert what they learn in those novel situations into "habitual" or "instinc-tive" processing. The more "subliminally" or "habitually" they can work, the faster they can translate; but subliminal translation pro-ceeds in a fruitful back-and-forth shuttle movement with conscious, analytical experience, the processing of new situations that require alert awareness and thus bring about change and growth.

One of the fundamental assumptions behind this book is that learning is most effective when it is learner-centered – which is to say, when each learner (each student, but the teacher as well) has experiences and makes discoveries on his or her own, and those experiences and discoveries arise out of and are tied back into his or her previous experience and knowledge as well. For this book to work at its peak effectiveness in the classroom, the teacher has to be willing to enter into a learner-centered environment – to work with his or her students to create that kind of environment. This means:

- The teacher is not the source of all knowledge, but a facilitator of students' learning experiences, and a learner along with the students.
- The students are not passive recipients of knowledge or knowhow but its active generators, and thus teachers along with the teacher.
- There are no right or wrong "answers" or solutions to the discussion topics or exercises given at the end of each chapter; they are designed to help groups of learners draw on what they already know in order to develop effective strategies for finding out things that they don't yet know, and each group will get different things from doing them.
- Not all the discussion topics and exercises will work with all groups, since people are different; the teacher must be prepared to "fail" with some topics and exercises, and to try something else instead.

For centuries it was assumed that learning is simply a matter of being presented with facts and imprinting them on one's memory. An authority, usually a teacher, tells the learner the facts and the learner takes possession of them, "stores" them in memory for later recall. This assumption is still very much alive today, of course, as is clear from countless classrooms in which the teacher lectures and the students take notes in order later to be able to store the facts in memory for the final exam. The Brazilian educator Paulo Freire (1970) calls this approach to education the "banking method": the assumption is that the learner's brain is a bank account into which the teacher makes factual "deposits." Learning is simply the passive intake of information.

This pedagogy has been questioned for as long as pedagogies have been discussed – well over two thousand years – by those who argue that people learn best not by listening passively and memorizing what they hear but by doing things, actively participating in a process. This "hands-on" pedagogy lies behind the practical translation seminars that make up the bulk of translator training programs: if you learn to translate best by translating, then the best way to teach students how to translate is to give them texts and have them translate them into another language.

These two approaches to teaching, learning-by-listening and learning-by-doing, have often been seen as the polar opposites that cover the field: either you lecture and expect students to take notes and pass "objective" exams on the material covered in class, or you set them a practical task and give them feedback on how well they complete it, assuming that the act of completing the task will teach them at least as much as the feedback.

The two approaches have also been labeled "good" and "bad": depending on one's pedagogical philosophy,

- either lecturing is "good"
  (because it is the most efficient way to cover large amounts of material for large numbers of students in a short period of time)
- and practical seminars are "bad"
  (because they are inefficient – they are time-consuming and require a very low student-teacher ratio – and because it is hard to rank students on their practical "experiences" in objective, i.e. numerical, ways)
- or practical seminars are "good"
  (because people learn by doing)
- and lecturing is "bad"
  (because passive listening and rote memorization are the least effective way to store information in memory).

Historically, the former attitude favoring lecturing over practical seminars has been thought of as "conservative" and the latter, favoring practical small-group work over lecturing, has been thought of as "progressive." Recent empirical studies of learning have shown, however, that this opposition is misleading. People *can* learn extremely well by listening passively while someone else talks. And while hands-on experience is unquestionably an effective channel of learning, there are ways of structuring that experience in classrooms that block its effectiveness.

This research shows that the most important factor in the effectiveness of various teaching methods for learning is what is called "brain-compatibility" – how well the teaching method "fits" the way the brain actually learns.

Lecturing

Thus, for example, at the broadest and most obvious level, what makes a lecture effective as a teaching tool is not its "coverage," how much information the lecturer is able to squeeze into an hour and a half, but how interesting it is. Some lectures can be so fascinating that the audience does not notice the passage of time; others can be so dull that everyone is falling asleep after the first five minutes.

Some defenders of traditional lectures will admit that, yes, alas, some lecturers are not particularly riveting; but one must not forget, they will add, that part of the blame lies with the students. Students must make an effort to be interested as well. Even the most brilliant speaker cannot get through to someone who is determined to be bored; and one can hardly expect teachers to compete with the blandishments of MTV. If students are not willing to make the effort to take an interest in the lecturer's ideas, they should not be in the class – or, possibly, in the university at all.

And there is some truth to this. It *is* possible to block interest in a subject. But there are some hard scientific realities behind students' interest in (and enhanced ability to learn from) an exciting, enthusiastic lecture and instant rejection of a boring, monotonous one:

1 *Modulation of voice, gesture, posture.* The brain is built to pay particular attention to change, and to sink into a less focused and attentive state when things don't change, or change is minimal. That is why we notice moving things against an unchanging background; why our fingers constantly seek out a wound or sunburn or other change in our skin, and our tongues constantly find their way back to the hole where a tooth was recently pulled out. It is also why lullabies put children (and sometimes parents) to sleep: melodies without sudden changes in pitch, volume, or timbre are physiologically soporific. A speaker who does not change her or his volume or pitch or rhythm, who stands stock still and maintains a poker face, will similarly put listeners to sleep. It is possible to fight this sleepiness, but extremely difficult; it is a physiological function that is hard-wired into the human brain.

2 *Personal enthusiasm, fervor, commitment.* Due to the power of the brain's limbic system to shape our thought and behavior, emotions are physiologically very contagious. This "contagion" is very difficult to resist: when everyone is crying or laughing, it requires enormous emotional energy to keep from doing the same (see Robinson 1991: 5ff.). The rapid transfer of emotional states from one body to another explains how attitudes, prejudices, taboos, fears, and the like are passed on from generation to generation: children pick them up from their parents, often without the mediation of words. It explains how the mood of a whole group of people can shift almost instantaneously. It also explains why an enthusiastic speaker makes her or his audience feel enthusiastic as well, and why someone who speaks with no emotion at all quickly numbs an audience into boredom.

3 *Examples, illustrations, anecdotes.* The neurological rule is: the more complex the neural pathways, the more effectively the brain functions. A synaptic firing sequence that only moves through three or four areas in the brain will always provoke less attention, excitement, thought, and growth in the learner than one that moves through several hundred, even several thousand. This is the problem with teaching (and writing) that adheres closely to a single method, like lists of general principles. There is nothing wrong with lists of general principles; but they only activate certain limited areas of the brain. When they are illustrated with anecdotes from the speaker's or other people's experiences, that not only activates new areas in the listener's brain; it also inspires the listener to think up similar events in her or his own experience, which again activates numerous new neural loops. From a speaking and writing viewpoint, the rule would say: the more specificity and variety, the better. Vague, general, and repetitive phrasings will always be less interesting and provocative than specific, detailed, and surprising phrasings.

4 *Relevance.* This is closely related to the importance of illustrating general claims with detailed observations, examples, and anecdotes. The brain is a merciless pragmatist: because it is faced with millions more stimuli than it can ever process, it must screen out things that it perceives as irrelevant to its needs. Sometimes it is forced to shut out even very interesting stimuli,

because they overlap with more relevant stimuli that must be attended to first. Speakers and writers who build bridges to their listeners' and readers' experience are often condemned by traditionalists for "pandering" to their audience; much better, in these people's minds, to present a subject in its most logical, systematic, and objective form and let listeners and readers build their own bridges. While that works for specialists who have spent years building such bridges, discovering the relevance of a subject to their own lives, it does not work at all for beginners who have no idea what possible connection it might have to their experience.

5 *State of mind (brain waves).* It is common knowledge that we need to be in a receptive state of mind before we can take in new information. Most people also recognize that it is difficult to perform even the simplest analytical or other processing operations in certain mental or physical states – when worried, or feverish, or angry, or hungry. It should be obvious, for example, that a listener forced to sit through a boring lecture might well grow angry and become even less receptive to the lecture than otherwise; or that a listener who is enjoying a lecture will relax into a receptive frame of mind and will be more open to the new ideas presented in it than otherwise. What may not be so obvious is that the most receptive state of mind is not full alertness, as we have been taught to believe, but a relaxed, dreamy reverie state that our teachers have branded "not paying attention" or "daydreaming" – the so-called "alpha" state. Many of the exercises in this book use music and relaxation to help students get into this receptive frame of mind.

6 *Multimodal experience.* As we will see in Chapter 3, the rule regarding the complexity of neural pathways applies equally to the channels through which information comes: information presented through a single voice (as in the traditional lecture) is received and processed far less effectively than information presented through several voices (as in discussion, team-teaching, or taped materials); and information presented through voice alone is received and processed far less effectively than information presented through voice, music, visual material, and various tactile and kinesthetic experiences.

Small-group work

Most educators agree that human beings learn better by doing than by listening. The most effective lectures, therefore, will also get the audience involved in doing something actively, even if it is only a thought exercise. By this logic, practical hands-on small-group seminars ought to be the perfect pedagogical tool.

But again, it's not so much the tool itself that makes the difference as how you use it. Many small-group exercises and discussions are just as boring as sitting in a monotonous lecture. Students given a boring task to perform or topic to discuss in a group will quickly shift to more interesting topics, like their social life; or, if forced to stay on task, will go through the required steps grudgingly, resentfully, and thus superficially and mechanically, learning next to nothing. For small-group work too, therefore, it is important to take into consideration how the brain functions:

1 *Variety*. Variety is the spice of life for good physiological reasons: when things don't change, the brain ignores them. Traditional teachers have begun to blame television for young people's short attention spans and need for constant change and excitement; but it really isn't television's fault, nor is it even a new phenomenon. It is a deepseated human need, part of the brain's evolutionary structure. A classroom that uses lots of small-group work will only be interesting and productive for students if the nature of the work done keeps changing. If students are repeatedly and predictably asked to do the same kind of small-group work day after day (study a text and find three things to tell the class about it; discuss a topic and be prepared to summarize your discussion for the rest of the class), they will quickly lose interest.

2 *Collaboration*. It might seem as if this should go without saying: when students work together in small groups, of course they are going to collaborate. But it is relatively easy for one student in a group to assume the "teacher's" role and dominate the activity, so that most of the other students in the group sit passively watching while the activity is completed. This is especially true when the group is asked to come up with an answer that will be checked for correctness or praised for smartness: when the teacher

puts pressure on groups to perform up to his or her expectations, their conditioned response will be to defer to the student in the group who is perceived as the "best" or "smartest" – the one who is most often praised by the teacher for his or her answers. Collaboration means full participation, a sense that everyone's contribution is valued – that the more input, the better.

3 *Openendedness*. One way of ensuring full participation and collaboration is by keeping group tasks openended, without expecting groups to reach a certain answer or result. The clearer the teacher's mental image is of what s/he expects the groups to produce, the less openended the group work will be; the more willing the teacher is to be surprised by students' creativity, the more they will collaborate, the more they will learn, and the more they will enjoy learning. Openended tasks leave room for each student's personal experience to emerge – an essential key to learning, as students must begin to integrate what is coming from outside with what they already know. When the successful completion of a task or activity requires every student to access his or her personal experience, also, whole groups learn to work together in collaborative ways rather than ceding authority to a single representative. (All of the topics for discussion and exercises in this book are openended, with no one right answer or desired result.)

4 *Relevance*. Group work has to have some real-world application in students' lives for it to be meaningful; it has to be meaningful for them to throw themselves into it body and soul; they have to throw themselves into it to really learn. This emphatically does not mean only giving students things to do that they already know! Learning happens out on the peripheries of existing knowledge; learners must constantly be challenged to push beyond the familiar, the easy, the known. Relevance means simply that bridges must constantly be built between the known and the unknown, the familiar and the unfamiliar, the easy and the challenging, the things that already matter to students and the things that don't yet matter but should.

5 *State of mind*. This follows from everything else – part of the point in making group work varied, collaborative, open-ended, and relevant is to get students into a receptive frame of mind – but

it is essential to bear in mind that these things don't always work. An exercise that has worked dozens of times before with other groups leaves a whole class full of groups cold: they sit there, staring at their books, doodling on their papers, mumbling to their neighbors, rolling their eyes, and you wonder whatever could have happened. Never mind; stop the exercise and try something else. No use beating a dead horse. There are many receptive mental states: relaxed, happy, excited, absorbed, playful, joking, thoughtful, intent, exuberant, dreamy. There are also many non-receptive mental states: bored, distracted, angry, distanced, resentful, absent. The good teacher learns to recognize when students are learning and when they are just filling a chair, by remaining sensitive to their emotional states.

6   *Multimodal experience.* It is often assumed that university classrooms are for intellectual discussions of important issues – for the spoken and written word. Drawing, singing, acting, dancing, miming, and other forms of human expression are for the lower grades (and a few selected departments on campus, like art or theater or music). Many university teachers will feel reluctant to use many of the exercises in this book, for example, because they seem inappropriate for university-level instruction. But the brain's physiological need for multimodal experience does not disappear after childhood; it continues all through our lives. Studies done on students' retention of material presented in class have shown that the more senses a student uses in processing that material, the better s/he will retain it (see Figure 9). The differences are striking: students who only hear the material (for example, in a lecture), retain only 20 percent of it. If they only see it (for example, in a book), they retain 30 percent of it. If they see it and hear it, by reading along in a book or rereading lecture notes, or if the lecture is accompanied by slides or other visual aids, they retain 50 percent of it. If in addition to seeing it and hearing it they are able to talk about it, in class discussions or after-class study groups, retention goes up to 70 percent. And when in addition to seeing it, hearing it, and talking about it, they are able to do something with it physically, act it out or draw a picture or sing a song about it, retention soars to 90 percent. Undignified? Perhaps. But what is more important, dignity or learning?

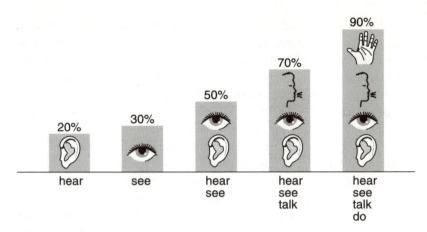

FIGURE 9 Channels of learning
Source: Adapted from Irmeli Huovinen's drawing in Vuorinen 1993: 47

Some teachers may find these "shifts" in their teaching strategies exciting and liberating; for others, even a slight move in the direction of a more student-centered classroom may cause unpleasant feelings of anxiety. To the former, the best advice is to do whatever feels right: use the book as a springboard or muse rather than as a straitjacket; let the book together with your students and your own instincts lead you to an approach that not only works but keeps working in different ways. To the latter, the best advice is to try this approach in small doses. Teachers can use the book more traditionally, by having students read the chapters and take exams on the subject matter, with perhaps an occasional teacher-led discussion based on the discussion topics at the end of every chapter. But the true core of the book is in the exercises; it is only when teachers let students try out the ideas in the chapters through multimodal experiences with the exercises that the book will have its full effect. If, however, the exercises – and the "less academic" classroom atmosphere that results from their extensive use – arouse all your suspicions or anxieties, teach the book mostly traditionally, but let the students do one or two exercises. And keep an open mind: if they enjoy the exercises, and you enjoy watching them enjoy themselves, even if you are not convinced that they are learning anything of value, try a few more. Give the exercises a fair chance. They really do work; what they teach is valuable, even if its value is not immediately recognizable in traditional academic terms.

All the discussion topics and exercises presume a decentered or student-centered classroom, in which the teacher mainly functions as a facilitator of the students' learning experiences, not as the authority who doles out knowledge and tests to make sure the students have learned it properly. Hence there are no right or wrong answers to the discussion topics – no "key" is given here in the appendix for teachers who want to use these topics as exam questions – and no right or wrong experiences to derive from the exercises. Indeed I have deliberately built in a tension between the positions taken in the chapters and the discussion topics given at the end of the chapters: what is presented as truth in the chapter is often questioned in the discussion topics at the end. The assumption behind this is that human beings never accept anything new until they have tested it against their own experience. The assumption that facts or precepts or theories can or should simply be presented as abstract universal truths for students to memorize is based on a faulty understanding of human neural processing. The brain simply does not work that way.

Tied to this brain-based pedagogical philosophy is the progress in Chapters 5–10 (and in Chapter 11 backwards) through the three phases of Charles Sanders Peirce's "duction" triad: abduction (guesses, intuitive leaps), induction (practical experience), and deduction (precepts, theories, laws). The idea here is that precepts and theories are indeed useful in the classroom – but only when they arise out of, and are constantly tied back to, intuitions and practical experiences. The second half of the book integrates a number of different translation theories – especially linguistic, functional, descriptive, and postcolonial ones – into an experiential approach to becoming a translator by helping students to experience the steps by which a theorist derived a theory, or by having them redraw and rethink central diagrams to accommodate divergent real-world scenarios. Everyone theorizes; it is an essential skill for the translator as well. What turns many students off about translation theory, especially as it is presented in books and articles and many classrooms, is that it tends to have a "completeness" to it that is alien to the ongoing process of making sense of the world. The theorist has undergone a complex series of steps that has led to the formulation of a brilliant schema, but it is difficult for others, especially students without extensive experience of the professional world of translation, to make the "translation" from abstract schemas to practical applications, especially to problem-solving strategies. The wonderful thing about the *act* of schematizing complex problems visually or verbally is the feeling of things "locking into place," "coming together," "finally making sense": you have struggled with the problem for weeks, months, years, and finally it all comes into focus. Presented with nothing more than the end-product of this process, however, students aren't given access to that wonderful feeling. Everything just seems "locked into place" – as into prison.

In this sense *theorizing* translation is more important for the translation student than *theories* of translation as static objects to be studied and learned. Our students should become theorists themselves – not merely students of theories. This does not mean that they need to develop an arcane theoretical terminology or be able to cite Plato and Aristotle, Kant and Hegel, Benjamin and Heidegger and Derrida; what it means is that they should become increasingly comfortable thinking complexly about what they do, both in order to improve their problem-solving skills and in order to defend their translational decisions to agencies or clients or editors who criticize them. Above all they need to be able to shift flexibly and intelligently from practice to precept and back again, to shuttle comfortably between subliminal functioning and conscious analysis – and that requires that *they* build the bridges rather than standing by passively while someone else (a teacher, say, or a theorist) builds the bridges for them. This does not mean reinventing the wheel; no question here of handing students a blank slate and asking them to theorize translation from scratch. All through Chapters 6–10 existing theories will be explored. But they will be explored in ways that encourage students to find their own experiential pathways through them, to build their own bridges from the theories back to their own theorizing/translating.

> *Seventy-five percent of teachers*
> *are sequential, analytic presenters*
> *that's how their lesson is organized . . .*
> *Yet 100% of their students*
> *are multi-processors*

(Jensen 1995a: 130)

1 External knowledge: the user's view

The main idea in this chapter is to perceive translation as much from the user's point of view as possible, with two assumptions: (1) that most translation theory and translator training in the past has been based largely on this external perspective, and (2) that it has been based on that perspective in largely hidden or repressed ways. Some consequences of (1) are that many traditional forms of translation theory and translator training have been authoritarian, normative, rule-bound, aimed at forcing the translator into a robotic straitjacket; and that, while this perspective is valuable (it represents the views of the people who pay us to translate, hence the people we need to be able to satisfy), without a translator-oriented "internal" perspective to balance it, it may also become demoralizing and counterproductive. A consequence of (2) is that important parts of the user's perspective, especially those of timeliness and cost, have not been adequately presented in the traditional theoretical literature or in translation seminars. Even from a user's external perspective, translation cannot be reduced to the simplicities of "accurate renditions."

Discussion

1 Just what else might be involved in translation besides "strict accuracy" is raised in this first discussion topic. The ethical complexities of professional translation are raised in more detail in Chapter 2 (p. 30–3); this discussion can serve as a first introduction to a very sensitive and hotly contested issue. The more heavily invested you are in a strict ethics of translation, the harder it will be for you to let the students range freely in this discussion: you will be tempted to impose your views on them. It is important to remember that, even if your views reflect the ethics and legality of most professional translation, students are going to have to learn to make peace with those realities on their own terms, and an open-ended discussion at this point, when the stakes are low, may help them do so. Also, of course, traditional ethics do not cover all situations; they are too narrow. As professionals, students will have to have a flexible

enough understanding of the complexities behind translation ethics to make difficult decisions in complicated situations.

2 Here it should be relatively easy to feed students little tidbits of information about the current state of machine translation research and let them argue on their own.

Exercises

1 This exercise works well in a teacher-centered classroom; it is a good place to start for the teacher who prefers to stay more or less in control. Stand at the board, a flipchart, or an overhead projector (with a blank transparency and a marker) and ask the students to call out the stereotyped character traits, writing each one down on the left side of the board, flipchart, or transparency as you hear it. Then draw a line down the middle and ask the students to start calling out user-oriented ideals, writing them down on the right side as you hear them. When they can think of no more, start asking them to point out similarities and discrepancies between the two lists. Draw lines between matched or mismatched items on the two sides. Then conduct a discussion of the matches and mismatches, paying particular attention to the latter. Try as a group to come up with ways to rethink the national characteristics that *don't* match translator ideals so that they are positive rather than negative traits. The idea is to shift students' focus from the external perspective that sees only problems, faults, and failings to an internal perspective that seeks to make the best out of what is at hand. The students must not only be able to believe in themselves; they must be able to capitalize on their own strengths, without feeling inferior because they do not live up to some abstract ideal.

Another way to run this exercise is in small groups: break the class up into groups of four or five and have each group do the exercise on its own; then bring them all together to share their discoveries with the whole group.

2 This can be done as a demonstration exercise in front of the class: ask for volunteers, have them plan what they're going to do, and do it while the other students watch; then discuss the results with

the whole class. Or it can be done in smaller groups, each group planning and enacting their own dramatization. A demonstration exercise leaves the teacher more control, but also gives fewer students the actual experience.

3 Here the important thing is pushing the students to generate as much complexity as possible. Some groups may be tempted to set up a tidy one-to-one correspondence between the specific types of reliability listed in the chapter and specific translation situations; encourage them to complicate this sort of neat tabulation, to find problems, conflicts, differences of opinion and perception, etc. Professionals need considerable tolerance for complexity; this exercise is designed to begin building that tolerance.

4 Here the temptation may be to settle things too quickly and easily. Set a minimum time limit: their negotiations must last at least ten or fifteen minutes. The longer they negotiate, the more complications they will have to imagine, present, and handle.

2 Internal knowledge: the translator's view

This chapter offers the first tentative statement of a position that will be developed throughout the book: the internal viewpoint of the practicing translator. It is an attempt to reframe the user's requirements – reliability, timeliness, and cost – in terms that are more amenable to translators' own professional self-perceptions: as professional pride, income, and enjoyment.

Discussion

1 This first discussion topic is designed to help students address a common misperception: that translators translate, period. Many student translators believe implicitly that there are clear boundaries between translation and other text-based activities, and that they will never be asked to cross those boundaries – or if they are, that they should naturally refuse. This is a chance for you to correct these misperceptions with anecdotes from your own experience and knowledge of the professional field; but those

anecdotes will have the greatest impact on students if they are presented as obstacles to their simplistic notions, problems for them to digest, rather than as truths that bring the discussion to a halt.

2 Here again, your own anecdotes will be helpful – especially ones that complicate an oversimplistic assumption about "improving" a text.

Exercises

1 Choose a source text, not too difficult, and mark it off in increasing increments, 10 words more each time: at word 10, word 30 (20-word interval), word 60 (30-word interval), etc. These intervals will be very artificial, of course; sometimes you will have to include a single word from a sentence, or a larger segment of a sentence. An example from this chapter:

> These are the questions we'll be exploring throughout the book [A: 10 words]; but briefly, yes, translators and (especially) interpreters do all have something of the actor in them, the mimic, the impersonator [B: 20 words], and they do develop remarkable recall skills that will enable them to remember a word (often in a foreign language) that they have heard only once. Translators and interpreters are [C: 30 words] voracious and omnivorous readers, people who are typically in the middle of four books at once, in several languages, fiction and nonfiction, technical and humanistic subjects, anything and everything. They are hungry for real-world experience as well, through travel, living [D: 40 words] abroad for extended periods, learning foreign languages and cultures, and above all paying attention to how people use language all around them: the plumber, the kids' teachers, the convenience store clerk, the doctor, the bartender, friends and colleagues from this or that region or social class, and so on. Translation [E: 50 words] is often called a profession of second choice: many translators were first professionals in other fields, sometimes several other fields in succession, and only turned to translation when

they lost or quit those jobs or moved to a country where they were unable to practice them; as translators they often mediate between former colleagues in two or more different language [**F: 60 words**] communities. Any gathering of translators is certain to be a diverse group, not only because well over half of the people there will be from different countries, and almost all will have lived abroad, and all will shift effortlessly in conversation from language to language, but because by necessity translators and interpreters carry a wealth of different "selves" or "personalities" around inside them, ready to be reconstructed on the computer [**G: 70 words**] screen whenever a new text arrives, or out into the airwaves whenever a new speaker steps up to the podium. A crowd of translators always seems much bigger than the actual bodies present.

Hand the text out to the students with the segments marked, so they can glance at the next or previous segment briefly; this will enable them to figure out the best way to translate partial sentences in a given segment.

Insist that they use the full five minutes each time: when they are translating segment A (10 words), this will mean working hard to generate enough "work" to be doing for the entire five-minute period. As the segments get longer, they may feel pressured to squeeze a few more words into the five-minute period; insist that they stop immediately when you tell them to stop.

Help them pace themselves through the translation. Call off the minutes, saying "First minute's up, move on to the next two words; second minute's up, etc." (In the second segment, you will be giving them four words per minute; then six, then eight, etc.) As you increase the speed, insist that they stay with it. Have people pay attention to their feelings as they stick with a certain speed: are they bored? As the speed increases, do they feel their stress levels rising?

As each person begins to hit intolerable stress levels, they should quit translating and wait until everyone is done.

When everyone is finished, take ten or fifteen minutes to let the whole group discuss what happened, what people felt as they proceeded; whether the slower translators felt guilt or shame as they dropped out; whether the faster translators felt a competitive need to be better than everyone else, and so suppressed feelings of stress in order to "win the race."

Be sure and stress that there is no one "optimum" speed for translators; it would be all too easy to turn this exercise into an opportunity for gloating and humiliation. Nor is it a good idea to collect the students' translations, or to compare "error rates" in class. The idea here is not competition, but experience: each student should be able to explore his or her own speed and attitudes about rapid translation in a safe environment.

2   Either bring in a source text or have the students themselves bring one in from a translation seminar or actual translation task. Then set up the situation:

They are to imagine themselves as simultaneously "here" and somewhere else. The "here" is the classroom; the somewhere else is a place or time when they experienced burnout, or were very close to burning out. Talk them through it: have them remember an experience of burnout or near-burnout; have them summon up the feelings they felt then. As they begin to relive the desperation of that time, begin to shift them imaginatively "back" into the classroom as well, so that while they imagine themselves in that other place and time they are also in front of you, where they are required to translate the text in front of them. They don't actually have to do the translation; but they have to try to convince themselves that they have to, and perhaps even put pencil to paper in the first attempt to do the translation. Create as much realistic pressure as you can: they must finish the translation by the end of the class period; they will be graded on their performance, and their grade on this "test" will constitute 50 percent of their grade for the term; errors will not be tolerated; no distinction will be made between minor and major errors; two errors will constitute failure. All errors will be read aloud to the class, and the other students will be encouraged to ridicule the "bad" translator.

All through this experience they should be monitoring their feelings about this pressure with one part of their mind while feeling them with another.

After fifteen to twenty minutes of the "desperate" part of the exercise, move to the "happy" or "hopeful" part. Tell them to stand up, shake themselves, stretch, jog in place, walk around, get a drink of water, etc. Then have them sit back down and work in groups – except that this time all the pressure is off, no deadlines, no grades. Also, they are to come up with the funniest "wrong" translation – an assignment that will guarantee a good deal of fun.

Leave ten to fifteen minutes at the end of class to discuss their feelings about the two different translation experiences. Have them ponder whether either situation is a "realistic" one – and whether, even if they are never actually required to translate in this or that exact way, it might be possible for them to *put* themselves into one of the two mental states they experienced in the exercise, by worrying too much, or by sharing difficult translation experiences with coworkers or friends.

This exercise can also be done entirely in small groups; in this case the students themselves will be expected to "inflict" the symbolic burnout on each other, each student pushing the others to remember and feel as much burnout as possible, threatening them with terrible things if they fail, and then focusing those desperate feelings on the text, as if they were required to translate it by the end of class. Once again, leave time at the end of class to discuss the experience with the whole group.

Students can also be asked to explore their experience through other channels: by drawing or diagraming it, acting it out in their small groups, telling stories, etc.

3 The translator as learner

We don't know nearly enough about translators. Who are they? What kinds of childhood did they have? What got them interested in languages? Do they prefer to learn languages from books, in classrooms, in relationships, in the "native" country? Where do they work? How do they work? And so on.

This book makes many generalizations about translators, and how people become translators. Because so little sociological research has been done on translators and translator populations, these generalizations are highly problematic: based on the author's own experience and anecdotes told by friends, colleagues, and students, or postings to Lantra-L. Are translators really like this or that? Is this really the way people become translators?

Generally speaking, whenever a student disagrees with some generalization this book makes about translators – "This isn't true of me, or of any of the other translators I know!" – it is worthwhile to stop and discuss the differences. Sometimes they will be so minor as not to be worth extensive discussion. Sometimes they will stem from a discrepancy between some translator ideal with which the student identifies strongly and a specific claim this book makes about the professional realities of translation: the importance of sublimation for rapid translation, for example. In these latter cases the teacher may agree with the book, but will want to get the student to make the discovery on her or his own, by working through her or his own experience.

But sometimes the discrepancies will arise from the fact that the complex variety of translators is far greater than any generalization could ever hope to capture. People translate for many different reasons, get very different satisfactions from the job, hate different aspects of it, etc. And this chapter is devoted to some of those differences.

Implications of learning-style theory for teaching

Traditional teaching methods favor a certain rather narrow learning-style profile:

- field-independent (willing to work in artificial contexts such as the classroom)
- structured-environment (a lesson plan, a set beginning and ending time, desks in rows and columns, a teacher with authority and students trained to submit to that authority)
- content-driven (it doesn't matter how a thing is taught)
- sequential-detailed/linear (take everything one step at a time and assume that everyone will learn each step as it comes along and be ready to move on to the next one)
- conceptual/abstract (it is more effective for both time-management and learning to formulate rules and processes out of complex practical experience and present them to students in abstract theoretical forms)
- externally-referenced (students learn best by submitting to the teacher's authority)
- matching (counterexamples, deviations, problem areas, conflicted issues, contradictions, arguments should be avoided in class, as

they only distract students from the main point being taught, which is a unified body of knowledge that they are expected to internalize); and

- analytical-reflective (translation proceeds most effectively when translators have been taught a set of precepts, which they then thoughtfully apply to every text they receive *before* they actually begin translating it).

And as the chapter suggests, this approach does work with some students. Some people do prefer to learn this way. Many, however, do not. It has traditionally been assumed that those who do not learn effectively in the established ways are inferior students and should either "shape up" (learn to conform to accepted teaching and learning methods) or "drop out" (go do something else with their lives). Brain research over the past two or three decades has shown, however, that *everyone's* brain thrives on far more variety and change than traditional teaching methods have allowed – and that learners often scorned as "stupid" or "slow" or "disruptive" are no less intelligent or creative than the "good" students favored by a traditional classroom (Sylwester, 1995, Caine and Caine 1994). In this light, narrowly conventional teaching methods are quite simply counterproductive. They discriminate against large groups of learners, and that is inequitable; but even more importantly, they severely limit society's access to the capabilities and ideas of its members, and that is wasteful.

A more progressive classroom, therefore, one that remains open to the widest possible variety of learning styles, will be structured rather differently than the traditional one: it will

- keep field-dependent and field-independent learning in a fruitful tension, switching frequently between hands-on experience in natural contexts and more academic, conceptual, abstract, theoretical learning in artificial contexts
- keep contextual-global and sequential-detailed learning too in a fruitful tension, switching frequently between intuitive and inferential formulations of the "big picture" and sequential analyses of minute details
- model and encourage a constant shifting between external and internal referencing, helping students to test the pronouncements of external authorities (including the teacher) against their own

experience and to test their own opinions against the systems and ideas of translation theorists

- both match and mismatch, encouraging students to seek out both similarities and dissimilarities, conformities and deviations, accepted models and problems with those models, and to explore the connections between them

- keep the environment flexible, allowing people to move around in the classroom, stand up or sit down or lie down, according to their own preferences; it will sometimes be noisy, sometimes quiet; different types of music will be played

- be relationship-driven, with the teacher and all the students being recognized as important contributors to the learning process, and as much responsibility placed on the students as on the teacher for learning; and

- be multisensory and multimodal, using as many different input channels as possible, including visualization and dramatization as well as open-ended conversation.

Discussion

1 This topic offers an opportunity to discuss any reservations you or your students may be having about the exercises in this book, here in connection with memory research. We develop many procedural memories in university classrooms: how to act when we walk in, how to interact with students or the teacher, etc. Students can formulate some of those procedural memories that they have developed in and for university classrooms, and reflect on their attitudes toward the exercises in this book in terms of those habits. And what procedural memories have you developed for the classroom? Even the most innovative teachers, who are constantly changing their teaching style in response to student needs, have procedural memories or "ruts" that govern whole large segments of their teaching. What are yours?

2 This is a chance to get students to discuss their experience as translators and the routines they've developed to help them do their work more effectively: typing skills, terminology management, transfer patterns, interpreting skills, etc. This is not only to

help them develop those routines further; it is also to help them develop professional pride in their skills, professional self-esteem.

3   Many people are strongly convinced that becoming aware of what they do and why is not only unnecessary or irrelevant, but actively harmful. They may say that this chapter, and perhaps the book as a whole as well, is a waste of time – time better spent learning to transfer specific words and phrases from one specific language to another. They may be so attached to subliminal processing that they are afraid that too much awareness will slow them down – even, ironically enough, when one of the ideas to which they are subliminally attached is that they translate consciously and analytically, not subliminally. Most of us are trained not to delve too deeply into the inner workings of things, especially our own minds – we are afraid of what we will find, what skeletons will come tumbling out of the closet. This discussion topic provides a chance to air some of these feelings. This early in the semester you may not yet know which students are most and which least receptive to this approach; the less receptive ones may well feel that discussing their negative attitudes is just as big a waste of time as everything else in the book, but they can be encouraged to articulate their attitudes as carefully as possible. Other students may feel excited and empowered to find themselves in several different learning styles, and so to learn more about themselves.

4   The problem, of course, is that the simplifications that are so helpful in directing our attention to specific subareas of our behavior also distort the complexity of that behavior. Everyone has at least a little of every "learning style" ever analyzed. It is therefore utterly false for anyone to say "my learning style is X." It is almost certainly X, Y, and Z, and a lot of other letters as well. The kinds of simplifications associated with logical or analytical thinking are extremely useful in screening out vast segments of a field so as to concentrate on a single thing at once; but it is very easy to become so enamored of the simplified image that emerges from such thinking that we forget the bigger and more complex picture.

This discussion topic, therefore, encourages you and your students to explore the tensions between simplified and complex perceptions of things in terms of the learning styles examined in the chapter. Some people, sequential-analytical learners, will find the chapter's simplified "grid" of learning styles very attractive; others, global-contextual learners, may feel very uncomfortable with all the minute distinctions that seem to ignore so many gray areas. "But I'm *all* of these things!" they may protest. "I'm this way in some moods, that way in others!" Encouraging students to reconsider the material in the chapter in this broader, more complex way will give your global-contextual learners a chance to express their dissatisfaction with the chapter's presentational style and to brainstorm about alternative ways of studying learning styles, and thus give them a chance to learn the material through more comfortable channels. (Global-contextual learners may feel more comfortable with Figure 1 on pp. 60–1; certainly visual ones will.) This discussion may also cause sequential-analytical learners some distress; they may react by calling more global-contextual approaches too vague and impressionistic to be of any use to anybody, and by dismissing this discussion topic as a waste of the class's time. This, of course, provides you and the other students with an excellent example of the importance of learning styles.

5   This topic is likely to be of greatest interest to students who are unsympathetic to the book's approach: it will allow them to express their sense (which is quite true) that this isn't the whole truth about translation, it's only a single perspective. But it also encourages more sympathetic students to think critically not only about the specific models offered and claims made in this book, but about their learning processes in general – especially in relation to "authoritative" knowledge, facts or procedures presented to them by authorities (like you and me). Many of them will have been taught to memorize vocabulary by staring at a word list on a piece of paper, or perhaps by mumbling the words out loud to themselves; this book argues that that method is less effective than learning vocabulary in real human social contexts. Which is true for *them?* Do they learn well both ways, but differently? What difference does it make for them to "experience" some learning styles through prepared tests (exercises 4–5), others through tests they make up themselves (exercise 6)?

You may even want to ask them to reformulate the main points in this book through their own learning styles. What would the book be like then? Would it be a textbook at all? (Some might prefer for it to be more like technical documentation, or a cook-book, or rules to a board game, or a collection of aphorisms or Zen koans, or a single pithy reminder that they could tape to their computer monitor.)

6   The clear and present danger here, of course, is that students will feel obliged to describe you as their teacher-ideal. We're all susceptible to flattery – only a sociopathic monster does not want to be liked and admired, and a good number of us secretly hope our students will think us the very best teacher they ever had – and since we hold several forms of power over our students (the power to give grades, to give or withhold praise, to ridicule, etc.), it is usually in our students' best interests to butter us up. There are, however, two problems with this: one is that students learn nothing from such exercises (except perhaps that you too are a sucker for flattery); the other is that they know that such shams have nothing to do with their learning, everything to do with your ego. The higher you let them build your self-esteem, therefore, the lower you drop in their esteem. The only way to come out of this sort of discussion with any respect (not to mention getting your students to think critically), in fact, is to encourage them to tell you straight out, or even to hint obliquely at, what *you* could be doing better.

One way to achieve this, at least in some cultures, is to have the students first discuss their preferences in teachers and teaching styles in smaller groups, and then bring their findings to the whole group. (In many cultures, students' deference toward teachers is too deeply ingrained for them ever to utter a word of criticism against their teacher. There, this sort of exercise may just be an exercise in futility, better skipped altogether.) Whole-group beha-vior is public behavior, subject to the strictest restraints: a student speaking up in front of the whole class knows that s/he has to please you without losing her or his classmates' respect. In small groups, it is easier for students to build up a small measure of student solidarity, which may provide enough peer-support that it becomes possible to express some carefully worded criticism of your teaching.

7   The general answer here is: become more active. Play a more active role in the class. Just what that "activity" means will depend largely on who their teacher is and what kind of school

culture they've been raised in. In an extremely authoritarian classroom, for example, being more active may mean paying more attention – and then the important question would be how that is done. (Do you just tell yourself to pay more attention? If you're falling asleep, do you pinch yourself, rub the sleep out of your eyes, try to move your body in small ways? Or do you look for something in the lecture that connects with your personal experience?) In less structured environments, it might mean talking more in class, negotiating with the teacher about the type of classwork and homework assigned, even helping to teach the class. There are numerous ways of becoming more active; each one, depending on the specific classroom environment in which it is applied, will require a different balancing act between the student's needs (for relevance, connection, active engagement, etc.) and the teacher's needs (for control, respect, dignity, etc.).

Exercises

1 This exercise could be done very briefly in the context of discussion (while discussing topic 1 or 2, for example): you could ask the students to do the exercise individually, on their own, in about five minutes, and then return to the discussion to share their experiences with the rest of the class. (The need for specific hands-on experiences for learning to be effective is a good example of one of the points made in this chapter, and a strong justification for the book's heavy emphasis on exercises.) Or you could divide them up into groups before the discussion begins, letting them do the exercise with three or four other students; then when it comes time to share their experiences in the large-group discussion they will have the solidarity of their small group to support them in joining in the conversation.

2 Here students are asked to enter into a fairly typical collaborative translation situation and pay attention to what is going on in their own heads and in their interactions with fellow students in terms of memory and learning. Learning-style theorists would say that the most important experience for students to pay attention to will be mismatches: the places where other students' translations differ from theirs, and why. Mismatches generate "problems," and

problems force students to focus on the nature of an interaction. Encourage them to pay special attention to even the smallest mismatches or differences that arise.

This exercise also anticipates a process that is central to Chapters 5–10: the inductive process of generating working theories out of practical experience.

3   This can be run as a long-term project – lasting two or three weeks, say. You can encourage students either to work on their own or to form their own groups, as they please, and to work both in and out of class to develop interesting teaching methods to try out on the other students. You may or may not want to provide them with behind-the-scenes help – private meetings, visual aids (videos, slides, posters, etc.), secondary sources on effective teaching strategies – but if you provide some students with such help, you'd better provide it to all who want it.

It may also be necessary to prepare the class for the evaluation process. Some school cultures will encourage the other students to be very harsh; other school cultures will require that nothing but positive feedback be given. Neither extreme is particularly helpful; and students may need some help in learning to mix praise with constructive criticism. (Depending on your students, how responsible and thoughtful you think they are, it may help the process to ask them to decide on a grade or mark for the presenter(s); then again, this sort of "official" grading procedure can also destroy all spontaneity and enjoyment in the evaluation process.)

Be sure and give students a chance to discuss the meaning or significance of this exercise – to step back from their immediate or "gut" reaction to a teaching presentation ("Great!" "It was horrible!") to a more careful weighing of the various responses. An enjoyable lesson may be superficial; an apparently boring lesson may require a quieter receptivity for its true value to emerge. Make sure students try out several different perspectives on the various presentations.

And above all: if the students overwhelmingly prefer a certain approach that is significantly unlike yours, but also amenable to your personality, consider giving it a try – *with* this class.

4–5   These tests are typically very popular with students. It is excit-
       ing to find more out about yourself, and the exercises use a
       series of testing formats familiar from many popular magazines
       ("rank your sex life!"). To save class time you can assign one
       or more tests as homework; but they are considerably more
       enjoyable in class, with you reading the questions aloud and
       each student answering individually on paper, or with the stu-
       dents taking the tests in small groups. Most people seem to find
       it more interesting to explore individual differences with others
       present. It is also important, of course, to discuss the findings
       afterward: were the students surprised at what they found? How
       well do the test results fit with other things they know about
       themselves? How might they want to develop certain "second-
       ary" learning styles that showed up in the tests but were not as
       heavily emphasized or "preferred" as certain others?

       This chapter in general and these three exercises in particular
       also offer many potential research avenues for students to
       pursue at any level: they can take one or more of the tests to
       translators they know (or even some that they do not know) and
       study the results. With considerable additional research into
       learning styles, the tests could also be adapted to research at
       the M.A. or Ph. D. levels.

6   This exercise will require a great deal of creativity from your
       students; if you have time, it might be best to give them several
       weeks to work on it, as small-group projects. If that is imprac-
       tical, you might want to divide the students into groups of four
       or five in class, giving each group a learning-style test (a–f) and
       letting them have twenty to thirty minutes to plan their strategy:
       choose a test format, divide up the work among the various
       group members, exchange phone numbers or e-mail addresses,
       etc. Then have them give the test to the whole class the next
       day.

       As they work on their tests, encourage them to draw on many
       different use situations from everyday life, including as many
       pertaining to translation as possible.

7–8   These two modification exercises probably require more time
       than a single class period: students should probably be given a
       night or two (possibly even a week) to work on one, alone or
       in a group. Both exercises are likely to appeal to internally

referenced and intuitive-experimental students, who may have been chafing at having to do exercises invented and directed by someone else. But the creative process of modifying exercises will benefit the others in the group as well: even if the idea and act of taking charge of this sort of classroom activity may make some feel uneasy, it is the best way for them to explore the practical consequences of their own learning styles.

4 The process of translation

This chapter presents the general theoretical model on which the whole book is based; an additional topic for class discussion might deal with what good theoretical models are, how they help us, and also how they restrict our imaginations, how they block us from seeing other things that might be equally important but according to the model don't "exist." The main idea is that professional translators shuttle back and forth between "subliminal" translation, which is fast and largely unconscious, and alert, analytical translation, which is slow and highly conscious. The former mode is made up of lots of experiences of the latter mode: every time you solve a problem slowly, painstakingly, analytically, it becomes easier to solve similar problems in the future, because you turn the analytical process into a subliminal one. Also, one of the things you "sublimate" is the sense that certain types of textual features cannot be handled subliminally: they set off "alarm bells" that bring you up out of the "fast" mode and initiate the "slow" one.

Some students may shy away from the theoretical model – especially, perhaps, the terms, such as abductive/inductive/deductive. Since those terms will appear throughout the third section, it is important to deal with any feelings of mistrust or rejection students may have toward them at this point – especially by talking about them in an open-ended way, without trying to ram the terminology or the model down anyone's throat. A good approach here might be to discuss your own reservations about them – you are not likely to feel entirely comfortable either, since you didn't think them up yourself, and talking about the process by which you tested them against your own experience and partly overcame your mistrust, partly decided to set it aside, may help. If some student(s) cannot get over their mistrust, reassure them by saying that suspicion of theoretical frameworks is an important part of critical thinking, and encourage them to continue to critique the model as they proceed in the book. It is not essential for the students to accept the model as "true," or the best possible one; only that they agree to use it provisionally as *one* explanation of translation.

Discussion

One possible scenario: when scholars theorize a process, they have to be as conscious as they can in order to become aware of details, their connections to other details, any discrepancies or conflicts between details and different parts of the explanatory model, etc. It is quite natural, then, for them to project this conscious analytical state onto the process they're studying, and assume that the people engaged in it – in this case, translators – are doing much the same sort of thing they are doing when they theorize it. In this reading, the one crucial detail of which the theorists do not become conscious would be the critical *differences* between theorizing and translating – the fact (if it is one) that translators work much less consciously than theorists.

Another, more radical scenario: it only *seems* natural for theorists to project their own conscious, analytical state onto translators because that is the state in which, traditionally in the rationalist West, all important human processes are supposed to take place. Because we have been taught to idealize total alert consciousness and to associate with that state certain rational, logical, analytical processes, we "see" it in any human activity that we similarly want to idealize. If translation, then, is a respectable profession, translators *must* work rationally, logically, analytically, consciously; and, contrariwise, if anyone says that they don't, that constitutes an attack on the respectability of the profession. In this interpretation, rationalist ideals condition "empirical" perception to the point where we think we see what we want to see.

And one more step: perhaps theorists do not work as consciously and analytically as they like to think either. This would explain the fact (if it is a fact) that translation theorists have been so unable or unwilling to "see" translator behavior that doesn't fit their explanatory model. In this interpretation, the model does their thinking for them; because they have internalized or "sublimated" the model, it seems as if they are thinking consciously, analytically, etc., but in fact they are only the channels through which the model imposes itself on the world.

A good argument could also be made for the interpretation that the model developed in this book works in much the same way: that it arises less out of a "true" empirical perception of the way translators actually translate, and more out of the author's personal unconscious predilections, or what Chapter 3 would call his "learning styles." Discussion topic 5 in Chapter 3 (p. 84) raises this very possibility. If you want to advance this last argument in class, you may want to review Chapter 3 and the suggestions for teachers for that particular exercise.

Exercises

1   This exercise can be (1) run by the teacher, with all the students participating at once, calling out suggestions of habits that run their lives; (2) done in small groups, with each group responsible for coming up with a list of ten or so habits that they rely on in their day-to-day living; or (3) done individually, as homework, with each student going home to think about the question and coming to class the next day prepared to discuss it. This third approach could also be set up as a research project: each student goes and talks to the people who know him or her best, parents, spouses, lovers, roommates, and asks them to list his or her habits – irritating and otherwise. However the material on habits is collected, be sure and give students a chance to air and discuss them with the whole class.

Students can also be asked to present their findings through other channels than the auditory: by drawing "habit diagrams" of their typical day, by dramatizing their habits, etc.

2   This exercise could take the same forms as exercise 1: whole-group discussion run by the teacher, small-group work, individual homework or research project. The process here will be slightly different, however, since in this exercise the students are not just noticing habits, but exploring memories of how they came to be habits. The similarity between the two processes should also be clear, however: since habits are things that we rarely notice, we

may need other people's help to *see* them at all, to realize that this or that thing we do is highly habitualized.

Again, various visual or dramatic channels might be used to present findings.

3   This exercise can be done fairly quickly, in class discussion (either with the full group or in smaller groups), just to give students some sense of the variety of linguistic problem areas in their language combination – and, of course, of their own awareness of those problems, their own sense of the alarm bells that do (or should) go off. Or it could be turned into a longer project, involving the keeping of a translator's log or journal as they work on translations for other classes and the analysis and/or classification of the problem areas that they find in their own work. Be sure and get them to reflect on and articulate what it feels like when an "alarm bell" goes on in their head while translating.

5 Experience

This chapter is about experience, the translator's experience of the world in general, of language, people, and so on – an introduction to the series of experiences in Chapters 6–10. What this emphasis on "experience" may not make immediately clear, however, is that it is also about learning. In almost every way, experience *is* learning. We learn only through experience – whether that experience is in the classroom or out. We learn things by listening to other people talk about them, reading about them, having them happen to us, or making them happen. People talk to us about things in lectures, on the television and the radio, in church, on the telephone, in cafes and restaurants and bars, in streets and stores, in living rooms and kitchens and bedrooms. We can learn in all of those places. We read about things in books – textbooks and novels, encyclopedias and nonfiction paperbacks, dictionaries and travel books, humor and collections of crossword puzzles – magazines and newspapers, letters and faxes and e-mail, usenets and the World Wide Web. Things happen to us at work and at home, with other people and alone, with lovers and spouses and friends and total strangers; the things that happen are wonderful or devastating, earth-shaking or trivial, things that we plan and things that take us by surprise, things that we want to tell others about and things that we are ashamed to tell anyone. We make things happen by wanting to learn something specific (play a musical instrument, learn a foreign language) or by vaguely craving a change in a humdrum life; with ideas (democracy, love, salvation, change) and with objects (guns, blueprints, fire).

These are obvious channels of learning, of course – but a surprising number of students believe that learning only takes place in the classroom. It seems to be a part of school culture in many parts of the world (possibly even everywhere) to believe that school is the source and setting of all learning; that beyond the classroom walls (in street or popular culture, in families and workplaces and bars) lies ignorance. If you have students who believe this, their learning outside of school is probably entirely unconscious. But even in school much of what we learn is unconscious: that teacher X is an ignoramus who doesn't know how to teach, teacher Y is sad and lonely and bitter, hates kids, and burned out years ago, and teacher Z is a pedagogical genius who should be in the history books; that learning is not supposed to be fun ("no pain, no gain"); that "good" students always (act as if they) agree with the teacher and only "bad" students dare to disagree; that a teacher who encourages you to disagree or argue with him or her, or to develop independent and original views on things, probably doesn't really mean it, and will punish you in subtle ways if you act on such encouragement; or that (in teacher Z's classroom) learning is exciting, challenging, chaotic, unpredictable, and mostly enjoyable, but may also make you angry or anxious; that being a teacher would be the worst fate you can imagine (if many of your teachers are like teacher Y) or the greatest job on earth (if even a few of your teachers are like teacher Z). All of this is learned in school – but neither the teachers teaching it nor the students learning it realize that this learning is going on.

Depending on how comfortable you are with challenges to your teacherly authority, you might even want to get your students to talk about the unconscious lessons you've been teaching them. Of course, the more uncomfortable you are with such things, the stronger these lessons will have been, and the more adamantly the students will refuse to enumerate them for you – unless you let them do so anonymously (by writing a list of five things they've learned from you that you didn't know you were teaching, for example). The more comfortable you are with such discussions, the more likely it is that you have them with your students all the time anyway: they are powerful channels of critical thinking, self-reflection, metalearning – of getting students to reflect critically on how and when and why they learn, so that they can maximize the transformative effect of their learning all through their lives.

The important thing to bear in mind through Chapters 5–10 is that inductive experience remains the best teacher – far more effective than deduction, the use of rules and laws and abstract theories. Students cannot be expected to internalize an entire deductive system of translation in the abstract and then go out and start translating competently. In fact, without hands-on exercises and other practical experiences they cannot be expected even to *understand* an entire deductive system of translation – not because they are students, but because they are human, and human beings learn through doing. Deduction can be a powerful and productive prod to learning; it can force people to rethink a rigid or narrow position, or to return to their ordinary lives with a fresher eye for novel experiences, things that their previous assumptions could not explain. But the prod is only part of the learning process, which must continue long after the prodding is done – and continue specifically in ways that build bridges between "knowing that" and "knowing how," knowing something in the abstract and being able to do something in the real world.

Discussion

1–4   Remember that there are no right answers here. These are questions that people are likely to feel very strongly about, to the point of believing that their position is not only right but the only possible one. Those who can really only learn foreign languages well by living in the country are going to insist that that is the only legitimate way to become a translator; those who are very good at learning languages from books or classes, and indeed have learned several languages that way (and perhaps have never left the country in which they were born) will disagree strongly. Some people have very strong opinions on the issue of how to improve your native language: lots of grounding in grammar classes and strict prescriptive rules; a thorough familiarity with the great classics in the language; total immersion in pop and street culture; or simply a good ear. There are good translators who started off in language classes or a foreign country and only later, as professional translators, started learning a technical subject or specialization; and there are good translators who started off as engineers or lawyers or medical students and only later began to work with languages. Some will argue that you should never accept a job in a language combination for which your ability is not absolutely tiptop professional – never into a foreign language, never out of a language that you only know slightly, etc. – and some that it doesn't really matter how well you know the language, you can always have your work checked. Let them fight it out – the main thing being not to reach a conclusion but to explore the implications of thinking either way, and (especially) of basing a general principle on one's own experiences and preferences.

5   There are two fairly well-defined camps on this question. On the one hand, you have people arguing that there is no room for intuition at all, you either know the word or phrase or you don't, and if you don't, you should find out – not "guess," which is how this camp tends to portray intuition. On the other hand, you have people (like the author of this book) arguing that intuition is inevitable, that all translators rely on intuition constantly, and that even "knowing" a word or a phrase is largely or even entirely an intuitive act. If any middle ground is to be found, it may be that translators tend to begin more tentatively, afraid to trust *either* their intuitions or their knowledge, and to grow in confidence with practice – an important point to stress because a rigid condemnation of all intuition may well frighten off the less confident students, who *know* they don't know enough to translate with total certainty (nobody does).

6   This is another very general discussion topic aimed at exploring the pedagogical assumptions underlying this book – which are stated vis-à-vis this topic in the Introduction, namely, that it is important to chart out a middle ground between the two extremes raised in the topic. Practical/experiential learning (abduction/induction) needs to be sped up with various holistic

methods; precepts and abstract theories (deduction) needs to be brought to life experientially.

Exercises

1   This exercise can be done either by individual students on their own (in class or at home) or by small groups of students working together. For example, the students could work in pairs, each partner telling the other his or her experiences of cultural change. The advantage of this latter approach is that some students working alone may not be able to remember any changes – or may never have been to a foreign culture – and other people's memories may help them remember or imagine such changes. If none of your students has ever been to a foreign culture, of course, the exercise will not work very well – unless you adjust it for knowledge of foreign cultures through foreign-language classrooms, television, etc.

2–4   These exercises are designed to bridge gaps between traditional pedagogies based on grammatical rules and dictionaries and the more experientially based pedagogy offered here. Many precept-oriented teachers, theorists, and students of translation react with contempt to the notion that intuition plays a significant role in translation, claiming instead that "craft" or "professionalism" always entails a fully conscious and analytical following of precepts. The idea here is that intuition is never pure solipsism or subjectivity; it always works in tandem with analytical processes, in part driving those processes (we have an intuitive sense for how to proceed analytically), in part serving as a check on those processes (we sense intuitively that an analysis is leading us in the wrong direction, producing results that run counter to experience of the real world), and in part being checked by those processes (analysis can show us how and where and why our intuitions are wrong and must be retrained).

For the three exercises you will need to find source texts for the students to work on – or you can ask them to bring source texts from other classes. All three exercises could be done with a single source text; or you could move on to a new source text with each exercise. The advantage of using a new text for each one is that students may grow bored with the same text and find less and less to talk about in it with each exercise.

6 People

In a people-oriented book, this chapter and the next are the most people-oriented of all. They make a case for teaching not only terminology but all translation skills through a person-orientation. (See also the introduction to Chapter 7 here in the appendix for further comments.)

Discussion

The consequences of this topic are intensely practical. Some people (philosophically they are called "foundationalists") would argue that the only way it is ever possible for us to understand each other is if the rules are stable, transcendental (i.e., exist in some otherworldly "realm of forms" rather than constantly being reinvented based on actual usage), and thus "foundational" – provide a firm foundation for communication to rest upon. One practical consequence of this belief is that rules become primary in the classroom as well: students must be taught grammar and vocabulary in the abstract, first and foremost, and applications later, if at all ("if we have time . . ."). Drill grammar and vocabulary in the A and B languages, and students will have an excellent foundation for translation skills. Similarly, translation theories must be taught in the abstract as well, so that students are given a systematic theoretical foundation for practice. If possible, of course (again, "if we have time . . ."), they should be given a chance to apply those theories to practice, to test them in practice, or to derive the theories inductively; but if we don't have time (and somehow we never do), well, that's all right too.

If we want to explore other possibilities in the classroom, it is also important to explore other theoretical possibilities for communication, because foundationalists in the department (teachers and students alike) will say, "If you don't start with the rules, with the abstract theories, with *system*, no communication will be possible at all, everything will fall apart, the students won't learn anything, etc."

I developed a countertheory in *The Translator's Turn* (1991); if you're interested in pursuing this theoretical issue at length, you may want to read the first chapter of that book. Generally, however, the "antifoundationalist" or "postfoundationalist" view is that usage (experience of language in actual use situations, writing and speaking) is primary, and the rules are reductive fictions deduced from perceived patterns in usage. People can communicate without absolutely stable rules partly because speech communities regulate language use, and try to make sure that when someone says "dog" everyone thinks of or looks at a canine quadruped; but partly also – and this is important because a speech community's regulation never works completely or perfectly – people can communicate because they work hard at it, restating things that are misunderstood, explaining and clarifying.

Exercises

1–5 These exercises are all designed to help students experience what I have called the "somatics" of language: the fact that we store the meanings of words, phrases, registers, and so on in our bodies, in our autonomic nervous systems, and that our bodies continue to signal to us throughout our lives how and what we are going to mean by those things (Robinson 1991). This means simultaneously that the meanings of "dog" and "cat," taboo words, lower-class words and phrases, baby talk, foreigner talk, and shaming words will all have been shaped powerfully by our speech communities, and thus regulated in collective ways (this is what I call "ideosomatics"); and that those meanings will have acquired more peripheral idiosyncratic ("idiosomatic") meanings as well, through the personal experiential channels by which they reached us (specific dogs and cats, our parents' and teachers' and other adults' attitudes toward swearing and lower-class language, etc.).

All five exercises are typically very enjoyable for students. All five can usually be done in a single hour-long class session.

7 Working people

This chapter maps out an approach to terminology (and related linguistic phenomena such as register) through the interpersonal contexts of its actual use: working people talking. In comparison with the traditional terminology studies approach, this person-oriented focus has both advantages and disadvantages. One of its main disadvantages is that it is difficult to systematize, because it varies so widely over time and from place to place, and therefore also difficult to teach. One of its main advantages is that it is more richly grounded in social experience, and therefore, because of the way the brain works, easier to learn (to store in and retrieve from memory).

This unfortunate clash between ease of teaching and ease of learning creates difficulties for the contextualized "teaching" of terminology, of course, in terms of actual situational real-world usage. A systematized terminology, abstracted from use and presented to students in the organized form of the dictionary or the glossary, seems perfectly suited to the traditional teacher-centered classroom; it is easily assigned to students to be "learned" outside of class, "covered" or discussed in class, and tested. The only difficulty is that the terms learned in this way are harder to remember than terms learned in actual working situations – and, unfortunately, those situations are hard to simulate in class (they are better suited to internships).

The traditional middle ground between learning terminologies from dictionaries and learning terms in the workplace is learning terms from texts: students are handed specialized texts and the teacher either goes over the key terms or has the students find them and perform certain exercises on them. This has the advantage of giving students a use-context for the words, so that instead of learning terms per se, they are learning terms in context. The problem here too is that black marks on a page provide a much more impoverished context than the actual workplace, making these words too hard to remember. Clearly, if the teacher is going to use specialized texts in the classroom, s/he should give the students multimodal exercises to perform on them, such as exercises 1–3 in this chapter. As we saw in Chapter 3, experiencing a thing through several senses not only makes the experience richer and more powerful; it physiologically, neurologically makes it easier to remember and put into practice later. Above all, these exercises give students the abductive experience of having to guess at or construct cohesive principles or imaginative "guides" to a translation – an experience that will stand them in good stead even when they are very familiar with the terminology in the source text. The "cohesion" of any text is always an imaginative construct, something the reader builds out of her or his active imagination; the only real difference between an "abductive" construct such as we've been considering here and an "inductive" construct based on more experience is that the latter is based on more experience, and is thus more likely to be convincing, sound "natural."

One solution to the problem of simulating the workplace in the classroom, of course, is to *leave* the classroom: make a field trip to a local factory where terms found in a source text are used, or to a hospital, or an advertising agency. Go directly to the source. Have students take copious notes or carry a tape recorder. Everywhere stress interpersonal connections, getting to know the people who do the jobs, not just the words they use. The words flow out of the people, are part of the people, part of who they are as professionals, and how they see themselves as part of the working world.

Back in the classroom, try exercise 2 – but with the field trip experience. See how much can be recalled through the use of various visual, auditory, tactile, and kinesthetic projections. Exercise 2 is designed to help people recall experiences long past, along with the words that originally accompanied them; but it can also be used to store more recent experiences in vivid ways that will facilitate later recall.

Discussion

1   This question, of course, gets at the heart of the pedagogical philosophy undergirding this book, and as such may provide a good opportunity to get students talking about the kind of learning experience the book is channeling for them, and how they are responding to it. While most people would agree that experientially based learning is more powerful and effective and realistic, even more "natural," than abstract, systematic, or theoretical learning, the latter is nevertheless still considered more "appropriate" for the university classroom (or for that matter any classroom), and some students will continue to feel

uneasy about bringing an experiential component into the realm of abstract theorizing. Most likely, however, the students who feel most uneasy about multimodal experientially based methods in the classroom will also have strong beliefs in the importance of experience *outside* the classroom, and can be engaged in fruitful discussion of the apparent contradictions or conflicts between these two views. Why should the classroom be different? Just because it always has been?

2–3   These questions address two of the most potentially inflammatory statements in the chapter; as discussion topics they provide a chance for students to air their disagreement – and, more importantly, to explore the precise nature of their disagreement *or* agreement.

Some will want to claim, for example, that translators are not fakers or pretenders but highly trained professionals whose work involves a great deal of imitation – which would be quite true. But precisely how do these two ways of formulating the work of translators differ? Only in the amount of professional self-esteem each seems to reflect or project outward to the user community?

Similarly, some will want to insist that the translator *never* pretend to know how to write in an unfamiliar register, but that s/he instead always *learn* first, and *then* imitate. But again, are these two positions really so far apart? Isn't the difference between them mostly one of self-presentation? Certainly for nontranslating users – clients, especially – it may be more effective to present oneself as an expert in a certain register. But is it really essential to maintain that particular form of self-presentation among other translators?

The value of talking about translation as "faking," it seems to me, is that it builds tolerance for the transitional stages in becoming a translator (and, perhaps, a sense of humor, always a good thing!) in translators themselves – especially student translators, who are nervous about having to be experts all of a sudden. Nobody becomes an expert all at once; they only pretend to, while they're learning. Making the jump from beginner to expert seem sudden and drastic, something that happens overnight, may well have the effect of frightening some future translators out of the field.

Exercises

1 For this exercise, students should bring a bilingual dictionary with
   them in class; you will need to bring a tape or CD and something
   to play it with.
      Write up a series of word lists in the students' source or target
   language. (This exercise works differently, but equally well, in
   both directions.) Each list should contain five words of medium
   difficulty that do not quite fit into a single coherent discourse or
   register. For example:

   demonstrator, ordinance, signpost, escalator, plastique
   venerable, vehicular, venereal, vulnerable, virtual
   cylinder, antislip surface, counter, column, revolving door
   float, chute, flatbed, load limit, listserv
   jamb, jack, jig, joist, joint
   manifold, mandatory, manifest, mangle, manhole

   Print each list on a separate sheet of paper and photocopy enough
   for the whole class; or else write them on the board or overhead
   transparency. Then take the class through the following exercises,
   one with each list. (The exercise can be completed in about 30
   minutes if you rush, but works better if you allow 45–60 minutes.)

   (a) Have the students work on the first list (it doesn't matter
        which) with a dictionary, alone; encourage them to be as
        thorough and analytical as possible, even looking up words
        they know and choosing the meaning that they think most
        likely (but don't encourage them to construct a coherent
        context to facilitate the determination of "likelihood" –
        yet). Get them to put their facial muscles into "concentra-
        tion" mode: focused eyes, knitted brow, clenched jaw.
   (b) Next have them work on the second list, still alone, but now
        relaxing, getting comfortable in their chairs, visualizing
        every word, and building a composite image of all five words
        before translating.
   (c) With the third list, have them work alone again, and relaxing
        and visualizing again, but with classical (or other fairly

complex but enjoyable) music playing in the background as they translate.

(d) With the fourth list, start with relaxation, music, and visualization again, but now have the students break up into groups of three or four, discussing context and collectively creating a reasonable and realistic context for the words (imagining a professional context for them, telling a story about them, etc.) before translating them.

(e) With the fifth list, do everything as in (d), but now have the students mime the meanings of the words to each other before translating.

(f) With the sixth list, do everything as in (e), but this time have the students try to come up with the funniest possible *wrong* or *bad* translations.

The exercise can be completed in about 30 minutes if you rush, but works better if you allow 45–60 minutes. Even if you rush, be sure to allow 15–20 minutes after it is over to give students a chance to talk about what they were feeling as the moved from one step to the next. What difference did relaxation make? Music? (Some find music very distracting; others become many times more productive once the music starts playing.) Group work? Mime? Funny wrong translations?

Some, incidentally, may find the idea of doing wrong translations disturbing. Note, however, that the creative process is the same in both right and wrong translations, just a lot more fun, and thus also more productive – generates more possible versions – in the latter. Skeptics can also be directed to the findings of Paul Kussmaul (1995: 39ff.) in his think-aloud protocol research:

> It could be observed in the protocols, especially during incubation, when relaxation was part of the game, that a certain amount of laughter and fooling around took place amongst the subjects if they did not find their solution at once. This, in combination with the "parallel-activity technique" described above, also prevented them from being stuck up a blind alley, and promoted new ideas. Laughter can also be a sign of sympathetic approval on the part of a subject and may help to create the gratification-oriented condition postulated by neurologists.
>
> (1995: 48)

2   This exercise is obviously closely related to (1), differing primar-
    ily, in fact, only in using a whole text instead of a word list. (The
    word list, being simpler, is more "teachable"; the whole text is
    more realistic, and more complicated.) Elements from exercise
    (1) not listed here might in fact be added – especially music.
        Note the somewhat artificial distinction made in this exercise
    between "preparatory" or "pre-translation" activities (a–c) and
    "translation" (d–e). In real life these blur together, of course, but
    it is useful for students to realize what an important role "pre-
    translation" processes play in the act of translation – how essen-
    tial it is to "get in the right frame of mind" to translate something.

3   This exercise can be done by individual students or in small
    groups. Its purpose is to give them a different way of organizing
    dictionary-knowledge about terminology than simply looking up
    individual words, and to enhance their ability to remember what
    they find through this method, using visual representation.

4   The value of this exercise for future translators' knowledge of
    terminology should be obvious. What may not be quite so obvious
    is that it can also serve to develop connections in the working
    world that may one day mean employment for the graduate. This
    is essentially an ethnographic research method; expanded to
    research paper or MA thesis length (especially if the workplace
    they study is a translation division in government or industry), it
    can put students in touch with potential future employers.

8 Languages

This chapter is an attempt to reframe linguistic approaches to translation in terms of *students'* acts of dynamic theorizing – to offer
students analytical and imaginative tools with which to transform
static, formalistic, and heavily idealized linguistic theories into mental processes in which they too can participate. The chapter is based
on the dual assumption that (1) the use of language is primary, and is
steeped in specific language-use situations in which we try to figure
out what the other person is saying, gradually building up a sense of
the patterns and regularities in speech and writing; and (2) abstract
linguistic structures are deductive patterns that grow out of that
process of sense-making, *not* (as linguists beginning with Saussure

believe) ideal structures that exist prior to speech and are, alas, mangled by actual speakers. Abstract linguistic structures are the inventions of linguists trying to reduce the complexity of language to logical forms. And that is a perfectly natural part of language use. We always try to find patterns; and because language is too complex for the patterns we find, we always overgeneralize. Overgeneralization is not only a natural but also a valuable reaction to complexity; in this sense linguists perform an important function. It is essential, however, that we remember what we (and linguists) are doing, that we are overgeneralizing, reducing complexity to an artificial simplicity – that we not start believing, with Saussure and Chomsky and the linguistic tradition, that we are somehow uncovering the "true underlying structure" of language.

Discussion

1 This topic is obviously designed to let students explore some of the ideas introduced just above, in the introduction to this chapter's appendix entry. Depending on where you stand on the issue of "what language is" or "what linguists do," you may want to (1) articulate my assumptions as spelled out above as a target for student critiques (if you disagree with me strongly and want to encourage students to do the same); (2) articulate those assumptions as something for students to think about and consider as an interesting (but not necessarily correct) alternative to linguistic approaches, and an explanation for why the book says the things it says (if you're flexible and openminded about these things); (3) present my assumptions as the truth (if you're completely in agreement and want to encourage students to join you there); (4) some combination of the above. Personally, I'd prefer (2). But it's your classroom.

2 Here again, the notion that every overgeneralization about language, including linguistic analyses, is an overgeneralization is only "insulting" if we want to assume that linguistic analyses describe a true underlying reality called *la langue* or competence. If linguistics is just an interesting and useful way of reducing the complexity of language to a workable analytical simplicity – an intellectual fiction, of potentially great heuristic value – then it is

fundamentally no different from the overgeneralizations any of us come up with to explain the language we use.

Exercises

1–2 Both of these exercises are designed to encourage students to look closely at linguistic approaches to translation, one (Nida and Taber) more prescriptive, the other (Baker) more descriptive – specifically in terms of their own inductive processes, their own work toward formulating patterns and regularities in language and translation. Just as the deduction section of the chapter suggested ways in which the theories of Catford and Hatim and Mason might be loosened up, converted from rigid structures to learning processes – and in this sense Figure 6 on p. 178 is crucial – so too are these exercises designed to help students explore the learning processes behind Nida and Taber and Baker (and, by extension, the other linguistic translation theorists they read).

The main consideration here is this: students are all too often presented with theories as *faits accomplis*, prefabricated structures that they are expected to observe from a distance (sometimes a very short distance) and memorize. They are neither required nor allowed to test the theories against their own experience, much less attempt to derive the theories on their own. But we know that deriving things on one's own is the best way to learn them. This is, in fact, most probably what translators and translation students mean when they complain about theory: not so much that it has no practical application (though that is often how they express it), but that they are given no chance to explore or experiment with its practical applications. It is presented to them as an inert object to be internalized. Indeed, since academic decorum frowns on theorists explaining in detail how they arrived at a certain theoretical formulation, and especially on theorists leaving things open-ended, half-articulated (perhaps with the suggestion that readers finish the thinking process on their own), students and other readers are given the impression that there is nothing more to be said, nothing to add to or subtract from the formulation, and therefore no place into which the reader could insert himself or herself as a thinker-in-process.

(As Shoshana Felman (1983) notes wryly, J. L. Austin's willingness to remain in process with his thinking about speech acts in *How to Do Things with Words* (1962/1976) scandalized his followers, notably John Searle: Austin developed the distinction between constative and performative speech acts, realized that the distinction didn't really work, and so, halfway through his book, discarded it and started over. This is *not* how academic books are supposed to proceed! The advantage of Austin's approach from a student's or other critical reader's point of view, however, is that it leaves room for them to participate, join in the inductive process of moving from complexity to simplicity – rather than simply taking it or leaving it, or, worse, simply memorizing it.)

I should also note that this dynamic underlies my insistence on building into this book exercises and discussion topics that encourage students to explore how I put the book together and why I did it that way, and how they would do things differently had it been theirs to write. It is not that I am some sort of masochist, wanting to be attacked; it is rather that I believe that students learn best if they actively construct knowledge rather than passively receive it, and that *always* involves or requires the ability to analyze and challenge and criticize received wisdom.

9 Social networks

This chapter explores the social nature of translation: how translators interact with other people to learn (and keep learning) language, to develop and improve translation skills, to get and do translation jobs, to get paid for them, etc. Because this particular sociological approach to translation has been most powerfully developed by the German *skopos/Handlung* school, the chapter concludes with a brief exposition of their theoretical models, along with exercises designed to help students understand those models better.

1   The main stability lost in a shift from text-based to action-based theories is the notion of textual equivalence, which becomes a nonissue in *skopos/Handlung* theories. For people who believe that translation (and translation studies) is and should remain text-based, focused on stable structures of linguistic equivalence between a source text and a target text, this approach will seem not only impossibly vague and general but not really about translation at all. Translation studies, they believe, should be about *translation*, which is equivalence between texts – not about translators in some huge sociological context. The *skopos/Handlung* theorists, on the other hand, argue that those sociological contexts are precisely where such things as the type of equivalence desired are determined.

This also means, of course, that any claim to universality is lost: a focus on the sociological contexts in which equivalence is determined will inevitably relativize discussions of the "correct" translation, because different people in different contexts will expect different types of correctness. For people who prefer absolutes and universals, this relativism will seem dangerous – it will seem to be saying to students that anything goes. It doesn't, of course – in those real-world contexts, anything does *not* go, translation is very closely regulated by sociological forces – but the comforts of universal absolutes are indeed lost.

2   The idea here is to give students a chance to talk about their fears and anxieties, and to help them to work through them to a greater sense of confidence in their own abilities. Students who are inclined to heap abuse on such fears should be gently but firmly discouraged from doing so in class.

3   This is a good chance for you to do some proselytizing for your national and/or regional translator organization or union, and to encourage students to join, buy their literature, attend their conferences (even, perhaps, offer to present their projects from this class at those conferences). If you are personally active in that group, share your experiences with them. Figure out ways to get the students to attend a conference – does the department have funds to help students attend? Would a fund-raiser be possible?

4   Social groups are often thought of as airtight categories: each person will be a member of certain groups, and other people will be members of other groups, with no overlaps. Obviously, this is not the case. Not only will people who are members of different groups also at some level be members of the same group – at the highest level, of course, we're all members of the human race – but the boundaries between groups are often fuzzy. Racially, for example, there are probably as many people of mixed race as there are of "pure" ones (if indeed such a thing exists). Not only are there many people with dual nationalities; immigrants and people living in borderlands often have mixed national and cultural loyalties. Even gender is fuzzy: some men are more feminine, some women more masculine; gays, lesbians, and bisexuals blur the gender lines; and there is even a small group of hermaphrodites who are biologically both male and female.

5   This topic is aimed implicitly at this entire book, and specifically Chapters 5–10 of the book, which constitute a series of bridges between theories and practice. At the extremes of the discussion, some will argue that theorists should serve practice by telling translators how to translate (usually a highly unpopular position among translators, for obvious reasons, but one that some translators do nonetheless hold), while others will claim that theory is useless for practice and should not be studied at all. Once these extreme positions have been aired, it will be most fruitful to explore the middle ground between them: how can theories be *made* useful for practice? Do we have to rely on the theorists themselves for this, or is it possible to convert apparently useless theories into practically useful ones on our own, as readers? (Chapters 6–10 are attempts to achieve such conversions, and the exercises in those chapters are examples of them.)

Exercises

1–2   As I mentioned just above, these exercises are designed to help students work through translation theories in ways that will render them more useful for translation practice – and in the process also help students begin to theorize translation more complexly themselves. Both exercises, like the ones in

Chapters 8 and 10, are long, elaborate, and complicated, and will require quite a bit of time – even a whole week of class time – to work through. Since they serve to introduce students to the prevailing theories of translation in the world today, and do so in ways that make those theories accessible, interesting, and practical for everyday use, they should be worth the time.

10 Cultures

This chapter explores the significant impact culture has on translation – not only in making certain words and phrases (so-called *realia*) "untranslatable," but, as recent culturally oriented theorists have been showing, in controlling the ways in which translations are made and distributed. Its main focus is on these latter theorists: the school variously called polysystems, descriptive translation studies (DTS), and manipulation, as well as the newer feminist and postcolonial approaches.

Discussion

All four of these topics address the universalist positions that have dominated Western translation theory until the past few decades; first developed by the medieval Christian church, later secularized as liberal humanism, that universalism has most recently been propounded by theorists like Eugene Nida and Peter Newmark, and is likely to be one of the main theoretical assumptions brought to this class by your students. If so, the relativistic notions that have come to prevail in translation theory over the past two or three decades will provoke considerable resistance among them – and that resistance needs to be expressed and discussed. If you have time in your course to assign extended readings from these culturally oriented theorists, you may be able to deal with that resistance at greater length, and perhaps wear it down. If not, it is probably better not to try to convince students that these new theorists are right and they, the students, and 1600 years of hegemonic Western translation theory, are wrong. Most effective at this point is to raise the possibility that things are more complicated and difficult than the universalist position makes them seem.

1 This position ties in closely with the one raised in topic 1 of Chapter 6; refer to that discussion above for further ideas.

2 This is likely to be an unpopular view; the main idea in discussing it, again, should not be to convince students of it (I'm not convinced myself), but to get them to take it seriously enough, for long enough, to consider its implications. Imagine a professional situation in which that assumption did in fact control your every decision – what would that be like?

3 Depending on how hot the political-correctness fires have raged in your country, you may or may not want to open this can of worms at all. Perhaps the best way to avoid the kind of useless bickering that the topic typically seems to generate is to focus the discussion on whether the professional community does require the avoidance of discriminatory usage – and, when and where it does, how best to deal with that.

4 Since the first scenario is so blatantly tied to medieval Christianity, where it originated, some students who do actually believe in that model will feel uncomfortable defending it, and will want to modify it in secular ways. Helping them to articulate their modifications, and to explore just how different they are from the scenario as spelled out in the chapter, may in fact be a useful way of getting at the point being made: that we all still retain a powerful loyalty to the universalist model, which continues to affect our thinking about translation when we overtly resist or reject it.

Exercises

1–2 Like the exercises in Chapters 7–9, these are designed to help students work through recent translation theories in hands-on ways, thinking about them critically, applying them to their experience, etc. As before, you should probably devote at least a week to these two exercises alone.

11 When habit fails

This concluding chapter returns us to the issue of analysis, which has *seemed* to be neglected throughout the book – though in fact it has always implicitly been present. Analysis is obviously a crucial part of translation, and this chapter explores some of the reasons why. Because the model used in this book portrays the translator as someone who shuttles back and forth between conscious analysis (whenever a problem arises, whenever, to put it in Massimini and Carli's (1995) terms, the challenge exceeds the translator's skills) and internalized or sublimated but still analytical processing (most of the time), it may seem to some as if analysis is being relegated to the peripheries of the translator's work, made secondary, even irrelevant. This could not be farther from the truth.

The key to successful translator training, I've been arguing, is to move from the painfully slow analytical processes that are typically taught in classrooms to the fast subliminal processes that most translators rely on to make a decent living – and the best way to do that is to learn to internalize those slow analytical processes, so that they operate unconsciously, by "second nature." At the same time, however, we must not lose sight of the fact that problem areas in a source text *always* force professional translators out of their "fast" modes and into the "slow" modes of conscious analysis – and this chapter explores that latter.

Discussion

1–2 Both topics, clearly, give students one more chance to discuss the model developed throughout the book, the practical pedagogical consequences of which they have been experiencing throughout the course.

Exercise

This exercise can be done by individual students, or they can work in pairs, one student reading the text to the other and monitoring the "translator's" physical changes – eyes widen, posture straightens, etc. You can also generate your own versions of these "problematic" source texts by finding or writing relatively simple texts and making some absurd change in them about ten lines from the top.

Works cited

Alkon, Daniel (1992) *Memory's Voice*. New York: Harper-Collins.

Anderson, Kristine K. (1995) "Revealing the Body Bilingual: Quebec Translation Theorists and Recent Translation Theory." *Studies in the Humanities* 22.1–2 (December): 65–75.

Asher, James J. (1985) *TPR Student Kit: 4 in 1*. Los Gatos, CA: Sky Oaks.

Austin, J. L. (1962/1976) *How to Do Things with Words*. Edited by J. O. Urmson and Marina Sbisa. Reprinted London: Oxford University Press.

Baker, Mona (1992) *In Other Words: A Coursebook on Translation*. London: Routledge.

Bassnett, Susan (1991) *Translation Studies*. Revised edition London and New York: Routledge.

Bennett, Milton J. (1993) "Towards Ethnorelativism: A Developmental Model of Intercultural Sensitivity." In R. Michael Paige, ed., *Education for the Intercultural Experience*. Yarmouth, ME: Intercultural Press. 21–71.

Berman, Antoine (1984/1992) *L'Épreuve de l'étranger: culture et traduction dans l'Allemagne romantique*. Paris: Gallimard. Translated by S. Heyvaert as *The Experience of the Foreign: Culture and Translation in Romantic Germany*. Albany: SUNY Press.

Bochner, Stephen, ed. (1981) *The Mediating Person: Bridges Between Cultures*. Cambridge, MA: Schenkman.

Bourdieu, Pierre (1986) *Distinction: A Social Critique of the Judgement of Taste*. Translated by Richard Nice. London and New York: Routledge.

Brislin, Richard W. (1972) "Expanding the Role of the Interpreter to Include Multiple Facets of Intercultural Communication." In Larry A. Samovar and Richard E. Porter, eds, *Intercultural Communication: A Reader*. Belmont, CA: Wadsworth. 233–40.

Buzan, Tony (1993) *The Mind Map Book: Radiant Thinking*. London: BBC Books.

Caine, Geoffrey, Renate Nummela Caine, and Sam Crowel

(1994) *MindShifts: A Brain-Based Process for Restructuring Schools and Renewing Education*. Tucson, AZ: Zephyr Press.

Calvin, William H. (1996) *How Brains Think: Evolving Intelligence, Then and Now*. New York: Basic Books.

Carbo, Marie, Rita Dunn, and Kenneth Dunn (1986) *Teaching Students to Read through Their Individual Learning Styles*. Englewood Cliffs, NJ: Prentice-Hall.

Catford, J. C. (1965) *A Linguistic Theory of Translation: An Essay in Applied Linguistics*. London: Oxford University Press.

Chamberlain, Lori (1988) "Gender and the Metaphorics of Translation." *Signs* 13: 454–72. Reprinted in Lawrence Venuti, ed., *Rethinking Translation*. London and New York: Routledge, 1992. 57–74.

Cheyfitz, Eric (1991) *The Poetics of Imperialism: Translation and Colonization from The Tempest to Tarzan*. New York: Oxford University Press.

Chomsky, Noam (1965) *Aspects of the Theory of Syntax*. Cambridge, MA: MIT Press.

Chukovskii, Kornei (1984) *The Art of Translation: Kornei Chukovskii's The High Art*. Translated by Lauren Leighton. Knoxville: University of Tennessee Press.

Copeland, Rita (1991) *Rhetoric, Hermeneutics, and Translation in the Middle Ages: Academic Traditions and Vernacular Texts*. Cambridge: Cambridge University Press.

Csikszentmihalyi, Mihaly (1990) *Flow: The Psychology of Optimal Experience*. New York: Harper & Row.

Csikszentmihalyi, Mihaly (1995) "The Flow Experience and Its Significance for Human Psychology." In Mihaly Csikszentmihalyi and Isabella Selega Csikszentmihalyi, eds, *Optimal Experience: Psychological Studies of Flow in Consciousness*. New York: Cambridge University Press. 15–35.

Delabastita, Dirk, and Lieven d'Hulst (1993) *European Shakespeares: Translating Shakespeare in the Romantic Age*. Amsterdam and Philadelphia, PA: John Benjamins.

Dhority, Lynn (1992) *The ACT Approach: The Use of Suggestion for Integrative Learning*. Philadelphia, PA: Gordon & Breach.

Díaz-Diocaretz, Myriam (1985) *Translating Poetic Discourse: Questions on Feminist Strategies in Adrienne Rich*. Amsterdam and Philadelphia, PA: John Benjamins.

Dryden, Gordon, and Jeannette Vos (1993) *The Learning Revolution: How to Learn Anything At Least Five Times Faster, Better, Easier*. Rolling Hills Estates, CA: Jalmar Press.

Duff, Alan (1989) *Translation*. Oxford: Oxford University Press.

Ellis, Roger, ed. (1989) *The Medieval Translator: The Theory and Practice of Translation in the Middle Ages*. Cambridge: Brewer.

Ellis, Roger, ed. (1991) *The Medieval Translator 2*. London: Centre for Medieval Studies, Queen Mary and Westfield College, University of London.

Ellis, Roger, ed. (1996) *The Medieval Translator/Traduire au Moyen Age*. Turnhout, Belgium: Brepols.

Ellis, Roger, and Ruth Evans, eds (1994) *The Medieval Translator 4*. Binghamton: Medieval and Renaissance Texts and Studies, SUNY.

Even-Zohar, Itamar (1979) "Polysystem Theory." *Poetics Today* 1.1–2: 283–305.

Even-Zohar, Itamar (1981) "Translation Theory Today: A Call for Transfer Theory." *Poetics Today* 2/4: 1–7. Reprinted as "Translation and Transfer." *Poetics Today* 11.1 (1990): 73–8.

Felman, Shoshana (1983) *The Literary Speech Act: Don Juan With J. L. Austin, or Seduction in Two Languages.* Translated by Catherine Porter. Ithaca, NY: Cornell University Press.

Finlay, Ian F. (1971) *Translating.* London: Teach Yourself Books.

Fitzgerald, Thomas K. (1993) *Metaphors of Identity: A Culture-Communication Dialogue.* Albany: SUNY Press.

Freire, Paulo (1970) *The Pedagogy of the Oppressed.* Translated by Myra Bergman Ramos. New York: Continuum.

Fuller, Frederick (1973) *A Handbook for Translators (With Special Reference to International Conference Translators).* Gerrards Cross, UK: C. Smythe.

Gallagher, Winifred (1994) *The Power of Place: How Our Surroundings Shape Our Thoughts, Emotions, and Actions.* New York: Harper-Perennial.

García Yebra, Valentín (1989a) *En torno a la traducción: teoria, critica, historia.* Madrid: Editorial Gredos.

García Yebra, Valentín (1989b) *Teoria y practica de la traducción.* Madrid: Editorial Gredos.

García Yebra, Valentín (1994) *Traducción: historia y teoria.* Madrid: Editorial Gredos.

Gardner, Howard (1985) *Frames of Mind: The Theory of Multiple Intelligences.* New York: Basic Books.

Gardner, Howard (1993) *Multiple Intelligences: The Theory in Practice.* New York: Basic Books.

Gentzler, Edwin (1993) *Contemporary Translation Theories.* London and New York: Routledge.

Godard, Barbara (1989) "Theorizing Feminist Discourse/Translation." *Tessera* 6 (Spring): 42–53.

Goleman, Daniel (1995) *Emotional Intelligence.* New York: Bantam Books.

Gorlée, Dinda L. (1994) *Semiotics and the Problem of Translation: With Special Reference to the Semiotics of Charles S. Peirce.* Amsterdam and Atlanta, GA: Rodopi.

Gramsci, Antonio (1971) *Selections from the Prison Notebooks.* Translated and edited by Quintin Hoare and Geoffrey Nowell-Smith. New York: International Publishers.

Grice, Paul (1989) *Studies in the Way of Words.* Cambridge, MA: Harvard University Press.

Griffin, Em (1994) *A First Look at Communication Theory.* 2nd edition. New York: McGraw-Hill.

Grinder, Michael (1989) *Righting the Educational Conveyor Belt.* Portland, OR: Metamorphous Press.

Gudykunst, William B., and Young Yun Kim (1992) *Communicating With Strangers: An Approach to Intercultural Communication.* 2nd edition. New York: McGraw-Hill.

Gutt, Ernst-August (1992) *Relevance Theory: A Guide to Successful Communication in Translation.* Dallas and New York: United Bible Societies.

Hampden-Turner, Charles (1981) *Maps of the Mind.* New York: Macmillan.

Hart, Leslie (1975) *How the Brain Works: A New Understanding of Human Learning.* New York: Basic Books.

Hart, Leslie (1983) *Human Brain and Human Learning.* White Plains, NY: Longman.

Hatim, Basil, and Ian Mason (1990) *Discourse and the Translator.* London and New York: Longman.

Hermans, Theo, ed. (1985) *The Manipulation of Literature: Studies in Literary Translation.* London: Croom Helm.

Hewson, Lance, and Jacky Martin (1991) *Redefining Translation: The Variational Approach.* London: Routledge.

Holmes, James S. (1975) *The Name and Nature of Translation Studies.* Amsterdam: Translation Studies Section, Department of General Literary Studies, University of Amsterdam.

Holz-Mänttäri, Justa (1984) *Translatorisches Handeln: Theorie und Methode.* Helsinki: Finnish Academy of Sciences.

Hoopes, D. S. (1981) "Intercultural Communication Concepts and the Psychology of the Intercultural Experience." In M. D. Pusch, ed., *Multicultural Education: A Cross-Cultural Training Approach.* Intercultural Network. 10–38.

Hymes, Dell (1972) "On Communicative Competence." In J. B. Pride and Janet Holmes, eds, *Sociolinguistics: Selected Readings.* Harmondsworth, UK: Penguin. 269–93.

Jacquemond, Richard (1992) "Translation and Cultural Hegemony: The Case of French-Arabic Translation." In Lawrence Venuti, ed., *Rethinking Translation.* London and New York: Routledge. 139–58.

Jensen, Eric (1988a) *SuperTeaching: Master Strategies for Building Student Success.* Del Mar, CA: Turning Point.

Jensen, Eric (1988b) *Introduction to Accelerated Learning.* Del Mar, CA: Turning Point.

Jensen, Eric (1995a) *Brain-Based Learning and Teaching.* Del Mar, CA: Turning Point.

Jensen, Eric (1995b) *Learning Styles of the 1990s.* Del Mar, CA: Turning Point.

Kim, Young Yun (1988) *Communication and Cross-Cultural Adaptation: An Integrative Theory.* Clevedon and Philadelphia: Multilingual Matters.

Krashen, Steven, and Tracy D. Terrell (1983) *The Natural Approach: Language Acquisition in the Classroom.* Englewood Cliffs, NJ: Alemany Press/Regents/Prentice-Hall.

Krings, Hans (1986) *Was in den Kopfen von Übertsetzern vorgeht: Eine empirische Untersuchung zur Struktur des Übersetzungsprozesses an fortgeschrittenen Französisch-lernern.* Tübingen, Germany: Gunther Narr.

Krontiris, Tina (1992) *Oppositional Voices: Women as Writers and Translators of Literature in the English Renaissance.* London and New York: Routledge.

Kussmaul, Paul (1995) *Training the Translator.* Amsterdam and Philadelphia: John Benjamins.

Lefevere, André (1992) *Translation, Rewriting, and the Manipulation of Literary Fame.* London: Routledge.

Levine, Suzanne Jill. (1992) *The Subversive Scribe: Translating Latin-American Literature.* St. Paul: Graywolf.

Lörscher, Wolfgang (1991) *Translation Performance, Translation Process, and Translation Strategies: A Psycholinguistic Investigation*. Tübingen, Germany: Gunther Narr.

Lotbinière-Harwood, Susanne (1991) *Re-belle et infidèle: la traduction comme pratique de reéctriture au féminin/The Body Bilingual: Translation as a Re-Writing in the Feminine*. Montreal: Editions du Remue-menage.

Lozanov, Georgi (1971/1992) *Suggestology and Outlines of Suggestopedy*. Translated by Marjorie Hall-Pozharlieva and Krassimira Pashmakova. Philadelphia, PA, Reading, UK, Paris, Montreuz, Tokyo, Melbourne: Gordon & Breach.

Maier, Carol (1980) "Some Thoughts on Translation, Imagination and (Un)academic Activity." *Translation Review* 6: 25–9.

Maier, Carol (1984) "Translation as Performance: Three Notes." *Translation Review* 15: 5–8.

Maier, Carol (1989): "Notes after Words: Looking Forward Retrospectively at Translation and (Hispanic and Luso-Brazilian) Feminist Criticism." In Herman Vidal, ed., *Cultural and Historical Grounding for Hispanic and Luso-Brazilian Feminist Literary Criticism*. Minneapolis: University of Minnesota Press. 625–53.

Margulies, Nancy (1991) *Mapping Inner Space: Learning and Teaching Mind Mapping*. Tuscon, AZ: Zephyr Press.

Massimini, Fausto, and Massimo Carli (1995) "The Systematic Assessment of Flow in Daily Experience." In Mihaly Csikszentmihalyi and Isabella Selega Csikszentmihalyi, eds, *Optimal Experience: Psychological Studies of Flow in Consciousness*. New York: Cambridge University Press. 266–87.

McCarthy, Bernice (1987) *The 4MAT System: Teaching to Learning Styles with Right/Left Mode Techniques*. Arlington Heights, IL: Excel.

Miller, George A. (1973) *Communication, Languages and Meaning: Psychological Perspectives*. New York: Basic Books.

Minh-Ha, Trinh T. (1994) "Other than Myself/My Other Self." In George Robertson, Melinda Mash, Lisa Tickner, Jon Bird, Barry Curtis, and Tim Putnam, eds, *Travellers' Tales: Narratives of Home and Displacement*. London and New York: Routledge. 9–26.

Newmark, Peter (1987) *A Textbook of Translation*. New York: Prentice-Hall.

Nida, Eugene A. (1985) "Translating Means Translating Meaning: A Sociosemiotic Approach to Translating." In Hildegund Bühler, ed., *Der Übersetzer und seine Stellung in der Öffentlichkeit / Translators and Their Position in Society / Le Traducteur et sa place dans la societé*. Vienna: Wilhelm Braunmüller. 119–25.

Nida, Eugene A., and Charles Taber (1969) *The Theory and Practice of Translation*. Leiden, The Netherlands: E. J. Brill.

Niranjana, Tejaswini (1992) *Siting Translation: History, Post-structuralism, and the Colonial Context*. Berkeley and Los Angeles: University of California Press.

Nord, Christiane (1991) *Text Analysis in Translation: Theory, Methodology, and Didactic Application of a Model for Translation-Oriented Text Analysis*. Amsterdam: Rodopi.

Ostrander, Sheila, and Lynn Schroeder (1991) *SuperMemory*. New York: Carol & Graf.

Padilla, Amado M., ed. (1980) *Acculturation: Theory, Models and Some New Findings*. Boulder, CO: Westview.

Peirce, Charles Sanders (1931–66) *Collected Papers of Charles Sanders Peirce.* Edited by Charles Hartshorne, Paul Weiss, and Arthur W. Burks. 8 vols. Cambridge, MA: Belknap Press of Harvard University Press.

Picken, Catriona, ed. (1989) *The Translator's Handbook.* 2nd edition. London: Aslib.

Pym, Anthony (1992a) *Translation and Text Transfer: An Essay on the Principles of Intercultural Communication.* Frankfurt am Main: Peter Lang.

Pym, Anthony (1992b) "The Relations between Translation and Material Text Transfer." *Target* 4.2: 171–89.

Pym, Anthony (1993) *Epistemological Problems in Translation and Its Teaching: A Seminar for Thinking Students.* Calaceite (Teruel), Spain: Caminade.

Pym, Anthony (1995) "Translation as Transaction Cost." Meta 40.4: 594–605.

Rafael, Vicente L. (1988/1993) *Contracting Colonialism: Translation and Christian Conversion in Tagalog Society under Early Spanish Rule.* Ithaca, NY: Cornell University Press. Revised edition. Durham, NC: Duke University Press..

Reiß, Katharina (1976) *Texttyp und Übersetzungsmethode: Der operative Text.* Kronberg, Germany: Scriptor Verlag.

Reiß, Katharina, and Hans J. Vermeer (1984) *Grundlegung einer allgemeinen Translationstheorie.* Tübingen, Germany: Niemeyer.

Rener, Frederick M. (1989) *Interpretation: Language and Translation from Cicero to Tytler.* Amsterdam and Atlanta, GA: Radopi.

Rey, Alain (1995) *Essays on Terminology.* Translated and edited by Juan C. Sager. Amsterdam and Philadelphia, PA: John Benjamins.

Rheingold, Howard (1988) *They Have a Word for It: A Lighthearted Lexicon of Untranslatable Words and Phrases.* New York: Tarcher.

Roberts, Paul William (1997) "My Translation Problem." *Lingua Franca* 7.1 (December/January): 69–75.

Robinson, Douglas (1986) "Metapragmatics and Its Discontents." *Journal of Pragmatics* 10: 359–78.

Robinson, Douglas (1991) *The Translator's Turn.* Baltimore, MD: Johns Hopkins University Press.

Robinson, Douglas (1995) "Theorizing Translation in a Woman's Voice: Subversions of the Rhetoric of Patronage, Courtly Love, and Morality by Early Modern Women Translators." *Translator* 1.2 (November): 153–75.

Robinson, Douglas (1996) *Translation and Taboo.* Dekalb, IL: Northern Illinois University Press.

Robinson, Douglas (1997a) *Translation and Empire: Postcolonial Theories Explained.* Manchester, UK: St. Jerome.

Robinson, Douglas, ed. (1997b) *Western Translation Theory From Herodotus to Nietzsche.* Manchester, UK: St. Jerome.

Rose, Colin (1987) *Accelerated Learning.* New York: Dell.

Rose, Steven (1992) *The Making of Memory.* New York: Anchor/Doubleday.

Sager, Juan C. (1990) *A Practical Course in Terminology Processing.* Amsterdam and Philadelphia, PA: John Benjamins.

Samuelsson-Brown, Geoffrey (1993) *A Practical Guide For Translators.* Cleveland, PA, and Adelaide: Multilingual Matters.

Schiffler, Ludger (1992) *Suggestopedic Methods and Applications.* Philadelphia, PA: Gordon & Breach.

Sechrest, Lee, Todd L. Fay, and S. M. Zaidi (1972) "Problems of Translation in Cross-Cultural Communication." In Larry A. Samovar and Richard E. Porter, eds, *Intercultural Communication: A Reader.* Belmont, CA: Wadsworth. 223–33.

Seguinot, Candace Lee Carsen (1989) *The Translation Process.* Toronto: H. G. Publications.

Simon, Sherry (1995) *Translation and Gender.* London and New York: Routledge.

Snell, Barbara M., ed. (1983) *Term Banks for Tomorrow's World: Translation and the Computer 4.* London: Aslib.

Snell-Hornby, Mary (1995) *Translation Studies: An Integrated Approach.* Revised edition Amsterdam and Philadelphia, PA: John Benjamins.

Steiner, George (1975) *After Babel: Aspects of Language and Translation.* London: Oxford University Press.

Sylwester, Robert (1995) *A Celebration of Neurons: An Educator's Guide to the Human Brain.* Alexandria, VA: ASCD.

Tannen, Deborah (1990) *You Just Don't Understand: Women and Men in Conversation.* New York: Morrow.

Taylor, E. (1988) *Subliminal Learning.* Salt Lake City, UT: Just Another Reality.

Tommola, Hannu, ed. (1992) *EURALEX '92.* Studia translatologica ser. a, vol. 2. Tampere, Finland: University of Tampere.

Toury, Gideon (1995) *Descriptive Translation Studies and Beyond.* Amsterdam and Philadelphia, PA: John Benjamins.

Venuti, Lawrence (1995) *The Translator's Invisibility.* London and New York: Routledge.

Vermeer, Hans J. (1989) *Skopos und Translationsaustrag.* Heidelberg: Institute für Übertsetzen und Dolmeschen, Universität Heidelberg.

Vinay, Jean-Paul, and Jean Darbelnet (1958/1977) *Stylistique comparée du français et de l'anglais: méthode de traduction.* Reprinted Montreal: Beauchemin.

von Flotow, Luise (1997) *Translation and Gender: Feminist Theories Explained.* Manchester, UK: St. Jerome.

Vuorinen, Ilpo (1993) Tuhat tappaa opettaa. Naantali, Finland: Resurssi. vol. 1 in the Moreno Institute of Finland publication series.

Weick, Karl. (1979) *The Social Psychology of Organizing.* Reading, MA: Addison-Wesley.

Wilss, Wolfram (1977/1982) *Übersetzungswissenschaft: Probleme und Methode.* Stuttgart: Klett. Translated by Wilss as *The Science of Translation.* Stuttgart: Gunter Narr Verlag.

Wilss, Wolfram (1996) *Knowledge and Skills in Translator Behavior.* Amsterdam and Philadelphia, PA: John Benjamins.

Wittgenstein, Ludwig (1958) *Philosophical Investigations.* Translated by G. E. M. Anscombe. Oxford: Basil Blackwell.

Index

abduction (Peirce) 94, 98–101,
104–7, 110, 113, 118, 123, 148,
150–1, 164–5, 248, 260, 264, 274,
303; about cultural difference
226–7; linguistic 164–5; and
people 131, 132
accelerated learning (Lozanov) 264
actor, translator as 27, 148–51
agency-freelancer relations 14–16,
39, 117, 134–6
alarm bells 106, 249, 292
Alkon, Daniel 91
analytical-reflective (learning style)
76, 80–2, 90, 284
Anderson, Kristine 236, 244
approaches to translation; cultural 3,
95, 222–38, 264; descriptivist
(DTS) 206, 313; feminist 78,
226–8, 233, 235–6, 313;
functional/action-oriented 205,
206–11; linguistic 3, 75, 162–89,
192–3, 264, 302, 308, 309;
manipulation school 205–6, 313;
person-centered 128–60, 300;
polysystems 192, 205–6, 313;
postcolonial 192, 225–7, 233–5,
313; psychological 3, 75, 95, 264;
skopos/Handlung 192, 205,
206–11, 310; social 3, 95,
264; sociolinguistic 75;
terminological 3, 117, 146–8, 151,
156–8, 163, 264, 302; translation
studies 205
Aristophanes 239–42

Aristotle 275
Asher, James J. 62, 91
ATSA-L 16
auditory (learning style) 57, 60,
68–70, 87–9, 91, 156, 264
Austin, J.L. 189, 310
authorities on translation 257–9,
287

Baker, Mona 184–9, 309
"banking method" (Freire) 265
Bassnett, Susan 232, 244
Beckett, Samuel 218
belles infidéles, les (Ménage) 242–4
Benis, Michael 36
Benjamin, Walter 275
Bennett, Milton J. 231, 244
Benny Hill Show, The 225
Beowulf 225
Best Way of Translating From One
Language to Another, The
(Dolet) 253
Bidani, Avi 255
Blackburn, Paul 77
Bochner, Stephen 143
Bourdieu, Pierre 150
brain function 156, 173–4, 249–50;
and computer comparisons 168;
and learning 263, 274, 284
Brain-Based Learning and
Teaching (Jensen) 59
Brislin, Richard W. 23
burnout 40, 45–6, 281–2
Buzan, Tony 91

Caine, Geoffrey 91, 284
Calvin, William H. 50
Carbo, Marie 91
Carli, Massimo 251, 315
Catford, J.C. 75, 163, 174–9, 189, 309
Chamberlain, Lori 235–6, 242, 244
Chaucer, Geoffrey 225
Cheyfitz, Eric 234, 244
Chomsky, Noam 189, 308
Chukovskii, Kornei 163, 189
Cicero, Marcus Tullius 121, 162
Como agua para chocolate (Esquivel) 215
CompuServe 16, 146, 203
conceptual/abstract (learning style) 60, 73, 75–6, 89–90, 283–4
concrete (learning style) 60, 73, 76, 89–90
content-driven (learning style) 60, 65–6, 89–90, 283
Copeland, Rita 222, 255
cost of translation 7, 19–21, 28
Crawford, Tony 255
Crowel, Sam 91
Csikzentmihalyi, Mihaly 43, 96, 137
Cuesta, Ana 197
cycles (Weick) 101–4

Darbelnet, Jean 76, 163, 189, 257
deduction (Peirce) 94, 98–101, 104–7, 110, 120, 122, 123, 132, 138, 172–4, 175, 248, 264, 274; as checking the rules 253; needs to be brought to life 299; and social activity 204; and terminology studies 156
Delabastita, Dirk 232, 244
Delisle, Jean 199
derHovanessian, Diana 118
Derrida, Jacques 275
Dhority, Lynn 91
Diaz-Diocaretz, Myriam 78, 236, 244
Dickens, Charles 225
Discourse and the Translator (Hatim/Mason) 174–82

Dolet, Etienne 253
Dryden, Gordon 91
Duarte, King 253
Duff, Alan 46
Dunn, Kenneth 91
Dunn, Rita 91
d'Hulst, Lieven 232, 244

Ellis, Roger 222, 244
En attendant Godot (Beckett) 218
enactment (Weick) 100–2
enjoyment in translation 21, 26, 28, 40–3, 49, 103
equivalence 9, 18, 79–80, 163, 192–3
Esquivel, Laura 215
Essay on the Principles of Translation, An (Tytler) 253
ethics of translation 22, 26, 29, 30–3, 44, 168, 203
Eurodicautom 258
Evans, K.-Benoit 256
Evans, Ruth 222, 244
Even-Zohar, Itamar 205, 232, 244
experience (Peirce) 94, 95–100, 103–7, 110–24, 134, 148, 264, 295–7; and professional credibility 194–5
external perspective on translation (Pym) 6–7, 21, 276
externally-referenced (learning style) 61, 76, 77–9, 89–90, 283–4

Felman, Shoshana 189, 310
field-dependent (learning style) 60, 62–3, 284
field–independent (learning style) 60, 62–3, 283–4
Finlay, Ian F. 46
First Look at Communication Theory, A (Griffin) 100
Fitzgerald, Thomas K. 143
FLEFO 16, 146, 154, 155, 194, 219, 227, 251
flexible environment (learning style) 61, 63–4, 84–7, 285

flow (Csikzentmihalyi) 41–3, 96, 137, 251–2
Flow Experience and its Significance for Human Psychology, The (Csikzentmihalyi) 43
Francœur, Lucien 78
Freire, Paulo 265
Frere, John Hookham 240
Freud, Sigmund 156
Fuller, Frederick 262

Gallagher, Winifred 55, 83, 91
Garcia Yebra, Valentin 163, 189
Gardner, Howard 57–9, 91
Gender and the Metaphorics of Translation, The (Chamberlain) 242
Gentzler, Edwin 232, 244
global-contextual (learning style) 61, 73–4, 82, 90, 284, 287
Godard, Barbara 78, 236, 244
Goleman, Daniel 53, 136–8
Gorlée, Dinda L. 108, 125
Gramsci, Antonio 224
Grice, Paul 165–6, 189
Griffin, Em 100, 101
Grinder, Michael 91
Grundlegung einer allgemeinen Translationstheorie (Reiß/Vermeer) 213–16
Gudykunst, William B. 231, 244
Gutt, Ernst-August 23

habit (Peirce) 50, 94, 96–100, 103–7, 112, 264, 294; and alarm bells 246
habitus (Bourdieu) 150, 151
Hampden-Turner, Charles 91
Hart, Leslie 91
Hatim, Basil 163, 174–82, 309
Hegel, G.W.F. 275
hegemony (Gramsci) 224
Heidegger, Martin 275
Hermans, Theo 205, 232, 244
Hewson, Lance 23
Hindrichs, Vladimir 36

Holmes, James S. 205, 232, 244
Holz-Mänttäri, Justa 23, 74, 205, 216–19
Hoopes, D.S. 231, 244
How Brains Work (Calvin) 50
How To Do Things With Words (Austin) 310
howlers 113–14, 130, 223
Humboldt, Wilhelm von 163
Huovinen, Irmeli 273
Hymes, Dell 189

impulsive-experimental (learning style) 61, 76, 80–2, 90
In Other Words (Baker) 184–9
income from translation 26, 28, 33–40, 103
independent/dependent/interdependent (learning styles) 61, 64–5
induction (Peirce) 94, 98–101, 104–7, 110, 118, 123, 131, 133, 135, 173–4, 175, 248, 264, 274, 303; as best teacher 297; as checking alternatives 259; and cultural immersion 228; and functional approaches 206; linguistic 167; and the translator community 202; and working people 152
instinct (Peirce) 96–100, 103–7
intelligent activity, translation as 49–51
intercultural communication (ICC) 231–2
internal perspective on translation (Pym) 6–7, 21, 25–44, 278
internally-referenced (learning style) 61, 76, 77–9, 89–90, 284, 291–2
Internet 117, 120, 146, 203
interpreting 67, 69, 71, 73, 77, 78–9, 94, 133, 149; chuchotage 64; conference 75, 140; court 74, 75, 80, 139; escort 64, 74; simultaneous 64, 80, 164
intuition in translation 13–18, 82, 248, 261; *see also* abduction

intuitive-experimental (learning
style) 61, 292
involvement in the profession 26,
29, 30

Jacquemond, Richard 234–5, 244
Jensen, Eric 59, 62, 65, 66, 73, 76,
91, 275
Jerome (Eusebius Hieronymus)
120–1, 204–5

Kant, Immanuel 275
Kim, Young Yun 143, 231, 244
kinesthetic (learning style) 57, 60,
66, 70–3, 87–9, 91, 156, 264
Krashen, Steven 62, 91
Krings, Hans 143
Krontiris, Tina 236, 244
Kussmaul, Paul 125, 148, 196, 306

Lantra-L 16, 120, 140, 146, 154,
155, 194, 219, 227, 251, 282
learning 49–91, 94, 103, 139, 156,
282, 296; and experience 110; and
memory 51–2, 181; state-
dependent 55
learning styles 59–91, 123, 136,
283–5, 286, 289
LeDoux, Joseph 53
Lefevere, André 75, 80, 205, 232,
233, 239–42, 244
letter to Pammachius (Jerome)
120–1, 204
Levine, Suzanne Jill 31, 78, 236, 244
Like Water For Chocolate
(Esquivel) 215
Lindsay, Jack 240, 241
linguistic 'places' (Catford) 175,
177–8
"Logic and Conversation" (Grice)
165
Lörscher, Wolfgang 108
Lotbinière-Harwood, Susanne 31,
78, 236, 244
Loyal Counselor, The (Duarte) 253
Lozanov, Georgi 1, 62, 264
Luther, Martin 205

Lysistrata (Aristophanes) 239–42

machine translation 22, 43–4
Maier, Carol 236, 244
Maine, J.P. 240
Margulies, Nancy 91
Martin, Jacky 23
Mason, Ian 163, 174–82, 309
Massimini, Fausto 251, 315
matching (learning style) 61, 76,
79–80, 89–90, 283, 285
Maurer, Werner 15
McCarthy, Bernice 76, 91
memory 51–7, 139, 146, 173–4;
bodily 49; and learning 51–2;
representational 52–3, 83;
procedural 52–3, 82, 83, 115;
intellectual 53; emotional 53–4;
and context 54–6
Ménage, Gilles 242
Menkes, Gabor 167
Miller, George A. 143
Minh-Ha, Trinh T. 230, 244
mismatching (learning style) 61, 76,
79–80, 89–90, 285, 289–90
multimodal teaching 57, 264, 269,
272, 285, 303
multiple intelligences (Gardner)
57–9, 136; emotional 136–8;
personal 58, 64, 136–8

Neuro-Linguistic Programming 66
Newmark, Peter 76, 163, 257, 313
Nida, Eugene, A. 75, 163, 182–4,
189, 203, 309, 313
Niranjana, Tejaswini 234, 244
Nord, Christiane 205, 207–11
Nummela Caine, Renate 91, 284

Ostrander, Sheila 91
overgeneralization 169–70, 182,
308–9
O'Neill, Marla 154

Padilla, Amado M. 231, 244
pedagogy of translation 2, 82, 124,
147–8, 263–75; and brain function

274; and lecturing 266–9; and
small groups 266, 270–2
Peirce, Charles Sanders 93, 96–101,
108, 113, 131, 206, 264, 274
Philosophical Investigations
(Wittgenstein) 128
Piaget, Jean 50
Picken, Catriona 46, 262
Plato 275
political correctness 227–8, 233, 239
Pound, Ezra 77
power differentials 106, 234–5
Power of Place, The (Gallagher) 55
professionalism in translation 14, 22,
94, 103, 197; and pride 26, 28–33
project management 26, 33, 39
psychoanalysis 139, 156
Pym, Anthony 6, 12, 23, 74, 80,
198–201, 224–5, 244, 260

Rafael, Vicente 234, 244
raising the status of the profession
26, 33–4, 39–40
Rawlinson, Haydn J. 154–5
Reiß, Katharina 74, 205, 213–16
relationship-driven (learning style)
61, 65–6, 89–90, 285
reliability 7–16, 18, 19–21, 26, 28,
41, 45, 49; as professional pride
29; textual 8–12; translator's
12–16
retention (Weick) 100–2
reticular activation 249–50, 259
Rey, Alain 160
Rich, Adrienne 78
Richter, Werner 131
Robinson, Douglas 46, 66, 71, 74,
80, 121, 143, 166, 193, 229, 236,
244, 301
Rogers, Benjamin Bickley 240
Rose, Colin 87, 91
Rose, Stephen 91
rules, of translation 94, 120–2, 124,
162, 173–4, 175, 182, 248, 254–8;
Weick on 101; *see also* deduction
Rychlewski, Alex 255

Sager, Juan 160
Samsonowitz, Miriam 15
Samuelsson-Brown, Geoffrey 46
Sapir, Edward 163
Saussure, Ferdinand de 224, 308
Schiffler, Ludger 91
Schroeder, Lynn 91
Searle, John 310
Sechrest, Lee 231
Seguinot, Candace Lee Carsen 108
selection (Weick) 100–2
sequential-detailed/linear (learning
style) 61, 73, 74–5, 90, 283–4
Shakespeare, William 225
Simões, Jussara 37
Simon, Sherry 80, 236, 244
Snell, Barbara M. 160
Snell-Hornby, Mary 232, 244
*Social Psychology of Organizing,
The* (Weick) 100
specialist vs. general source texts
198–202
speech acts (Austin) 310
speed in translating 2, 26, 28, 33, 41,
34–40, 45, 49, 96, 103, 279–81
Stratford, Philip 80–81
structured environment (learning
style) 61, 63–4, 84–7, 283
Subversive Scribe, The (Levine) 31
suggestopedia (Lozanov) 264
Sylwester, Robert 91, 284
*Systematic Assessment of Flow in
Daily Experience, The*
(Massimini/Carli) 251

Taber, Charles 75, 182–4, 189, 309
Tannen, Deborah 226
Taylor, E. 91
Terrell, Tracy D. 62, 91
Text Analysis in Translation (Nord)
207–11
Textanalyse und Übersetzen (Nord)
207
theories of translation *see*
approaches to translation
theory vs. theorizing 120–2, 181,
275; as subliminal 105, 293–4

Theory and Practice of Translation, The (Nida/Taber) 182–4
timeliness in translation 7, 16–19, 26
Tommola, Jorma 160
Toury, Gideon 75, 205, 232, 244
TRANSLAT 16
Translating Means Translating Meaning (Nida) 203
translation, advertising 8–9, 80, 117, 122–3, 139, 215; analytical 2, 95, 119, 246–8, 261, 265, 292; Bible 8, 16, 121, 182–4, 233; for children 9; commercial 74; conscious 2, 49, 95, 261, 262; film-dubbing 37, 69; legal 80, 147, 149; literary 8, 16, 74, 80, 117; medical 80, 139, 147, 149; medieval 122, 193, 222; scientific 74; subliminal 2, 50, 95, 103, 105, 119, 246, 247, 261, 262, 264, 292; technical 23, 74, 80, 215; unconscious 2, 49
Translation and Text Transfer (Pym) 204
Translation, Rewriting, and the Manipulation of Literary Fame (Lefevere) 233, 239–42
translator, associations/unions 30, 203; conferences 30, 203; discussion groups 203; *see also* Lantra-L, FLEFO

Translatorisches Handeln (Holz-Mänttäri) 216–19
Translator's Turn, The (Robinson) 301
Tytler, Alexander Fraser, Lord Woodhouselee 253

unrandomizing (Weick) 169

Venuti, Lawrence 77–8
Vermeer, Hans J. 74, 205, 213–16
Vinay, Jean-Paul 76, 163, 189, 257
Virgil (Publius Vergilius Maro) 180
visual (learning style) 57, 60, 66–8, 87–9, 91, 156, 264
von Flotow, Luise 236, 244
Vos, Jeannette 91
Vuorinen, Ilpo 273

Waiting for Godot (Beckett) 218
Wallace, Josh 255
Way, A.S. 239–41
Weick, Karl 93, 100-2, 108, 169, 254
Wheelwright, C.A. 239, 241
Whorf, Benjamin Lee 163
Wilss, Wolfram 75, 262
Wittgenstein, Ludwig 128, 140
Wong, Gloria 15
World Wide Web 117, 250, 295

Yoshimoto, Banana 235